From Paris to
New York by Land

Harry de Windt

Esprios.com

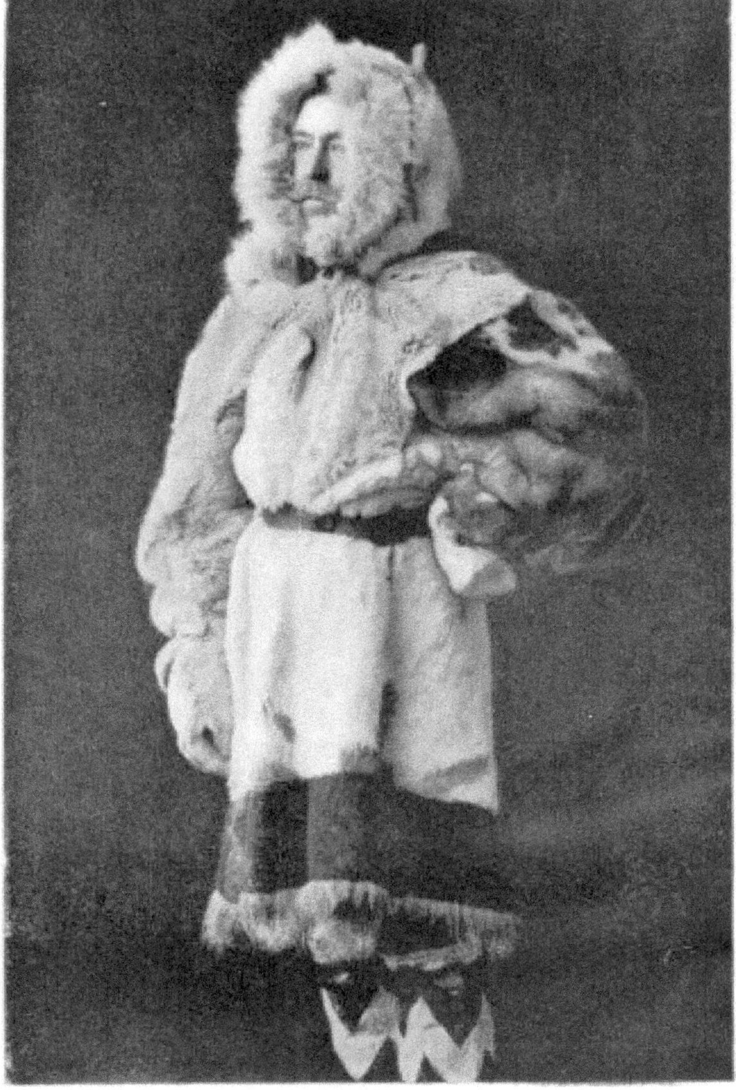

TO MY WIFE

PREFACE

Many who read the following account of our long land journey will not unnaturally ask: "What was the object of this stupendous voyage, or the reward to be gained by this apparently unnecessary risk of life and endurance of hardships?"

I would reply that my primary purpose was to ascertain the feasibility of constructing a railway to connect the chief cities of France and America, Paris and New York. The European Press was at the time of our departure largely interested in this question, which fact induced the proprietors of the *Daily Express* of London, the *Journal* of Paris, and the New York *World* to contribute towards the expenses of the expedition. Another reason is one with which I fancy most Englishmen will readily sympathise—viz., the feat had never before been performed, and my first attempt to accomplish it in 1896 (with New York as the starting-point) had failed half way on the Siberian shores of Bering Straits.

The invaluable assistance rendered by the United States Government in the despatch of a revenue cutter to our relief on the Siberian coast is duly acknowledged in another portion of this volume, but I would here express my sincere thanks to the "Compagnie Internationale des Wagonslits" for furnishing the expedition with a free pass from Paris to the city of Irkutsk, in Eastern Siberia. In America the "Southern Pacific" and "Wabash" Lines extended the same courtesies, thus enabling us to travel free of cost across the United States, as guests of two of the most luxurious railways in the world.

45 Avenue Kléber, Paris,
October 1903.

CONTENTS

PART I.—EUROPE AND ASIA
I. THROUGH EUROPE. THE TRANS-SIBERIAN RAILWAY.
II. THE PARIS OF SIBERIA
III. THE GREAT LENA POST-ROAD
IV. THE CITY OF THE YAKUTE
V. THE LAND OF DESOLATION
VI. VERKHOYANSK
VII. THROUGH DARKEST SIBERIA
VIII. AN ARCTIC INFERNO
IX. THE LOWER KOLYMA RIVER
X. A CRUEL COAST
XI. IN THE ARCTIC
XII. AMONG THE TCHUKTCHIS
XIII. AMONG THE TCHUKTCHIS (*contd.*)

PART II.—AMERICA.

XIV. ACROSS BERING STRAITS—CAPE PRINCE OF WALES
XV. AN ARCTIC CITY
XVI. A RIVER OF GOLD
XVII. DAWSON
XVIII. THE UPPER YUKON AND LEWES RIVERS. THE WHITE PASS RAILWAY
XIX. THE FRANCO-AMERICAN RAILWAY—SKAGWAY—NEW YORK

PART III.—APPENDICES.
I. APPROXIMATE TABLE OF DISTANCES, PARIS TO NEW YORK
II. LIST OF POST STATIONS BETWEEN IRKUTSK AND YAKUTSK
III. REINDEER STATIONS BETWEEN YAKUTSK AND VERKHOYANSK
IV. YAKUTE SETTLEMENTS BETWEEN VERKHOYANSK AND SREDNI-KOLYMSK

V.   SETTLEMENTS ON KOLYMA RIVER BETWEEN SREDNI-KOLYMSK AND NIJNI-KOLYMSK
VI. A SHORT GLOSSARY OF YAKUTE WORDS
VII. GLOSSARY OF VARIOUS DIALECTS IN USE AMONGST THE TCHUKTCHIS INHABITING THE COASTS OF N.E. SIBERIA
VIII. METEOROLOGICAL RECORD OF THE DE WINDT EXPEDITION

LIST OF ILLUSTRATIONS

HARRY DE WINDT
POOR YAKUTES
THE CHIEF OF POLICE, VERKHOYANSK
A VISITOR
CAPE DESPAIR
TENESKIN'S DAUGHTERS
ESKIMO GIRLS
CONSTRUCTING THE WHITE PASS RAILWAY

PART I
EUROPE AND ASIA

CHAPTER I

THROUGH EUROPE. THE TRANS-SIBERIAN RAILWAY.

The success of my recent land expedition from Paris to New York is largely due to the fact that I had previously essayed the feat in 1896 and failed, for the experience gained on that journey was well worth the price I paid for it. On that occasion I attempted the voyage in an opposite direction—viz., from America to France, but only half the distance was covered. Alaska was then almost unexplored and the now populous Klondike region only sparsely peopled by poverty-stricken and unfriendly Indians. After many dangers and difficulties, Alaska was crossed in safety, and we managed to reach the Siberian shores of Bering Straits only to meet with dire disaster at the hands of the natives of that coast. For no sooner had the American revenue cutter which landed us steamed away than our stores were seized by the villainous chief of the village (one Koari), who informed us that we were virtually his prisoners, and that the dog-sleds which, during the presence of the Government vessel, he had glibly promised to furnish, existed only in this old rascal's fertile imagination. The situation was, to say the least, unpleasant, for the summer was far advanced and the ice already gathering in Bering Straits. Most of the whalers had left the Arctic for the southward, and our rescue seemed almost impossible until the following year. When a month here had passed away, harsh treatment and disgusting food had reduced us to a condition of hopeless despair. I was attacked by scurvy and a painful skin disease, while Harding, my companion, contracted a complaint peculiar to the Tchuktchis, which has to this day baffled the wisest London and Paris physicians. Fortunately we possessed a small silk Union Jack, which was nailed to an old whale rib on the beach (for there was no wood), much to the amusement of the natives. But the laugh was on our side when, the very next morning, a sail appeared on the horizon. Nearer and nearer came the vessel, scudding close-reefed before a gale which had raised a mountainous sea. Would they see our signal? Would the skipper dare to lay-to in such tempestuous weather, hemmed in as he was by the treacherous ice? Had we known, however, at the time that the staunch little *Belvedere* was commanded by the late Capt. Joseph Whiteside, of New Bedford, we should have been spared many moments, which seemed hours, of intense anxiety. Without a thought of his own safety, or a valuable cargo of whales representing many thousands of pounds, this gallant sailor stood boldly in shore, launched a boat, which, after a scuffle with the natives and a scramble over floating ice, we managed to reach, and hauled us aboard the little whaler, more dead than alive. A month later we were in San Francisco, far from the fair French city we had hoped to reach, but sincerely grateful for our preservation. For twenty-four hours after our rescue no ship could have neared that ice-bound coast, and we could scarcely have survived, amidst such surroundings, until the following spring.

A glance at a map will show the route which I had intended to pursue in 1896, although, as this land journey has never before been accomplished (or even attempted), I was unable to benefit by the experience of previous explorers. From New York we travelled to Vancouver, thence across the now famous Chilkoot Pass to the Great Lakes and down the Yukon River to the sea, crossing Bering Straits in an American revenue cutter to the Siberian settlement of melancholy memory. From here I hoped to reach the nearest Russian outpost, Anadyrsk, by dog-sled, proceeding thence along the western shores of the Okhotsk Sea to Okhotsk and Yakutsk. The latter is within a couple of thousand miles of civilisation, a comparatively easy stage in this land of stupendous distances. Had I been able on this occasion to reach Anadyrsk, I could, all being well, have pushed on to Yakutsk, for Cossacks carry a mail, once a year, between the two places. But the connecting link between that miserable Tchuktchi village and Anadyrsk was missing, and so we had to submit to the will of fate.

Follow now on a map my itinerary upon the last occasion, starting from Paris to Moscow, and continuing from Moscow to Irkutsk by the Trans-Siberian Railway. Here we strike in a north-easterly direction to Yakutsk by means of horse-sleighs. Reindeer-sleighs are procured at Yakutsk, and we then steer a north-westerly course to Verkhoyansk. From Verkhoyansk we again proceed (still with reindeer) in a north-easterly direction to the tiny political settlement of Sredni-Kolymsk, where we discard our deer (for there is no more moss) and take to dog-sleds. A journey of nearly two months, travelling almost due east, brings us to East Cape Bering Straits, the north-easternmost point of Asia, and practically half way from Paris to our destination.

From here the journey is fairly easy, for the beaten tracks of Alaska now entail no great hardships. Remote Eskimo settlements like that at Cape Prince of Wales are naturally as primitive as those on the Siberian side, but once Nome City is reached, the traveller may proceed (in summer) to New York solely by the aid of steam.

I shall not weary the reader with details of my preparations. Suffice it to say that, although the minutest care and attention were lavished on the organisation of our food-supply, lack of transport in the Far North compelled me to abandon most of our provisions and trust to luck for our larder, which was therefore frequently very meagrely stocked. Indeed, more than once we were within measurable distance of starvation, but this was the more unavoidable in so far as, even at Moscow, I was compelled to abandon several cases of provisions on account of a telegram received from the Governor-General of Siberia. The message informed me that reindeer were scarce, dogs yet more so, and that, unless the expedition travelled *very* light, it could not possibly hope to reach even the shores of the Arctic Ocean, to say nothing of Bering Straits. Nevertheless, even at the outset of the journey I was blamed, and that by totally inexperienced persons, for abandoning stores so early in the day; a certain British merchant in Moscow expressing surprise that I should have "made such an egregious error" as to leave any provisions behind. I fancy most explorers have met this type of individual—the self-complacent Briton, who, being located for business or other purposes in a foreign or colonial city, never leaves it, and yet poses as an authority on the entire country, however vast, in which he temporarily resides. I can recall one of these immovable fixtures in India, who had never stirred from Bombay save in a P. and O. liner, but who was good enough to advise me how to travel through

From Paris to New York by Land

Central Baluchistan, a country which I had recently explored with some success! The Moscow wiseacre was perhaps unaware that during hard seasons in Arctic Siberia the outfit of an expedition must be strictly limited to the carrying capacity of dogs and reindeer. However, this gentleman's ignorance was perhaps excusable, seeing that his experience of Russian travel had been solely gleaned in a railway car between Moscow and the German frontier. I am told that the same individual severely criticised me for not travelling through Siberia in summer, thereby avoiding the severe hardships arising from intense cold. He was, of course, unaware that during the open season the entire tract of country north-east of Yakutsk is practically impassable owing to thousands of square miles of swamp and hundreds of shallow lakes which can only be crossed in a frozen condition on a dog-sled. Even the natives of these regions never attempt to travel between the months of May and September.

Paris is my home, and I am not ashamed to own that, like most Parisians, I suffer, when abroad, from a nostalgia of the Boulevards that a traveller were perhaps better without. It was therefore as well that our departure for New York took place on a dreary December day, when the beautiful city lay listless and despondent, swept by a wintry gale and lashed by gusts of driving sleet. The sky was sunless, the deserted thoroughfares rivers of mud mournfully reflecting bars of electric light from either side of the street. As my cab splashed wearily up the Rue Lafayette I thought that I had never seen such a picture of desolation. And yet it were better, perhaps, to remember Paris thus, than to yearn through the long Arctic night for the pleasant hours I had learned to love so well here in leafy June. Bright days of sunshine and pleasure in and around the "Ville Lumière!" cool, starlit nights at Armenonville and Saint Cloud! Should I ever enjoy them again?

"The De Windt Expedition" left Paris on December 19, 1901. Preliminary notices of the journey in the French Press had attracted considerable notice in Paris, and a small crowd of journalists and others had assembled at the Gare du Nord to wish us God-speed. We were three in number—myself, the Vicomte de Clinchamp (a young Frenchman who acted as photographer), and George Harding, my faithful companion on many previous expeditions. The

"Nord Express" was on the point of departure, but a stirrup-cup was insisted upon by some of De Clinchamp's enthusiastic compatriots, and an adjournment was made to the Buffet, where good wishes were expressed for our safety and success. After a hearty farewell the train steamed out of the station amidst ringing cheers, which plainly told me that Paris as well as London contained true friends who would pray for our welfare in the frozen North and welcome our safe return to "La Belle France."

Moscow was reached three days later, and here commenced the first of a series of minor but harassing delays which relentlessly pursued me throughout the Asiatic portion of the journey. While alighting from the train I was suddenly seized with such severe internal pains, accompanied by faintness and nausea, that on arrival at the Slaviansky Bazar (the best Hotel, by the way, in the place), I was carried to bed. The attack was inexplicable. Harding, ever a pessimist, suggested appendicitis, and a physician was hastily summoned. The medicine-man gravely shook his head: "You are very ill," he said, and I did not dispute the fact. "Can it be appendicitis?" I asked anxiously. "Appendicitis," replied the Doctor; "what is that? I never heard of the disease!"

Morning brought me some relief, and with a not unnatural distrust of Russian medical methods, I resolved to return at once to Berlin and consult Professor Bergmann. To abandon the journey was now out of the question, but our medicine-chest was up-to-date and I could at any rate ask the famous surgeon how to treat the dread disease should it declare itself in the wilds of Siberia. The next morning saw me back in Berlin, and by midday my mind was at rest. I was suffering from a simple rupture of long standing, but hitherto quiescent, which only required rest and proper treatment for at least a fortnight. "Then it must be in the train," I said, explaining the situation and the priceless value of time. So, after some discussion, I departed with the Professor's good wishes, which, however, were conveyed with an ominous shake of the head.

Two days later I arrived in Moscow, only to be confronted by another difficulty: our rifles, revolvers and ammunition had been seized at the Russian frontier, and at least a fortnight must elapse before we could obtain them. Moscow fortunately boasts of an excellent gun-maker, and I was able to replace our armoury with English weapons, though, of course, at a ruinous expense. But time was too precious to waste. We had now but a little over four months in which to reach Bering Straits, for by the middle of May the bays and estuaries of the Arctic begin to break up, and open water might mean imprisonment (and worse) on these desolate shores throughout the entire summer. So I purchased revolvers, two rifles and a fowling-piece at about five times their usual cost, and hoped that our troubles were over, at least for the present. I should add that the arms had left London six weeks previously, and that I was furnished with a special permit to introduce them into the country. But Russian methods are peculiar, and fortunately unique, I was unaware before our departure of the fact that if a gun is consigned direct from its English maker to a gunsmith in Russia it goes through without any trouble whatsoever. Otherwise, it may take six months or more to reach its destination.

The New Year was passed in Moscow, and a gloomy one it was. From an historical and picturesque point of view the city is intensely interesting, but otherwise it is a dull, dreary place. Russian cities, not excepting Petersburg, generally are, although the English novelist generally depicts them as oases of luxurious splendour, where love and Nihilism meet one at every turn, and where palaces, diamonds and silver sleigh-bells play an important part, to say nothing of that journalistic trump card, the Secret Police! I wish one of these imaginative scribes could spend a winter evening (as I have so often done) in a stuffy hotel reading-room, with a *Times* five days old, wondering whether the Russians will ever provide a theatre sufficiently attractive to tempt a stranger out of doors after nightfall. In summer it is less dismal; there are gardens and restaurants, dancing gipsies and Hungarian Tziganes, but even then the entertainment is generally so poor, and the surroundings so tawdry, that one is glad to leave them at an early hour and go sadly to bed.

The distance from Moscow to Irkutsk is a little under 4000 English miles, the first-class fare a little over a hundred roubles (or about £12), which, considering the journey occupies nine days or more, is reasonable enough. There are, or were, two trains a week,—the

"State" and Wagonlits expresses, which run alternately. The former is a Government train, inferior in every respect to the latter, which is quite as luxurious in its service and appointments as the trains run by the same company in Europe.

At 10 P.M., on January 4, we left Moscow, in a blinding snowstorm, a mild foretaste of the Arctic blizzards to come, which would be experienced without the advantage of a warm and well-lit compartment to view them from. For this train was truly an ambulant palace of luxury. An excellent restaurant, a library, pianos, baths, and last, but not least, a spacious and well-furnished compartment with every comfort, electric and otherwise (and without fellow travellers), rendered this first "étape" of our great land journey one to recall in after days with a longing regret. But we had nearly a fortnight of pleasant travel before us and resolved to make the most of it. Fortunately the train was not crowded. Some cavalry officers bound for Manchuria, three or four Siberian merchants and their families, and a few Tartars of the better class. The officers were capital fellows, full of life and gaiety (Russian officers generally are), the merchants and their women-folk sociable and musically inclined. Nearly every one spoke French, and the time passed pleasantly enough, for although the days were terribly monotonous, evenings enlivened by music and cards, followed by cheery little suppers towards the small hours, almost atoned for their hours of boredom.

Nevertheless, I cannot recommend this railway journey, even as far as Irkutsk, to those on pleasure bent, for the Trans-Siberian is no tourist line, notwithstanding the alluring advertisements which periodically appear during the holiday season. Climatically the journey is a delightful one in winter time, for Siberia is then at its best—not the Siberia of the English dramatist: howling blizzards, chained convicts, wolves and the knout, but a smiling land of promise and plenty even under its limitless mantle of snow. The landscape is dreary, of course, but most days you have the blue cloudless sky and dazzling sunshine, so often sought in vain on the Riviera. At mid-day your sunlit compartment is often too warm to be pleasant, when outside it is 10° below zero. But the air is too dry and bracing for discomfort, although the pleasant breeze we are enjoying here will presently be torturing unhappy mortals in London in the shape of a boisterous and biting east wind. On the other hand, the monotony after a time becomes almost unbearable. All day long the eye rests vacantly upon a dreary white plain, alternating with green belts of woodland, while occasionally the train plunges into dense dark pine forest only to emerge again upon the same eternal "plateau" of silence and snow. Now and again we pass a village, a brown blur on the limitless white, rarely a town, a few wooden houses clustering around a green dome and gilt crosses, but it is all very mournful and depressing, especially to one fresh from Europe. This train has one advantage, there is no rattle or roar about it, as it steals like a silent ghost across the desolate steppes. As a cure for insomnia it would be invaluable, and we therefore sleep a good deal, but most of the day is passed in the restaurant. Here the military element is generally engrossed in an interminable game of *Vint*[1] (during the process of which a Jew civilian is mercilessly rooked), but our piano is a godsend and most Russian women are born musicians. So after *déjeuner* we join the fair sex, who beguile the hours with Glinka and Tchaikovsky until they can play and sing no more. By the way, no one ever knows the time of day and no one particularly wants to. Petersburg time is kept throughout the journey and the result is obvious. We occasionally find ourselves lunching at breakfast time and dining when we should have supped, but who cares? although in any other clime bottled beer at 8 A.M. might have unpleasant results.

[1] Russian whist.

The Ural Mountains (which are merely downs) are crossed. Here the stations are built with some attempt at coquetry, for the district teems with mineral wealth, and in summer is much frequented by fashionable pleasure-seekers and invalids, for there are baths and waters in the neighbourhood. One station reminds me of Homburg or Wiesbaden with its gay restaurant, flower-stall, and a little shop for the sale of trinkets in silver and malachite, and the precious stones found in this region—Alexandrites, garnets and amethysts. But beyond the Urals we are once more lost in the desolate plains across which the train crawls softly and silently at the rate of about ten miles an hour. I know of only one slower railway in the world, that from Jaffa to Jerusalem, where I have seen children leap on and off the car-steps of the train while in motion, and the driver alight, without actually stopping his engine, to gather wildflowers! We cross the great Obi and Yenisei rivers over magnificent bridges of iron and Finnish granite, which cost millions of roubles to construct. Krasnoyarsk is passed by night, but its glittering array of electric lights suggests a city many times the size of the tiny town I passed through in a *tarantass* while travelling in 1887 from Pekin to Paris. So the days crawl wearily away. Passengers come and passengers go, but this train, like the brook, goes on for ever. Although the travelling was luxurious I can honestly say that this was the most wearisome portion of the entire journey. But all things must have an end, even on the Trans-Siberian Railway, and on the tenth day out from Moscow we reach (unconsciously) our destination—Irkutsk. For it is two o'clock in the morning and we are aroused from pleasant dreams in a warm and cosy bed to embark upon a drive of about three miles through wind and snow in an open *droshky*. But we are now in Eastern Siberia, and comfort will soon be a thing of the past.

CHAPTER II

THE PARIS OF SIBERIA

We arrived in Irkutsk on the eve of the Russian New Year, when business throughout the Empire comes to a standstill, and revelry amongst all classes reigns supreme. It was, therefore, useless to think of resuming our journey for at least a week, for sleighs must be procured, to say nothing of that important document, a special letter of recommendation, which I was to receive from the Governor-General of Siberia. But a resplendent *aide-de-camp* called at the hotel and regretfully informed me that State and social functions would keep his Excellency fully occupied for several days. It was hopeless, he added, to think of getting sleighs built while *vodka* was running like water amongst the people. So there was nothing for it but to await the end of the festival with patience, without which commodity no traveller should ever dream of visiting Asiatic Russia. He is otherwise apt to become a raving lunatic.

Irkutsk has several so-called hotels, the only one in any way habitable being the "Hotel Metropole," a name which has become suggestive of gold-laced porters and gilded halls. It was, therefore, rather a shock to enter a noisome den, suggestive of a Whitechapel slum, although its prices equalled those of the Carlton in Pall Mall. The house was new but jerry-built, reeked of drains, and swarmed with vermin. Having kept us shivering for half an hour in the cold, a sleepy, shock-headed lad with guttering candle appeared and led the way to a dark and ill-smelling sleeping-apartment. The latter contained an iron bedstead (an unknown luxury here a decade ago), but relays of guests had evidently used the crumpled sheets and grimy pillows. Bathroom and washstand were supplied by a rusty brass tap, placed, *pro bono publico*, in the corridor. Our meals in the restaurant were inferior to those of a fifth-rate *gargotte*. And this was the best hotel in the "Paris of Siberia," as enthusiastic Siberians have christened their capital.

Irkutsk now has a population of over 80,000. It stands on a peninsular formed by the confluence of two rivers, the clear and swiftly-flowing Angará (which rises in Lake Baikal to join the river Yenisei just below Yeniseisk), and the small and unimportant Irkut river. It is an unfinished, slipshod city, a strange mixture of squalor and grandeur, with tortuous, ill-paved streets, where the wayfarer looks instinctively for the "No-thoroughfare" board. There is one long straggling main street with fairly good shops and buildings, but beyond this Irkutsk remains much the same dull, dreary-looking place that I remember in the early nineties, before the railway had aroused the town from its slumber of centuries. Even now, the place is absolutely primitive and uncivilised, from an European point of view, and the yellow Chinese and beady-eyed Tartars who throng the business quarters are quite in keeping with the Oriental filth around, unredeemed by the usual Eastern colour and romance. On fine mornings the Market Place presents a curious and interesting appearance, for here you may see the Celestial in flowery silk elbowing the fur-clad Yakute and Bokhara shaking hands with Japan. The Irkutsk district is peopled by the Buriates, who originally came from Trans-Baikalia, but who have now become more Russianised than any other Siberian race. The Buriat dialect is a kind of *patois* composed of Mongolian and Chinese; the religion Buddhism. About every fourth Buriat becomes a Lama, and takes vows of celibacy. They are thrifty, industrious people, ordinarily of an honest, hospitable disposition, who number, perhaps, 300,000 in all. This is probably the most civilised aboriginal race in Siberia, and many Buriates now wear European dress, and are employed as Government officials.

The climate of Irkutsk is fairly good; not nearly so cold in winter as many places on the same latitude; the summers are pleasant and equable; but the fall of the year is generally unhealthy, dense fogs occasioning a good deal of pulmonary disease and rheumatism. The city, too, is so execrably drained that severe epidemics occasionally occur during the summer months, but in winter the dry cold air acts as a powerful disinfectant. In spring-time, when the river Angará is swollen by the break-up of the ice, inundations are frequent, and sometimes cause great destruction to life and property. Winter is, therefore, the pleasantest season here, for during dry warm weather the clouds of black gritty dust are unbearable, especially on windy days. Indeed, the dust here is almost worse than in Pekin, where the natives say that it will work its way through a watch-glass, no exaggeration, as I can, from personal experience, testify.

There was little enough to do here during our five days of enforced inactivity, and time crawled away with exasperating slowness, the more so that the waste of every hour was lessening our chance of success. But although harassed myself by anxiety, I managed to conceal the fact from de Clinchamp, whose Gallic nature was proof against *ennui*, and who managed to find friends and amusement even in this dismal city. In summer we might have killed time by an excursion to Lake Baikal,[2] for I retain very pleasant recollections of a week passed, some years since, on the pine-clad margin of this the largest lake in Asia, sixty-six times the area of the Lake of Geneva. Now its wintry shores and frozen waters possessed no attraction, save, perhaps, the ice-breaker used by the Trans-Siberian Railway to carry passengers across the lake, a passage of about twenty miles. But even the ice-breaker had met with an accident, and was temporarily disabled. So there was literally nothing to do but to linger as long as possible over the midday meal in the dingy little restaurant, and then to stroll aimlessly up and down the "Bolshaya," the main thoroughfare aforementioned, until dusk. This is the fashionable drive of the city, which on bright days presented an almost animated appearance. There is no lack of money in Irkutsk, for gold-mining millionaires abound, and I generally spent the afternoon watching the cavalcade of well-appointed sleighs dashing, with a merry clash of bells, up and down the crowded street, and sauntering amongst the groups of well-dressed women and brilliant uniforms, until darkness drove me back to our unsavoury quarters at the Metropole. My companions generally patronised the skating rink, a sign of advancing civilisation, for ten years ago there was not a pair of skates to be found throughout the length and breadth of Siberia. Thus passed our days, and the evenings were even longer and more wearisome. Once we visited the Opera, a new and beautifully-decorated house, but the performance was execrable, and "La Dame de Chez Maxim" unrecognisable in Russian dress. There were also other so-called places of amusement, which blazed with electric light from dusk till dawn, where refreshments were served at little wooden tables while painted harridans from Hamburg cackled suggestive songs to the accompaniment of a cracked piano. In these establishments we used to see the local millionaires (and there are many) taking their pleasure expensively, but sadly enough, amidst surroundings that would disgrace a *dive* in San Francisco. The company was generally very mixed, soldiers and flashily-dressed *cocottes* being alone distinguishable, by their costume, from the rest of the audience. For although the Siberian woman of the better class has learnt of late years to dress well, wealth makes no difference to the garb of mankind. All of the latter have the same dirty, unkempt appearance; all wear the same suit of shiny black, rusty high boots, and a shabby slouch-hat or peaked cap. Furs alone denote the difference of station, sable or blue fox denoting the mercantile Crœsus, astrachan or sheep-skin his clerk. Otherwise all the men look (indoors) as though they had slept in their clothes, which, by the way, is not improbable, for on one occasion I stayed with an Irkutsk Vanderbilt who lived in palatial style. His house was a dream of beauty and millions had been lavished on its ornamentation. Priceless pictures and *objets d'art*, a Paris *chef*, horses and carriages from London, and covered gardens of rare orchids and exotics. No expense had been spared to render life luxurious in this land of dirt and discomfort. Even my host's bedroom was daintily furnished, *à la* Louis XV., by a French upholsterer. And yet he slept every night, fully dressed, on three chairs! There is no accounting for tastes—in Siberia!

[2] "Lake Baikal is about twenty miles from Irkutsk. It is 420 miles in length, its breadth varying from ten to sixty miles. Its average depth is rarely less than 819 ft., but in parts the ground has been touched only at 4500 ft. The natives believe it to be unfathomable."—"Side Lights on Siberia," by J. Y. Simpson.

Although the "Bolshaya," in which most of the *café chantants* are situated, is bright with electric light, the back streets of the city are lit by flickering oil-lamps, and here the stranger must almost grope his way about after dark. If wise he will stay at home, for robbery and even murder are of frequent occurrence. A large proportion of the population here consists of time-expired convicts, many of whom haunt the night-houses in quest of prey. During our short stay a woman was murdered one night within a few yards of our hotel, and a man was stabbed to death in broad daylight on the busy

"Bolshaya." The Chief of Police told me that there is an average of a murder a day every year within the precincts of the city, and warned us not to walk out unarmed after dark. There was no incentive to drive, for the Irkutsk cab, or *droshky*, is a terrible machine, something like a hoodless bath-chair, springless, and constructed to hold two persons (at a pinch) besides the driver. There is no guard-rail, and it was sometimes no easy matter to cling on as the vehicle bumped and bounded, generally at full gallop, along the rough, uneven streets.

Three days elapsed before the business of the city was resumed and I was able to turn my attention to the purchase of sleighs. Fur coats and felt boots we were already provided with, but I had determined to obtain the Arctic kit destined to protect us from the intense cold north of Yakutsk from the fur merchants of that place. Finally, when the fumes of *vodka* had evaporated, at least a dozen sleigh-builders invaded my bedroom early one morning, for the Irkutsk papers had published our needs. The whole day was passed in driving about to the various workshops and examining sleighs, some of which appeared to have been constructed about the same period as the Ark. It was not easy to make a selection from the score of ramshackle *kibitkas* which were hauled out for my inspection, especially as I had a very faint notion of the kind of sleigh required for the work in hand. Fortunately, my friend the Chief of Police, white with rage and blazing with orders, burst into a yard as I was concluding the purchase of a venerable vehicle, which bore a striking resemblance to Napoleon's travelling carriage at Madame Tussaud's, and which would probably have come to pieces during the first stage.

"Son of a dog," furiously cried the official to the trembling coach-builder, "don't you know that this gentleman wishes to go to Yakutsk, and you are trying to swindle him into buying a 'Bolshaya' *coupé*!" And in less than a minute I was being whirled away towards the Police Station, where a number of the peculiar sleighs required for this journey are kept on hand for the convenience of travellers.

"That man is an infernal scoundrel," said the Chief of Police, when told that Napoleon's *barouche* was to have cost me 150 roubles. "I will give you a couple of good Yakute sleighs for half the money.

You can only use them on the Lena." And when I saw the primitive contrivances in question I no longer marvelled at their low price.

Let me describe the comfortless conveyance in which we accomplished the first two thousand miles of the journey across Siberia. A Yakute sleigh has a pair of runners, but otherwise totally differs from any other sleigh in the wide world. Imagine a sack of coarse matting about four feet deep suspended from a frame of rough wooden poles in a horizontal triangle, which also forms a seat for the driver. Into this bag the traveller first lowers his luggage, then his mattress, pillows, and furs, and finally enters himself, lying at full length upon his belongings. There is a thick felt apron which can be pulled completely over its occupant at night-time or in stormy weather. This sounds warm and comfortable, but is precisely the reverse, for after a few hours the porous felt becomes saturated with moisture (formed by bodily warmth and external cold), rendering the traveller's heavy garments damp and chilly for the remainder of the journey. There is nothing to prevent the *Koshma*, as this covering is called (*Cauchemar* would be a better name!), from resting upon the face during sleep, and frost-bitten features are the natural result. So far, therefore, as comfort is concerned a Yakute sleigh is capable of some improvement, for, even in fine weather, the occupant must raise himself up on his elbows to see anything but the sky above him, while in storms the damp, heavy covering casts him into outer darkness. Under the most favourable circumstances little is seen of the country travelled through, but, as the Chief of Police consolingly remarked, "Between here and Yakutsk there is nothing to see!"

Provisions were the next consideration, and these were obtained from a well-appointed store on the "Bolshaya." We now had but a dozen cases of condensed foods, &c., left, and these I wished to keep intact, if possible, for use in the Arctic regions. On the Lena road the post-houses were only from thirty to forty miles apart, but as they only provide hot water and black bread for the use of travellers, I laid in a good supply of canned meats, sardines, and tea to carry us comfortably, at any rate, through the first stage of the journey. With months of desolation before us our English tobacco was too precious to smoke in civilisation, so a few hundred Russian cigarettes were added to the list.

At last came the welcome news that the Governor-General would grant us an interview. Accompanied by an *aide-de-camp*, we drove to the Palace on the banks of the Angará, and were ushered into the presence of the Tsar's Viceroy, who governs a district about the size of Europe. General Panteleyéff was a middle-aged man, with white moustache, light blue eyes, and a spare athletic figure, displayed to advantage by a smart dark green uniform. The General is a personal friend of the Emperor, and the cross of St. Andrew and a tunic covered with various orders bore witness to their wearer's distinguished career. He received me most cordially, and asked many questions regarding the land-journey, which had apparently aroused considerable interest in Russian official circles. The General, however, had no great faith in the proposed line to connect his country with the New World.

"We have our hands too full in the Far East for the next century," he said, with a smile, "to meddle with Arctic railways."

His Excellency assured me of every assistance as far as Nijni-Kolymsk, the most remote Cossack outpost on the shores of the Polar Sea, on ordinary occasions a year's journey from St. Petersburg. "Beyond Kolymsk," he added, "I fear I cannot help you. The Tchuktchi region is nominally under my control, but even our own officials rarely venture for any distance into that desolate country. But you will first have to reach Nijni-Kolymsk, and even that is a voyage that few Russians would care to undertake; and beyond Nijni-Kolymsk you will have yet another two thousand miles to Bering Straits. Great Heavens! what a terrible journey! But you English are a wonderful people!" Here a secretary entered the apartment with a document, which the Governor rapidly scanned and then signed.

"Your Imperial passport," he said, placing the paper in my hand, "which will ensure civility and assistance from all officials you may meet as far as the Kolyma river. Beyond that you must rely upon yourselves and the goodwill of the natives, if you ever find them! May God preserve you all."

So saying, with a hearty shake of the hand, the General touched a bell, the *aide-de-camp* appeared, and I was re-conducted to my sleigh, rejoicing that nothing could now retard our departure. Amongst other privileges the passport ensured immediate relays of horses at the post-stations. As there are no less than one hundred and twenty-two of these (from fifteen to twenty-five miles apart) between Irkutsk and Yakutsk, and as the ordinary traveller is invariably delayed by extortionate postmasters, this clause was of the utmost importance. In many other ways also the document was a priceless one, and without it we could scarcely have reached the shores of America.

It may be that I have unduly underrated the attractions of Irkutsk to the average public. If so, the reader must remember that every hour of delay here was of importance and meant endless worry and vexation to the leader of an expedition which had not an hour to lose. There is no doubt that Irkutsk must in a few years become a teeming centre of commercial activity. The social aspects of the place will then no doubt improve under the higher civilisation introduced by a foreign element. The resources of this province are limitless, for the soil has up till now, minerally speaking, only been scratched by idle fingers. Further afield we hear of important discoveries of valuable minerals in Manchuria, while the output of gold in the Lena district has been trebled by modern machinery within the past four years. Coal has also been recently discovered within a short distance of Lake Baikal, and is already being exported in large quantities to the Pacific ports. Irkutsk has, no doubt, a great commercial future, but should I ever return there I shall, personally speaking, be quite satisfied to find a decent hotel. Such an establishment run on modern lines would certainly yield fabulous returns. At present the only available restaurant is that of the grimy and verminous Metropole, and even here the local millionaires cheerfully pay prices for atrocious food and worse wines which would open the eyes of a Ritz.

Perhaps the most pleasant memory which I retain of Irkutsk is a cheery little supper which was given in our honour by a Mr. Koenigswerther and his wife and brother on the eve of our departure. The travellers, who had only arrived that day, were visiting the city on business connected with the purchase of furs, and a chance word dropped in the purest French by Madame at the dinner-table linked our parties inseparably for the remainder of the evening; indeed, until the next day. Madame Koenigswerther, an attractive little *Parisienne*, seemed to cast a gleam of sunshine over the gloomy dining-room in which we had partaken of so many melancholy meals. The trip here from Paris had already imbued her with a passion for further exploration, and I verily believe that she would have accompanied the expedition to Yakutsk if not restrained by her less enthusiastic male companions. Bed on such an occasion was not to be thought of, so we visited the theatre and *café chantants*, ending the evening with a supper at the Metropole (previously ordered by the fur merchants) which proved that money, even in Irkutsk, will convert a culinary bungler into a very passable *chef*. Our departure for the North took place very early on the morning of January 19, and I have since heard that nothing would induce our merry little hostess to seek her couch until the tingle of our sleigh bells had died out on the frosty air.

"A New York!" she cried, as our horses sprang into their collars and dashed away down the frosty, silent street.

"N'ayéz pas peur! Nous arriverons," answered de Clinchamp, with a cool assurance which at the time excited my envy, if not admiration!

CHAPTER III

THE GREAT LENA POST-ROAD

The distance from Irkutsk to Yakutsk is about 2000 English miles, but the post-road by which we travelled during the first stage of the overland journey is, properly speaking, no road at all. After leaving Irkutsk the traveller crosses about 150 miles of well-wooded country, until the upper waters of the Lena river are reached.[3] In winter time the frozen surface of the latter connects the two cities, and there is no other way by land. A double row of pine branches stuck into the snow at short intervals indicate the track, and this is a necessary precaution, as the hot springs of the Upper Lena frequently render the ice treacherous and unsafe. A sharp look-out is, therefore, kept all along the line for overflows, and, when necessary, the road is shifted to avoid them, but notwithstanding these precautions, darkness and drunken drivers often cause fatal accidents. In summer time Yakutsk may be reached by small steamers plying from Ust-kutsk, on the Lena, about 250 miles by road from Irkutsk. The trip takes about a fortnight down stream, and three weeks in the reverse direction, but sand-bars frequently cause delays, rendered the more irksome by poor accommodation, stifling heat, and clouds of mosquitoes.[4]

[3] The Lena river has an estimated length of not less than 3000 miles. It rises in the Baikal mountains and flows north and east past the towns of Kirensk, Vitimsk, and Olekminsk to Yakutsk, thence it turns to the north-west and enters the Arctic Ocean, forming a wide delta. The Lena receives several large tributaries, viz., the Vitim, about 1400, the Olekma, about 800, and the Aldan, about 1300 miles long.

[4] This must be very slow travelling, for Dobell, the traveller, writes: "When I descended the Lena from Ust-kutsk in the spring of 1816, I was only fourteen days going to Yakutsk in a large flat-bottomed boat."

Most people in England have a very vague idea of the size of Siberia. It is only by actually visiting the country that one can grasp the harassing difficulties due to appalling distances and primitive modes of locomotion, especially when the traveller is bound for the Far North. I will, therefore, endeavour to convey to the reader, as briefly as possible, the area of this land of illimitable space, and cannot do so better than by quoting the graphic description given by the American explorer, Mr. George Kennan.[5] He says: "You can take the whole of the United States of America, from Maine to California and from Lake Superior to the Gulf of Mexico, and set it down in the middle of Siberia without touching anywhere the boundaries of the latter's territory; you can then take Alaska and all the countries of Europe, with the exception of Russia, and fit them into the remaining margin like the pieces of a dissected map. After having thus accommodated all of the United States, including Alaska, and the whole of Europe, except Russia, you will still have more than 300,000 miles of Siberian territory to spare. In other words, you will still have unoccupied in Siberia an area half as large again as the Empire of Germany." According to the census of 1897 the entire population of Siberia is little more than that of the English metropolis.

[5] "Siberia and the Exile System," by George Kennan.

A couple of Yakute sleighs sufficed for ourselves and entire outfit. I rode with de Clinchamp in the leading vehicle, while Harding and the bulk of the stores followed in the other. At first sight, the Yakute sleigh appears to be a clumsy but comfortable contrivance, but very few miles had been covered before I discovered its unlimited powers of inflicting pain. For this machine does not glide like a well-behaved sleigh, but advances by leaps and bounds that strain every nerve and muscle in the body. In anything like deep, soft snow it generally comes to a standstill, and the combined efforts of men and horses are required to set it going again. However, for the first three or four days, good progress was made at the rate of about 200 versts[6] in the twenty-four hours, for we travelled night and day. There was no incentive to pass the night in the post-houses, which were generally of a filthy description, although luxurious compared to the Yakute Yurtas and Tchuktchi huts awaiting us up North. On the Lena post-road, stages were only from fifteen to thirty miles apart, and with a fresh *troika* (three horses harnessed abreast) at such short intervals, our rate of speed for the first week was very satisfactory. Between

Irkutsk and the river Lena part of the road lies through dense forests, which are generally infested with runaway convicts, so we kept a sharp look-out and revolvers handy. Only a week before we passed through this region a mail-cart had been held up and its driver murdered, but I fancy news had filtered through that my expedition was well armed, and we therefore reached the Lena unmolested.

[6] A verst is two-thirds of an English mile.

The weather at Irkutsk had been comparatively warm, and we were, therefore, unprepared for the intense cold experienced only forty-eight hours after our departure. Although on the evening of the 19th the thermometer had registered only 10° below zero Fahrenheit, it suddenly sank during the night to 65° below zero, where it remained until the following evening. Oddly enough, a dense mist accompanied the fall of the mercury, rendering the cold infinitely harder to bear. Our drivers declared that this climatic occurrence was most unusual, and the fact remains that this was the lowest temperature recorded during the entire journey south of the Yakute Yurta of Yuk-Takh, several hundred miles north of Yakutsk. There we had to face 75° below zero, but then Yuk-Takh adjoins Verkhoyansk, the coldest place in the world. But the dry frosty air of even this remote settlement inconvenienced me far less than the chilly breeze of a raw November day on the Paris Boulevards with the mercury half a dozen degrees above the freezing-point. On the Lena this Arctic cold only lasted for about eighteen hours, and then slowly rose again, after remaining at about 50° below zero for a couple of days. The severest cold afterwards experienced south of Yakutsk was 51° below zero, and that only upon one occasion. Otherwise it varied from 2° above to 40° below zero, but even that was sufficient to convert our provisions into a granite-like consistency, and at first wearisome delays were occasioned at the post-stations by the thawing out of petrified sardines and tinned soup converted into solid ice. Milk, frozen and cut into cubes, was conveniently carried in a net attached to the sleigh, and this, with tea, was our sole beverage. For a case with a few bottles of Crimean claret, which we had taken to enliven the first portion of the journey, was found when broached to contain nothing but fragments of red ice and broken glass. Even some cognac (for medicinal purposes) was partly frozen in its flask. On the same day de Clinchamp, removing his mits to take a photograph, accidentally touched some metal on the camera, and his fingers were seared as though with a red-hot iron. Perhaps our greatest annoyance on this voyage was the frequent deprivation of tobacco, that heavenly solace on long and trying journeys. For at even 40° below zero nicotine blocks the pipe-stem, and cigar or cigarette freezes firmly to the lips. The moustache also forms a mask of solid ice, and becomes an instrument of torture, so much so that on the third day out on the Lena ours were mercilessly clipped.

The post-houses on this road are, as I have said, luxurious as compared to the accommodation found among the Arctic races of Siberia, but I fancy those accustomed to "roughing it," as the word is generally understood in England, would find even a trip as far as Yakutsk rather a trial. Of course, these establishments vary from the best, which are about on a par with the labourer's cottage in England, to the worst, which can only be described as dens of filth and squalor. All are built on the same plan. There is one guest-room, a bare carpetless apartment, with a rough wooden bench, a table, and two straight-backed wooden chairs, and the room is heated to suffocation by a huge stove, which occupies a corner of the room. The flimsy plank partition is unpapered, but generally plastered with the cheap, crudely coloured prints sold by pedlars. Some of these depicted events connected with our recent war in South Africa, and it is needless to add that the English troops were invariably depicted in the act of ignominious flight.[7] I purchased one, in which three distinguished British Generals were portrayed upon their knees imploring mercy of Mr. Kruger, and sent it to England, but it never reached its destination. This work of art had been "made in Germany."

[7] I was surprised by the interest displayed by the Russian settlers of this district anent the Boer War. In every village we were eagerly questioned as to how affairs in the Transvaal were progressing.

In every guest-room, however squalid, four objects were never missing: the sacred Ikon, portraits of the Tsar and Tsarina, and a printed copy of the posting rules. On the wall was generally also a bill of fare, in faded ink, which showed how many generations of travellers must have been duped by its tempting list of savoury dishes. I never could ascertain whether these had ever really existed in the far distant past, or whether the notice was a poor joke on the part of the proprietor. In any case, the *menu* we found was always the same: hot water, sour black bread, and (very rarely) eggs of venerable exterior, for although the inmates of these stations presumably indulge occasionally in meat, no amount of bribery would induce them to produce it for our benefit. Vermin was everywhere; night and day it crawled gaily over the walls and ceiling, about our bodies, and into our very food, and, although the subject did not interest us, a naturalist would have delighted in the ever-changing varieties of insect life. Of the latter, cockroaches were, I think, the most objectionable, for they can inflict a nasty poisonous bite. Oddly enough, throughout Siberia I never saw a rat, although mice seem to swarm in every building, old or new, which we entered. The Lena post-house has a characteristic odour of unwashed humanity, old sheep-skins and stale tobacco. Occasionally, this subtle blend includes a whiff of the cow-shed, which generally means that one or more of its youthful occupants have been carried indoors out of the cold. In winter there is no ventilation whatsoever, save when the heavy felt-lined door is opened and an icy blast rushes in to be instantly converted by the stifling heat into a dense mass of steam. Indoors it was seldom under 80° Fahrenheit, and although divested of heavy furs we would invariably awaken from a sleep of, perhaps, a couple of hours, drenched with perspiration, in which state we would once more face the pitiless cold. In England such extremes of temperature, experienced day after day, would probably kill the strongest man outright, but here they made no appreciable difference in our bodily health.

It was no doubt rough travelling along the Lena, and yet the pleasures of the journey far outweighed its ills. Before reaching the river our way lay across vast deserts of snow, with no objects visible save, at rare intervals, some tiny village almost buried in the drifts, its dark roofs peeping out here and there, and appearing at a distance like pieces of charcoal laid on a piece of white cotton-wool. Beyond these nothing but the single telegraph wire which connects Yakutsk with civilisation. Coated with rime it used to stand out like a jewelled thread against the dazzling sky, which merged imperceptibly from darkest sapphire overhead to tenderest turquoise on the horizon. Who can describe the delights of a sleigh journey under such conditions, or realise, in imagination, the charm and novelty of a wild gallop over leagues of snow behind game little Siberian horses, tearing along to the clash of yoke-bells at the rate of twenty miles an hour! In anything but a Yakute sleigh we should have been in an earthly paradise.

And on fine evenings, pleasanter still was it to lie in the sleigh snugly wrapped in furs, and watch the inky sky powdered with stars—Ursa Major (now almost overhead) sprawling its glittering shape across the heavens, and the little Pleiades twinkling like a diamond spray against dark velvet. At times I could make out every lonely peak and valley in the lunar world, and even distinguish far-away Polaris twinkling dimly over the earth's great mystery. The stars are never really seen in misty Europe.

But a week, ten days, elapses and so little progress is made in the alarming total of mileage that the heart sinks at the mere thought of the stupendous distance before us. Few villages are passed and these are invariably alike. A row of ramshackle huts; at one extremity the post-house with black and white *verst* post, at the other a rough palisade of logs about twenty feet high, enclosing a space from which a grey column of smoke rises lazily into the frosty air. The building is invisible, but it generally contains one or more unhappy exiles wending slowly towards a place of exile. Every village between Irkutsk and Yakutsk has its *Balogan*, or resting-place for political offenders, but in the Far North beyond the Arctic Circle prison bars become superfluous. Nature has taken their place.

There can be no doubt that, for monotony, this journey is unequalled. After a few days surrounding objects seemed to float by in a vague dream. Only the "scroop" of the runners and jingle of the sleigh-bells seemed to be hammered into the brain, for all eternity. And yet, even the bells in their own way were a godsend, for they were changed (with the yoke) at every station, and I liked to think that every one of the hundred and twenty-two stages were accompanied by a different tune! There were other drawbacks to complete enjoyment. On the whole, the weather was still and clear, but occasionally the sky would darken, down would come the snow, and we would flounder about, sometimes for hours, lost in the drifts. Logs frozen into the river, fissures in the ice, and other causes rendered upsets of almost daily occurrence, but it was generally soft falling. I remarked that as we proceeded further north the post-horses became wilder and more unmanageable, and it was often more than the drivers could do to hold them. Twice our sleigh was run away with, and once de Clinchamp and myself were thrown with unpleasant force on to hard black ice. On another occasion the *troika* started off while the driver was altering the harness, and went like the wind before we could clamber on to the box, seize the reins, and stop them. The unfortunate *yemstchik*[8] was dragged with them, and I expected to find the poor fellow a mangled corpse, but we pulled him out from under his team badly cut and bruised, but otherwise little the worse for the accident. He had clung like grim death to the pole, or the heavy sleigh must have crushed him.

[8] Driver.

During daylight we could afford to laugh at such trifles, but at night time it was a different matter. To tear through the darkness at a breakneck pace at the mercy of three wild, unbroken horses required some nerve, especially when lying under the *koshma* as helpless as a sardine in a soldered tin. For the first few days overflows were a constant menace, especially at night when sleep under the apron was out of the question, for any moment might mean a plunge through the ice into the cold dark waters of the Lena. I generally had a clasp-knife ready to slash asunder, at a moment's notice, the ropes which secured the apron to the sleigh. After a time I could lie in the dark and tell with unerring precision whether the sleigh was gliding over the river or the land, and whether, in the former case, the ice was black and sound or that dread element, water, was rippling against the runners. If so, out came the clasp-knife, and there was no more *koshma* for that night. During the first week we frequently passed places where hot springs had broken through the ice. One or two of these holes were quite near the track, and might well, on a dark night, have brought the expedition to an untimely end.

Talking of ice, we noticed a curious phenomenon in connection with it while journeying down the Lena. On clear sunny days the frozen surface of the river would appear to be sloping downwards at a perceptible gradient in the direction in which we were travelling; occasionally it would almost seem as though we were descending a fairly steep hill, had not the unrelaxed efforts of our teams suggested the optical delusion which, as long ago as 1828, was observed by Erman the explorer, who wrote: "I am disposed to think that this phenomenon was connected with the glistening and distortion of distant objects which I remarked not only in this part of the valley, but frequently also on the following days. This proved that the air was ascending from the ice and therefore that the lower strata were lighter than those above in which the eye was placed. Under such circumstances a plane perfectly horizontal and level in fact would appear depressed towards the horizon, or, in other words, it would seem to slope downwards." Scientists must determine whether this be the correct explanation of this strange deception of nature, which was often noticeable on the Lena, although we never observed it elsewhere.

We reached Ust-kutsk (the first town of any importance) on the sixth day. This place figures largely on most English maps, but it is little more than an overgrown village. A church with apple-green dome and gilt crosses, a score of neat houses clustered around the dwelling of an *ispravnik*,[9] perhaps a couple of stores for the sale of clothing and provisions, and a cleaner post-house than usual: such is a "town" on the banks of the Lena. With the exception of Ust-kutsk there are only three, Kirensk, Vitimsk, and Olekminsk, places of such little general interest that they are chiefly associated in my mind with the four square meals we were able to obtain during those three weeks of incessant travel. At Ust-kutsk, for instance, we refreshed the inner man with a steaming bowl of *schtchi* or cabbage soup followed by the tough and greasy chunks of meat that had been boiled in it, and the meal tasted delicious after nearly a week on black bread, an occasional salt fish and dubious eggs. Our own provisions were so hopelessly frozen that we seldom wasted the time necessary to thaw them out into an eatable condition.

[9] An official who combines the duties of Mayor and Chief of Police.

There are salt-mines near Ust-kutsk from which about 50,000 *poods*[10] are annually exported throughout the Lena province, and the forests around here contain valuable timber, but agriculture did not seem so prosperous here as in the districts to the north and south. Oddly enough the cultivation of the land seemed to improve as we progressed northward, as far as Yakutsk, where, as the reader will presently see, the most modern methods of farming have been successfully adopted by a very peculiar and interesting class of people.

[10] A "pood" is thirty-six English pounds

I was told that during the navigation season, from June until the latter end of September, Ust-kutsk is a busy place on account of the weekly arrival and departure of the river steamers. But lying silent and still in the icy grip of winter, this appeared to me to be the most desolate spot I had ever set eyes upon. And we left it without regret, notwithstanding that a darkening sky and threatening snow-flakes accompanied our departure, and the cold and hunger of the past few days had considerably lowered the high spirits in which we had left Irkutsk. Up till now monotony had been the worst evil to bear. In summer time the river as far as Yakutsk is highly cultivated, and smiling villages and fertile fields can be discerned from the deck of a steamer, but in winter, from a sleigh, nothing is visible day after day, week after week, but an unvarying procession of lime-stone, pine-clad cliffs, which completely shut out any scenery which may lie beyond them, and between which the bleak and frozen flood lies as inert and motionless as a corpse. Even at Ust-kutsk, nearly 3000 miles from the Arctic Ocean, the stream is as broad as an arm of the sea, which enhances the general impression of gloom and desolation. But in this world everything is comparative, and we little dreamt, when reviling the Lena, that a time was coming when we should look back even upon this apparently earthly Erebus as a whirlpool of gaiety.

When we left Ust-kutsk at about 3 P.M. night was falling fast, a proceeding which scattered snow-flakes followed with such vigour that only a few *versts* had been covered when we were brought to a standstill by a dense snowstorm, which, with a northerly gale, rapidly assumed the proportions of a blizzard. Providence has mercifully ordained that a high wind seldom, if ever, accompanies a very low temperature or on this occasion (and many others) we should have fared badly. But here and in the Arctic a fall of the glass was invariably accompanied by a rise of the thermometer, and *vice versâ*. During this, our first storm, it was only eight degrees below zero, and even then it was impossible to face the wind for more than a few moments at a time, for it penetrated our heavy fur coats as though they had been of *crêpe-de-chine,* and cut into the face like the lash of a cat-o'-nine-tails. I had never experienced such a gale (although it was nothing to those we afterwards encountered), for the wind seemed to blow from all points of the compass at once as we blundered blindly along through the deep snow, pushing and hauling at the sleighs as well as our numbed hands and cumbersome garments would permit. So blinding was the snow we couldn't see a yard ahead; so fierce the wind we could scarcely stand up to it. Suddenly both teams gave a wild plunge which sent us sprawling on our faces, and when I regained my feet the sleighs were upset and the horses, snorting with terror, were up to their girths in a snow-drift. I then gave up all hopes of reaching a station that night. For over an hour we worked like galley-slaves, and suddenly when we had finally got things partly righted, the wind dropped as if by magic, and one or two stars peeped out overhead. The rapidity with which the weather can change in these regions is simply marvellous. We often left a post-house in clear weather, and, less than an hour after, were fighting our way in the teeth of a gale and heavy snow. An hour later and stillness would again reign, and the sun be shining as before! We now quickly took advantage of the lull to push on, and in a few hours were rewarded by the glimmering lights of a post-house. We had reached the village of Yakurimsk and, being fairly exhausted by the cold and hard work, I resolved to stay here the night. This was our first experience of frost-bite (both faces and hands suffered severely), which is not actually painful until circulation returns, and care must then be taken not to approach a fire. I have always found that snow, vigorously rubbed on the frozen part, is the best remedy. The stage between Ust-kutsk and Yakurimsk was a short one, only about eighteen *versts*, but it took us six hours to make it. When we awoke next morning bright sunshine was streaming into the guest-room, which was older and filthier than usual. But it possessed a cracked and cloudy looking-glass which dimly reflected three countenances swollen and discoloured beyond recognition. For we had neglected to anoint our faces with grease (Lanoline is the best), but after this experience never neglected this essential precaution.

The postmaster at Yakurimsk, a decrepit Pole of benign but unwashed exterior, informed me that the woods around his village swarmed with bears, and that on payment of a few roubles for beaters he could ensure us a good day's sport. But although the offer was tempting I did not feel justified in risking the delay. Wolves had also been numerous, but had, as usual, confined their attacks to pigs and cattle. Before visiting Siberia I had the usual fallacious notion concerning the aggressiveness of this meek and much maligned animal. I remember, in my early youth, a coloured plate depicting a snow scene and a sleigh being hotly pursued at full gallop by a pack of hungry and savage-looking wolves. In the sleigh was a Cossack pale with terror, with a baby in his teeth and a pistol in each hand. I fancy that, in riper years, I must have unconsciously based my estimate of the wolf's ferocity on this illustration, for I have now crossed Siberia four times without being attacked, or even meeting any one who had been molested. The only wolf which ever crossed my path was a haggard mangy-looking specimen, which, at first sight, I took for a half-starved dog. We met in a lonely wood near Krasnoyarsk in Western Siberia, but, as soon as he caught sight of me, the brute turned and ran for his life!

Our drivers and horses were exchanged at every station so that the severe work of the previous night did not retard our progress after leaving Yakurimsk. The weather was fine and we made good headway until the 28th, on the afternoon of which day we reached the second town of Kirensk. A few miles above the latter the Lena makes a wide *détour* of fifty to sixty miles and the post-road is laid overland in a straight line to avoid it. It was a relief to exchange, if only for a few hours, that eternal vista of lime-stone and pines for a more extended view. The Kirensk mountains are here crossed, a range which, although of no great altitude, is precipitous and thickly wooded, so much so that in places the sleighs could scarcely pass between the trees. The climb was severe, but a lovely view over hundreds of miles of country amply rewarded our exertions. The glorious panorama of mountain, stream, and woodland stretching away on all sides to the horizon, intersected by the silvery Lena, was after the flat and dismal river scenery like a draught of clear spring water to one parched with thirst. Overhead a network of rime-coated branches sparkled against the blue with a bright and almost unnatural effect that reminded one of a Christmas card. A steep and difficult descent brought us to the plains again, and after a pleasant drive through forests of pine and cedar interspersed with mountain ash and a pretty red-berried shrub of which I ignore the name, we arrived, almost sorry that the short land trip was over, at Kirensk.

Although not the largest, this is the prettiest and cleanest-looking town on the Lena. Perhaps our favourable impressions of the place were partly due to the dazzling sunshine and still, delicious air. Dull skies and a fog would, perhaps, have made a world of difference; but as, under existing conditions, Kirensk afforded us the only interval of real rest and enjoyment on the Lena, we were proportionately grateful. And it was almost a pleasure to walk through the neat streets, with their gaily-painted houses and two or three really fine stores, where any article from a ship's anchor to a gramophone seemed to be on sale. A few mercantile houses and a busy little dockyard, with a couple of river-steamers in course of construction, explained the prosperous appearance of this attractive little town, which contrasted cheerfully with all others which we saw in Siberia. The inn was quite in keeping with its surroundings, and perhaps a longer time than was absolutely necessary was passed there, for *déjeuner* was served, not in the usual dark fusty room reeking with foul odours, but in a bright, cheerful little apartment with comfortable furniture and a table set with a white cloth and spotless china by a window overlooking the river. There was a mechanical organ, too, which enlivened us with "La Marseillaise" and "Loin du Pays" as a pretty waiting-maid in Russian costume served us with some excellent cutlets and an omelette, which were washed down with a bottle of Crimean wine. These culinary details may appear trifles to the reader, but they had already become matters of moment to us. And the sun shone so brightly that the claret glowed like a ruby in the glass as we drank to the success of the expedition and our friends in far-away France and England. And so susceptible is man to the influence of his surroundings that for one fleeting hour New York seemed no distance away to speak of!

After leaving Kirensk the horses were harnessed *gusem* or tandem fashion, for it is here necessary to leave the river and travel along its shores where the roadway becomes a mere track three or four feet wide through the forests. As our sleighs were unusually broad, this caused some trouble, and once or twice trees had to be felled before we could proceed. When Vitimsk was reached, on February 2, the drivers there flatly refused to embark upon a stage until the breadth of our sleighs had been reduced by at least one-third. Fortunately the weather changed for the worse, and snowstorms and a stiff Northern gale would have greatly impeded us, so that the lost time was not so precious as it might have been. There is no inn at Vitimsk, but the post-house was clean and comfortable, and the *ispravnik*, on reading the Governor's letter, also placed his house and services at my disposal, but I only availed myself of the latter to hasten the alteration to the sleighs. The only wheelwright in Vitimsk being an incorrigible drunkard, this operation would, under ordinary circumstances, have occupied at least a week; under the watchful eye of the stern official it was finished in forty-eight hours. Politically, I am a Radical, but I am bound to admit that there are circumstances under which an autocratic form of Government has its advantages.

Until Vitimsk was reached we had met but few travellers during our journey down the Lena, certainly under a score in all, which was fortunate, considering the limited accommodation *en route*. But at Vitimsk I was destined to come across not only an Englishman but a personal friend. The meeting, on both sides, was totally unexpected, and as on the evening of our arrival I watched a sleigh drive up through the blinding storm and a shapeless bundle of furs emerge from it and stagger into the post-house, I little dreamt that the newcomer was one with whom I had passed many a pleasant hour in the realms of civilisation. The recognition was not mutual, for a week of real Siberian travel will render any man unrecognisable. "Pardon, M'sieu," began the stranger, and I at once recognised the familiar British accent; "Je reste ici seulement une heure." "Faites, monsieur," was my reply. But as I spoke the fur-clad giant looked up from the valise he was unstrapping and regarded me curiously. "Well, I'm d — — d," he said, after a long pause, "if it isn't Harry de Windt." But Talbot Clifton had to reveal his identity, for months of hardship and privation, followed by a dangerous illness, had so altered his appearance that I doubt if even his mother would have recognised her son in that post-house at Vitimsk. Clifton had already passed a year among the Eskimo on the Northern coast of the American continent, when, in the summer of 1901, he descended the Lena as far as its delta on the Arctic Ocean. Here he remained for several months, living with the natives and accompanying them on their fishing and shooting expeditions. In the fall of the year he returned to Yakutsk, where he contracted a chill which developed into double pneumonia, and nearly cost him his life. My friend, who was now on his way home to England, had only bad news for us. The reindeer to the north of Yakutsk were so scarce and so weak that he had only just managed to struggle back there from Bulun, on the delta, a trifling trip compared to the journey we were about to undertake. Moreover, the mountain passes south of Verkhoyansk were blocked with snow, and, even if deer were obtainable, we might be detained on the wrong side of the range for days, or even weeks. All things considered, I would rather not have met Clifton at this juncture, for his gloomy predictions seemed to sink into the hearts of my companions — and remain there. However, a pleasant evening was passed with the assistance of tobacco and a villainous mixture, which my friend concocted with fiery *vodka* and some wild berries, and called punch. I doubt if, before this notable occasion, Vitimsk had ever contained (at the same time) two Englishmen, a Frenchman, and the writer, who may claim to be a little of both.

Talbot Clifton left early the next day, and before sunset the sleighs were finished and we were once more on the road. From Vitimsk I despatched telegrams to the Governor of Yakutsk and the London *Daily Express*, and was surprised at the moderate charges for transmission. Of course, the messages had to be written in Russian, but they were sent through at five and ten kopeks a word respectively.[11]

[11] A kopek is the one-hundredth part of a rouble; the value of the latter is about 2*s*. 1*d*.

Vitimsk is, perhaps, less uninteresting than other towns on the Lena, for two reasons. It is the centre of a large and important gold-mining district, and the finest sables in the world are found in its immediate neighbourhood. Up till four years ago the gold was worked in a very desultory way, but machinery was introduced in 1898, and last year an already large output was trebled. This district is said to be richer than Klondike, but only Russian subjects may work the gold.

Olekminsk (pronounced "Alokminsk") was now our objective point. I shall not weary the reader with the details of this stage, for he is probably already too familiar, as we were at this juncture, with the physical and social aspects of travel on the Lena. Suffice it to say that a considerable portion of the journey was accomplished through dense forests, during which the sleighs were upset on an average twice a day by refractory teams, and that the filthiest post-houses and worst weather we had yet experienced added to the discomfort of the trip. Blizzards, too, were now of frequent occurrence, and once we were lost for nearly eighteen hours in the drifts and suffered severely from cold and hunger. Nearing Yakutsk travellers became more numerous, and we met some strange types of humanity. Two of these, travelling together, are stamped upon my memory. They consisted of an elderly, bewigged, and powdered little Italian, his German wife, a much-berouged lady of large proportions and flaxen hair, with a poodle. We met them at midnight in a post-house, where they had annexed every available inch of sleeping space the tiny hut afforded.

A gale and gusts of sleet rendered further progress impossible for that night, and I was therefore compelled to break in upon the conjugal privacy of the couple and their faithful companion. Monsieur, who was sleeping on the floor, at once made room for us, but Madame, who (with the poodle) occupied the bench, fiercely resented the intrusion and threatened de Clinchamp, the first to enter the room, with summary vengeance if he did not at once retire. This my friend politely did, but it was so bitterly cold outside that I battered at the bolted door of the guest-room until the little Italian emerged, and volubly explained the situation. His massive consort, it appeared, invariably disrobed at night (even in a Lena post-house!), and was not prepared to receive visitors. Gallantry forbade further discussion, and we shared the postmaster's dark closet with his wife and five squalling children. The room, about ten feet by four, possessed the atmosphere of a Turkish bath, and an odour as though it had, for several months, harboured a thriving family of ferrets. But with a lady in the question there was nothing to be done. When we awoke next morning the strange couple had departed. I never saw them again, but from what I afterwards heard at Yakutsk their mission to that city was such a shady one that I question if "Madame's" modesty was not assumed for the occasion.

The remainder of the journey from here to Yakutsk was accomplished without further incident, and the town of Olekminsk so resembles its predecessors as to need no description. We reached the place late at night, but the *ispravnik* was more hospitably inclined than others we had met, and gave us supper while the teams were changed. One of the dishes would certainly have found favour in a Paris restaurant—a fish called "Nelma," which is found only in the Lena, and is served uncooked and in thin frozen slices. Ices and champagne terminated the little repast, which was presided over by our host's pretty wife. The only other guest was one Vassily Brando, a political exile, whose intimacy with the *ispravnik* was strangely at variance with all that I had heard and read concerning exiles in the remoter parts of Siberia. Brando, a Jewish-looking person with keen dark eyes, was undergoing a sentence of eight years here after the usual term of preliminary imprisonment in Europe. During his incarceration Brando had taught himself English, which he now spoke almost fluently. This exile told me that Olekminsk contained twenty other politicals, and was preferred to any other town or village on the Lena as a place of detention. Neither he nor his companions could travel for more than ten versts in any direction without a special permit from the Governor of Yakutsk, but, as the poor fellow pathetically remarked, "That's no great hardship!" The exiles at Olekminsk may frequently receive letters and communicate with their friends (under the supervision of the authorities), and the solace of modern literature is not denied them so long as it is not connected with Socialism. Brando was an ardent admirer of Rudyard Kipling, and could, I verily believe, have passed an examination in most of his works.

POOR YAKUTES.

We took leave of our kind host, Captain Bereskine, at midnight. It was bitterly cold (30° below zero), and I was, therefore, surprised when we alighted at the first post-house, after a long stage of thirty-five miles, to find our host smilingly awaiting us with sandwiches, cigarettes, and a bottle of cognac! He had passed us on the road, determined, even at considerable discomfort to himself, that we should travel, at any rate through his district, in comfort. Such a thing could never have occurred in any country but Siberia, where hospitality is looked upon (amongst Russians) as the first duty of man. Just imagine leaving your host on a cold winter's night in England to travel from London to Edinburgh and finding him waiting at, say, Hitchin to bid you a final farewell. But the *simile* is weak, for there is a vast difference between an open sleigh and a sleeping-car.

An interesting personality we afterwards met on the road to Yakutsk was Dr. Herz, the famous naturalist, whom we fortunately came across in a post-house, for it gave me an opportunity of a chat with the Doctor anent his now well-known discovery, the "latest Siberian Mammoth," which he was conveying in sections, packed in twenty sleighs, to Irkutsk. Dr. Herz gave us, like Talbot Clifton, very disheartening accounts of affairs north of Yakutsk. The Doctor had travelled here from the Kolyma river (our goal on the Arctic Ocean) only with the greatest difficulty on account of the scarcity of reindeer and the dangerous condition of the mountain passes. The task of conveying the mammoth, even as far as this point, had been an almost super-human one, but no trouble or expense had been spared in the preservation of this antediluvian monster, which is undoubtedly the most perfect specimen of its kind ever brought to light. The animal was found frozen into a huge block of ice, as it had evidently fallen from a cliff overhead, for the forelegs were broken and there were other signs of injury. The flesh of the mammoth (which measures about twenty feet high) was of a pinkish colour and as fresh, in appearance, as during the monster's lifetime, countless ages ago. Some grasses found in the mouth had been carefully preserved, and have since been analysed with the view of ascertaining the age of the prehistoric monster. Time was now of the greatest importance to Dr. Herz, for everything depended upon the arrival of his treasure in European Russia in a frozen condition. A few days of warm muggy weather nearing Europe might render futile the task of many months of hardship. So our interview was of short duration, but I am glad to say that the eminent Professor eventually met with success, and that his priceless addition to the treasury of natural history now occupies a niche of honour in the Imperial Academy of Science in Petersburg.

Nearing Yakutsk the country becomes unutterably wild and desolate. Forest trees are now replaced for miles and miles by low withered scrub and dwarf fir-trees on either side of the river. As we proceed the Lena gradually widens until it resembles a succession of huge lakes, where even our practised drivers have some difficulty in finding the way. The Russian language is now seldom heard, for in the villages a kind of native *patois* is spoken. And yet the country is more thickly populated than upriver, although the pretty Russian *isba* has given place to the Yakute *yurta*, a hideous flat-roofed mud-hut, with blocks of ice for window-panes, and yellow-faced weirdly clad inmates, with rough, uncouth manners and the beady black eyes of the Tartar. And one cold grey morning I awaken, worn out with cold and fatigue, to peer with sleepy eyes, no longer down the familiar avenue of ice and pine-trees, but across a white and dreary wilderness of snow. On the far horizon, dividing earth and sky, a thin drab streak is seen which soon merges, in the clear sunrise, into the faint semblance of a city. Golden domes and tapering fire-towers are soon distinguishable, and our driver grows proportionately loquacious as his home is neared. "Yakutsk!" he cries, with a wave of his short, heavy whip, and I awaken de Clinchamp, still slumbering peacefully, with the welcome news that the first important stage of our long land-journey is nearly at an end.[12]

[12] This was on February 14, 1902, and 7800 miles (out of a somewhat alarming total) now lay behind us. To reach this from Irkutsk we had employed 720 horses, at a cost of under £70 for both sleighs

CHAPTER IV

THE CITY OF THE YAKUTE

During our stay in Yakutsk we were the guests of the Chief of Police, an official generally associated (in the English mind) with mystery and oppression, dungeons and the knout. But Captain Zuyeff in no way resembled his prototype of the London stage and penny novelette. By rights our host should have been a cool cynical villain, always in full uniform, and continually turning up at awkward moments to harass some innocent victim, instead of which he was rather a commonplace but benevolent individual devoted to his wife and child and consumed with a passion for photography, which was shared by many of the exiles under his charge. I once had occasion to go to his office and found Zuyeff in his shirt sleeves, busily engaged in developing "Kodak" films with a political who had dined at his house the night before! But this would never have done for a transpontine audience.

Yakutsk (which was founded in 1633 by the Cossack Beketoff) presents, at a distance, a rather imposing appearance, quickly dispelled on closer acquaintance. For a more lifeless, depressing city does not exist on the face of this planet. Even Siberians call this the end of the world. The very name of the place suggests gloom and mystery, for the news that filters through from here, at long intervals, into civilisation is generally associated with some tragedy or disaster, such as the awful fate of poor de Long and his companions of the *Jeannette* in the Lena delta, or more recently the Yakutsk Prison Mutiny. The Tsar's remotest capital is composed mainly of time-bleached wooden buildings of gloomy appearance even on the brightest day. We saw Yakutsk at its best, for in summer time the dusty streets and dingy dwellings are revealed in all the dirt and squalor which were concealed from our gaze by a clean mantle of snow. There are no public buildings to speak of, but the golden domes of half a dozen fine churches tower over the dull drab town, partly relieving the sombre effect produced by an absolute lack of colour. Even the palace of the Governor is a mean-looking one-storied edifice, scarcely fit for the ruler of a province seven times the size of France! A Cossack stockade of great age faces the palace; and its dilapidated wooden walls are tottering with age, but are yet in keeping with most of the houses around them. There is a legend concerning this fort (erected by Cossacks in 1647) which may, or may not, be true. The natives granted these first settlers as much land, for the erection of a citadel, as they could encircle with a limited number of reindeer skins. But the wily Russians cut the skins into thin, very long strips and took possession of an extensive site for a town. At present Yakutsk is a city of the past, one may almost add of the dead, where ghosts walk in the shape of surly Russian traders clad in the fashion of a century ago, and sinister-looking fur-clad Yakutes. And yet the dead here may be said to live, for corruption is delayed for an indefinite period, so intense is the cold. Shortly before our arrival a young Russian girl was exhumed for legal purposes, and her body was found in exactly the same condition as when it was interred five years before. This however is scarcely surprising in a soil which is perpetually frozen to a depth of six hundred feet.

The uncanny sensation of gloom and despondency which here assails the traveller is not mitigated by the knowledge that, to reach Yakutsk you must slowly wade, as we had done, through a little hell of monotony, hunger, and filth. To leave it you must retrace your steps through the same purgatory of mental and physical misery. There is no other way home, and so, to the stranger fresh from Europe, the place is a sink of despair. And yet Yakutsk only needs capital, energy, and enterprise to convert her into a centre of modern commerce and civilisation. Gold abounds in all the affluents of the Lena; last year the output in the Vitimsk district alone was over a quarter of a million sterling, and the soil is practically untouched. Iron also exists in very large quantities, to say nothing of very fair steam coal near the delta; and there is practically a mountain of silver known to exist near the city. Lead and platinum have also been found in considerable quantities further afield. Were the Yakutsk province an American State the now desolate shores of the Lena would swarm with prosperous towns, and the city would long ere this have become a Siberian El Dorado of the merchant and miner.[13] As it is the trade of this place is nothing to what it could be made, in capable and energetic hands, within a very short space of time. Here, as everywhere else on the river, the summer is the busiest season. In

August a fair is held on the Lena in barges, which drift down the river from the Ust-kutsk with European merchandise of every description. In the fall the barges are towed back by steamers, exporting furs, fish, and ivory to the value of twenty million roubles, the goods brought in only amounting to about a twentieth part of that sum. Steamers run frequently in the open season both up and down the river as far as Bulun in the Arctic Ocean, which tiny settlement yearly exports large quantities of salt fish, furs, and walrus tusks.[14]

[13] In face of these natural resources it is satisfactory to note that a line from Irkutsk to Yakutsk could be laid with little difficulty.

[14] Steam navigation on the Lena river was introduced in 1885.

In former days before the Russians annexed the Amur river there was regular communication between Yakutsk and Okhotsk, on the sea of that name, but although the road, or rather track, still exists, it is now rarely used.[15] However, American and Chinese goods do occasionally find their way into Siberia by Okhotsk, for the latter is a free port, and if merchandise is destined for the Lena province, it is cheaper to send it in this way than *viâ* Vladivostok and the Amur, especially as steamers now visit the Sea of Okhotsk every summer, sailing from Vladivostok and making the round trip *viâ* Gijija, Ayan, and Okhotsk.[16] In winter time, when the track is in good condition, the trip from Okhotsk to Yakutsk occupies about a fortnight, with horse sledges. In summer the goods are carried over the mountains to the head of the Nelkan River, which is reached twice during the season by steamers plying from Yakutsk, a journey of two weeks up stream and about half the time down. The Nelkan district is said to be fabulously rich in gold, so much so that Mr. Siberikoff, a prominent Siberian millionaire, lately visited the place with a view to constructing a railway to connect Nelkan with Ayan, on the Sea of Okhotsk, a distance of about two hundred versts.[17] The line would be a costly one, but the country is said to be so rich, that no expense is to be spared in opening it up. Steamers also run from Yakutsk up to Viluisk, but the trade with this place amounts to very little, £5000 or £6000 in all, every summer. Near Viluisk is the Hospital for Lepers founded some years ago by the English nurse, Miss Kate Marsden. In view of the conflicting statements which have appeared in England regarding this institution it is only fair to say that the lady in question is still spoken of in Yakutsk with respect and affection, and that the infirmary, which after much suffering and hardship she contrived to organise, is still in a flourishing condition. In 1901 it contained more than seventy patients in charge of a physician, his two assistants and three sisters of charity.

[15] See projected railway route, chap. xix.

[16] The Port of Ola is now also called at.

[17] This line is now commenced. See chap. xix.

As for the climate here it is no better and no worse than other places in this latitude, although Yakutsk is said to be the coldest place in winter and the hottest in summer in the world. But this is probably a mistake, for I carefully searched records of the temperature kept daily for the past fifteen years, and found that the greatest summer heat experienced during that period was 78° Fahrenheit in the shade, which is cooler than an average English summer; 69° below zero appeared to be the greatest cold here between the months of October and March, while at Verkhoyansk we experienced 78° below zero, which is, I imagine, about as low as the thermometer can fall on this earth. Winter here begins in September, and by the first week in October the country is ice-bound, and semi-darkness and 55° to 65° below zero continue until the spring. In May the Lena breaks up, flooding the country for hundreds of miles and isolating Yakutsk for about a month, during which you can neither get to the city nor leave it.[18] During the three months of summer dust and clouds or mosquitoes render life almost unbearable. And yet Yakutsk is a paradise compared to a certain settlement, which I shall presently describe, within the Arctic circle.

[18] The Lena is not perfectly free from ice until the end of May or early in June. By October 20 it is generally frozen over. "It is a peculiarity of these northern rivers that their waters are mainly derived from the melting snows in June and July, when the Lena, for example, overflowing its banks, spreads here and there to a width of 60 miles or more." —("In the Lena Delta," by G. W. Melville.)

From Paris to New York by Land

The day following our arrival a lunch was given in our honour by the Governor at the Palace, a ramshackle old building, comfortably furnished, but with no attempt at ostentation. The household was more like that of an English country house, and there was none of the stateliness and ceremony here which characterised the Governor's Palace at Irkutsk. Nor was I sorry for it, for in this land of hunger and long distances man can well dispense with formality and etiquette. We sat down over a score to lunch, including half a dozen ladies, one, at least, of whom was young and attractive, and as daintily gowned as though she had just returned from a drive in the Bois de Boulogne. But Madame V—— the bride of a Government official had arrived here too recently to acquire the mildewed appearance (I can use no other term), which every woman seems to acquire after a prolonged residence in Yakutsk. The meal was a merry one and was followed by music and dancing until nightfall, when another repast was served. By the way, although the pangs of hunger had often assailed us on the road, the frequency of meals here was our greatest trial. For they seemed to continue at short intervals throughout the twenty-four hours. The house of our host, the Chief of Police, was, for Yakutsk, an extremely quiet and orderly one, and yet I never once succeeded in getting to bed before 4 o'clock in the morning, chiefly because the principal meal of the day was only served at midnight. Breakfast at 9 A.M. consisted of such dainties as black bread, smoked fish, and *cheese*! This was followed at mid-day by a heavier meal, where wines, beer, and fiery *vodka* played an important part. At 3 P.M. a dinner of several courses was discussed, and at 8 P.M. tea (accompanied by sweets and cakes) was again partaken of. The midnight supper aforementioned wound up the day. A sideboard in the dining-room was laid out with salt fish, ham, *caviar*, raw cucumber, &c., for snacks at odd moments! There was seldom more than about three or four hours sleep, but a siesta was generally indulged in from 4 to 7 P.M., and a stay of ten days here convinced me of the wisdom of this arrangement. Most of the men passed their evenings in gambling at cards, but the women appeared to have absolutely no occupation of a rational kind. The entire city only boasted of three pianos, but nearly every house possessed a gramophone, which generally provided the music after dinner, when the ladies would sit in a silent circle and listen to the ruthless assassination of Massénet and Mascagni, while the men played cards or walked up and down the room chatting and smoking, and frequently adjourning to the buffet, which in Yakutsk is seldom far distant. Once a month an amateur performance is given at the club, and we attended one of these entertainments, which was of a wearisome description, commencing at about 6 P.M. and lasting till long after midnight. Of course there was, as usual, plenty to eat and drink between the acts.[19]

[19] The Russian Admiral Von Wrangell (who visited Yakutsk in 1820) wrote: "The inhabitants are not in an advanced state of intellectual cultivation. They pass much of their super-abundant leisure in somewhat noisy assemblages where eating and drinking play a principal part. After dinner, which is a very substantial meal, and at which *nalivka*, a liquor made of brandy, berries, and sugar, is not spared, the gentlemen pass the afternoon with cards and punch, and the ladies gather round the tea-table."

As sometimes happens in this world men here are far better off than women, for the former are occupied during the day with their professional duties, and, if so inclined, they can obtain excellent fishing and shooting within a day's journey. The Verkhoyansk mountains can be reached in under a week, and here there are elk, wild sheep, and other big game, but for the unfortunate fair sex life is one eternal round of hopeless monotony. There is not even a regiment to enliven the dreariness of existence, for the garrison consists of about one hundred and fifty Cossacks, with only a couple of officers in command. Nor is there a newspaper; only a dry official journal printed once a month, while the telegrams received by the Governor are sent round to subscribers of one rouble per month. In summer it is possible to walk or drive about, notwithstanding the mosquitoes, but in spring or winter-time the women here are often kept indoors for days together by the floods or piercing cold. No wonder that physical strength is soon impaired by an idle life, stimulants, and the eternal cigarette, or that moral laxity should follow the daily contamination of spicy scandal and pernicious French literature. I have heard Siberians assert that Yakutsk is the most immoral city in the world, and (with a mental reservation regarding Bucharest) I felt bound to agree with them. For if only one-half of the tales which I heard concerning the gay doings of the *élite* here were true, then must the wicked little Roumanian capital "take" (to use a slang expression) "a back seat." Apparently this state of affairs has existed for some time, for when Admiral Melville, of the *Jeannette*, was here twenty years ago, searching the coast for his unfortunate shipmates, he attended a reception given on New Year's Eve by the Lieutenant-Governor, and was told by the latter that, "on that night, as on no other, every man had his own wife at his side instead of some other man's."[20]

[20] "In the Lena Delta," by G. W. Melville.

At the time of our visit Yakutsk contained under a score of political exiles, who seemed to be no worse off, socially, than any one else, for they moved freely about in society and were constantly favoured guests of the Chief of Police. The exiles, however, were not permitted to take part in the private theatricals I have mentioned, a restriction which caused them great annoyance. Their loud and unfavourable criticisms from the stalls on the evening in question were certainly not in the best of taste, and, to my surprise, they were not resented by the Governor's staff. This incident will show that, in Yakutsk at any rate, the "politicals" are treated not only with leniency but with a friendly courtesy, which on this occasion was certainly abused. Mr. Olenin, an exile whose term of banishment was expiring, told me that he had no fault whatever to find with Yakutsk as a place of exile, so much so that he had resolved not to return to Russia at the end of his sentence, but to remain here and complete an ethnological work upon which he was engaged. As will presently be seen (in the eighth chapter), I do not in any way hold a brief for the Russian Government, although I have occasionally been accused (in the English Press) of painting its prisons in *couleur de rose* for my own private ends. I simply state what I saw on this and subsequent occasions, and am glad to say that in Yakutsk the condition of the political exiles was as satisfactory as it could possibly be made in such a rigorous climate and amidst such cheerless surroundings.

I obtained from Mr. Olenin a plain and unvarnished account of the Yakutsk prison revolt, and subsequent "massacre," which aroused such indignation in England a few years ago. It was then reported that the political exiles here were subjected to such cruelty while in prison that they unsuccessfully tried to starve themselves and then mutinied, upon which both men and women were mercilessly butchered. As a matter of fact, at the commencement of the incident the exiles were not confined in prison at all, but were living in provisional liberty. What really happened was this. A party (numbering about half a dozen of both sexes), which was bound for Verkhoyansk, carried more baggage than usual, and the season being far advanced, the Governor of Yakutsk directed that the exiles should start forthwith without their belongings, which should be sent after them as soon as possible. Otherwise, he explained, the politicals might not reach their destination before the break-up of the roads, which would probably mean death from starvation or by drowning in the floods. But an angry discussion followed this edict, and as the politicals were assembling in the open street for departure a young student lost his temper and fired his revolver, killing a policeman. A general *mêlée* ensued, during which several persons were accidentally killed and wounded, for a large crowd had been attracted by the sound of firearms. The exiles, Füff, Minor, and Pik, were shot dead on the spot. A young woman, Madame Gouriévitch, about to become a mother, was bayoneted, and died in great agony. Finally, after a hard struggle, the culprits were secured and confined in the prison, where some of them did undoubtedly try to starve themselves in order to escape execution. The case was tried at Petersburg, and three of the ringleaders, Zotoff, Haussmann, and Bernstein, were duly hanged in the Yakutsk gaol. Zotoff, who had been badly wounded during the fight, had to be carried on his bed to the scaffold. The other exiles received long terms of imprisonment at the political prison at Akatui, where I saw and conversed with them in 1894.[21] The women were sent to Viluisk, but have since been liberated.

[21] For further details of this prison see "The New Siberia," by Harry de Windt. Chatto and Windus, London. 1896.

Criminal convicts here are also well cared for, although the prison, which contained about ninety inmates, was old and dilapidated, like almost every other building in the place. But the wards appeared to be fairly clean and well warmed, a comfortable infirmary adjoined the building, and also a home maintained by private subscriptions for the children of prisoners. Enforced idleness seemed to be the chief complaint from which the convicts were suffering, for during the long winter months it is naturally difficult to find them employment.

Being aware that Russian officials are seldom overpaid, the lavish style in which they entertained us astonished me, for provisions of all kinds must, I imagined, always be at famine prices in a town within measurable distance of the Arctic regions. But inquiry proved that I was entirely wrong, and that living here is as cheap, if not cheaper, than in Irkutsk. It used not to be so when, in former days, Yakutsk was surrounded by vast marshes, often submerged, and apparently quite useless for the purposes of cultivation.[22] But these are now converted into fertile plains of grain and pasture, this innovation being entirely due to the "Skoptsi," a religious sect exiled from European Russia, who, by dint of thrift and industry, have raised a flourishing colony on the outskirts of the city.[23] Cultivation was formerly deemed impossible in this inclement region, but now the Skopt exile amasses wealth while the Russian emigrant gazes disconsolately at the former's rich fields and sleek cattle, and wonders how it is all done. For the Skoptsi are up-to-date farmers, employing modern American machinery, which they import into the country *viâ* Vladivostok. And their efforts have been amply repaid, for in 1902 the sale of corn and barley, formerly unknown here, realised the sum of over a million roubles. Thirty years ago this district contained but few herds of cattle, and now nearly two million roubles' worth of frozen meat is annually exported to the various settlements up and down the river. The inhabitants of Yakutsk are also indebted to these industrious exiles for the fact that their markets are now provided with vegetables of most kinds, although only the potato was procurable some years ago. Now cabbages, beetroot, carrots, radishes, cucumbers, and lettuce are to be had in season at a reasonable price, to say nothing of delicious water-melons in August, but I could not find that any other kind of garden-fruit was grown here, although wild berries are both numerous and delicious.

[22] The explorer Dobell wrote: "In the autumn of 1813 I found that agriculture had advanced no further than Olekma (Olekminsk), 600 versts above Yakutsk."

[23] The Skoptsi faith, the practice of which is strictly forbidden in Russia, entails a life of absolute chastity. This sect can only acquire new members by election, since both sexes so mutilate their persons that they can neither beget nor bear children.

The Skoptsi exiles, who number about six hundred, inhabit a village called Markha about seven versts from Yakutsk. Every man and woman in the place (there are of course no children) is a Skopt. We visited Markha one bright morning, driving out with the Governor, his staff and several other officials in about a dozen sleighs in all. Breakfast had been prepared for us at the house of the wealthiest Skopt in the village, and we did justice to it with appetites sharpened by the drive through the keen frosty air. There was a breeze and the cold was piercing, but once indoors the sun streamed into the room with such force that I was compelled to move my seat away from a window. One might have been lunching in the late spring at Nice or Beaulieu. The scrupulous cleanliness of Markha after the dirt and squalor of most Siberian villages was striking. Our host's sitting-room contained even palms and flowers, artificial, of course, but cheerful to the eye. He himself waited on us during the meal, and continually plied his guests with champagne and other rare vintages, for the Skopt, although a miser at heart, is fond of displaying his wealth. Avarice is the characteristic of these people, although they are kind to their own poor. We visited an institution maintained solely by the village for the old and decrepit of both sexes, and this place would have done credit to a European city. On the way to this establishment we passed several windmills, a rare sight in Siberia, also a number of corn and saw mills driven by steam. The engines were of American make, also all the agricultural machinery, which was shown us with pardonable pride. In every shed we entered the cattle looked sleek and well fed, and the poorest and tiniest hut had its poultry yard. The Lena Province now contains over 300,000 head of cattle, and their number is yearly increasing. When the Skoptsi first came here, forty years ago, cows and oxen were numbered by the hundred.

Books and European newspapers were plentiful in all the houses we visited in Markha, and the Skoptsi with whom I conversed were men of considerable intelligence, well up in the questions of the day. But their personal appearance is anything but attractive. Most of the men are enormously stout, with smooth flabby faces and dull heavy eyes, while the women have an emaciated and prematurely old appearance. The creed is no doubt a revolting one, physically and morally, but with all his faults the Skopt has certain good points which his free neighbours in Yakutsk might do well to imitate.[24]

[24] When a Skopt dies, his property is confiscated by the State, but he generally finds means to dispose of his wealth in other ways. Occasionally it is buried in remote places, where it remains if not discovered by accident.

Although the Yakutes form the bulk of the population in Yakutsk (the entire province contains about a quarter of a million) they do not mix a great deal with the Russians, and we saw little of the better class. As a race the Yakutes are not interesting, while in appearance both sexes are distinctly plain, and often repulsive. The type is Mongolian; sallow complexion, beady eyes, flattened nostrils and wiry black hair. The men are of medium height, thick set and muscular, the women ungainly little creatures, bedizened with jewellery, and smothered with paint. Some marry Russians and assume European dress, which only adds to their grotesque appearance. Notwithstanding their defects the Yakutes are extremely proud of their birth and origin, and consider themselves immeasurably superior to the Russians, who, they say, are only tolerated in the country for commercial purposes. A Yakute is therefore mortally offended if you call his chief town by anything but its native name: "The City of the Yakute."

Many Yakutes grow wealthy in the fur, fish or ivory trades, and are so shrewd in their dealings that Russians have christened them the "Jews of Siberia." But although cunning and merciless in business matters this Siberian financier becomes a reckless spendthrift in his pleasures, who will stake a year's income on the yearly Yakutsk Derby (which takes place over the frozen Lena), or squander away a fortune on riotous living and the fair sex. All who can afford it are hard drinkers, and champagne is their favourite beverage. The men of all classes wear a long blouse of cloth or fur according to the season, baggy breeches and high deerskin boots,—the women loose flowing draperies adorned, in summer, with bright silks and satins, and in winter with costly sables. A lofty head-dress of the same fur is worn in cold weather. The poorer Yakute is a miserable mortal. He has no warlike or other characteristics to render him of any interest whatsoever, like, say his Tchuktchi brethren in the Far North. For the Yakute peasant is too stupid to be treacherous, and as cowardly as the Tchuktchi is brave, and, while his wealthier compatriots have learned to a certain extent the virtue of cleanliness, the poor Yakute is generally nothing but a perambulating bundle of filthy rags, the proximity of which, even in the open air, is almost unbearable. But this is only amongst the peasantry. The town-bred Yakutes are more civilised and cleanly in their habits, and many are employed by the Russians as domestic servants. All Yakutes pay a pole tax of four roubles to the Russian Government, those possessed of means paying in addition an income tax. Ten years ago taxes were levied in furs, but they are now paid in coin of the realm. I was surprised to find that these natives are self-governed to a certain extent; minor crimes, such as theft, petty larceny, &c., being judged by prominent men in the towns and the head-man of each village. Murder and more serious crimes are dealt with by a Russian tribunal in Yakutsk.

I shall not forget my surprise one day when nearing Yakutsk to overhear one driver apparently addressing another in pure Turkish, a language with which I am slightly acquainted. The mystery was explained by Captain Zuyeff, who told me that there is such a marked resemblance between the language in question and Yakute that a merchant from Constantinople would readily be understood in the market-places of this far-away frozen land. Many words are precisely similar, and the numerals up to ten are identical (see Appendix). On several occasions, while crossing the Yakute region, the natives failed to comprehend my meaning in Russian, but when I spoke in Turkish they at once understood me.[25]

[25] "This race is supposed to be a Turkish branch of the Turanian stock. Latham informs us that their language is intelligible at Constantinople, and that the majority of their words are Turkish;

observing, also, that their traditions bespeak for them a Southern origin. He says: 'The locality of the Yakutes is remarkable, it is that of a weak section of the human race pressed into an inhospitable climate by a stronger one, yet the Turks have ever been the people to displace others rather than be displaced themselves.'"—"Frozen Asia," by Professor Eden.

We experienced considerable difficulty in getting away from Yakutsk, indeed had I not possessed my invaluable passport the expedition would probably have remained there. For every day invitations came pouring in for days ahead, and the entertainers would not hear of a refusal. At last, however, firmness became necessary, and I insisted (being empowered by my magic document to do so) upon immediate preparations being made for our departure, although every official in the place urged me to abandon a project which they averred could only end in disaster. By suggestion of the Governor a Siberian Cossack from the garrison, Stepan Rastorguyeff, joined the expedition to accompany us so far as I should deem expedient, for our further progress now bristled with difficulties. This man was employed to escort political exiles to the distant settlement of Sredni-Kolymsk, near the Arctic Ocean, and was therefore acquainted with the best way of reaching that remote post, indeed he afterwards proved an invaluable addition to our party.

It seemed hard that fate should have selected this year of all others to render the journey from Yakutsk to the north almost an impossibility. In the first place reindeer were so scarce and weak that the 1800 odd miles to Sredni-Kolymsk (which can generally be accomplished, under favourable circumstances, in four or five weeks) might now take us three months to cover. In this case failure of the journey and a summer in this dreary settlement would be our fate; for from May until October, Sredni-Kolymsk is isolated by marshy deserts and innumerable lakes, which can only be crossed in a sled. Throughout the summer, therefore, you can neither reach the place nor leave it.

A still more serious matter was an epidemic which had been raging amongst the Yakutes of the far north, and a fear of which had driven the Tchuktchis (or natives of the coast) into the interior of their country and along the seaboard in an easterly direction until their nearest settlement was now nearly six hundred miles distant from Sredni-Kolymsk, at which place I had calculated upon finding these natives, and utilising them as a means of procuring food and lodging and guidance along their desolate coast. Now, however, over six hundred miles of ice without a stick of shelter or mouthful of food stared me in the face. It was also suggested that, if many of the Tchuktchis had perished from the dread malady the remainder might have retreated in a body inland, in which case death from starvation seemed an unpleasant but not unlikely contingency. For beyond the aforesaid six hundred miles lay another stretch of about 1600 miles more, before we could reach our destination: Bering Straits.

Lastly, Sredni-Kolymsk had itself suffered from so serious a famine that an expedition had lately been despatched from Yakutsk to the relief of the sufferers. Provisions there would therefore be unprocurable. Also, most of the dogs in the Kolyma district had perished from a scarcity of fish the previous season, and as dogs were our sole means of transport along the Arctic Coast, the reader will admit that, all things considered, my expedition did not leave Yakutsk under the rosiest of conditions!

Nevertheless I cannot hope to adequately repay the kindness shown by every official in Yakutsk, from the Governor downwards, during that trying time, for it was undoubtedly their timely assistance which eventually kindled the bright flame of success out of the ashes of a forlorn hope. As soon as it was realised that my resolve to proceed northward was inflexible, every man worked to further my ends as though he himself was embarking upon the hazardous trip. Even the Governor was continually concocting plans to render our voyage as easy as possible, and to that end despatched a Cossack three days ahead of us, so that reindeer might be forthcoming at the stations without delay. But his Excellency evidently looked upon the scheme as a mad one, and my daily anxiety was lest he should suddenly take the initiative, set the wires in motion with Irkutsk, and put a final stopper on our departure for America—overland.

We now disposed of our cumbersome Yakute sleighs and exchanged them for "nartas," or reindeer-sleds, each drawn by four deer. A "narta" is a long narrow coffin-shaped vehicle about 7 ft. long by 3 ft. broad, fitted with a movable hood, which can be drawn completely over during storms or intense cold. The occupant lies at full length upon his mattress and pillows, smothered with furs, and these tiny sleds were as automobiles to wheelbarrows after our lumbering contrivances on the Lena. A reindeer-sled is the pleasantest form of primitive travel in the world, over smooth hard snow; but over rough ground their very lightness makes them roll and pitch about like a cross Channel steamer, to the great discomfort of the traveller.

Furs were my next consideration, for here we discarded civilised clothing and assumed native dress. The reader will realise what the cold must have been when I say that we often shivered inside the covered sleighs (where, however, the temperature never rose above 10° below zero), under the following mountain of material: two pairs of Jaeger singlets and drawers, thin deerskin breeches and three pairs of thick worsted stockings. Over this a suit of Arctic duffle (or felt of enormous thickness), and a pair of deerskin boots reaching above the knee and secured by leathern thongs. Then a second pair of deerskin breeches and a garment called by the Yakutes a "kukhlanka," a long, loose deerskin coat reaching to the knees, with a hood of the same material lined with wolverine. Under this hood we wore two close-fitting worsted caps and a deerskin cap with ear flaps. Two pairs of worsted gloves and one of bearskin mits, reaching almost to the elbow, completed the outfit. I had hoped to procure furs for a moderate price in Yakutsk. But for some occult reason deerskins cost almost as much here as in Moscow. The good old days are past when peltry was so cheap and European goods so dear, that an iron cauldron fetched as many sable skins as it would hold! Stepan also insisted upon the purchase of a number of iron horse-shoes, which he explained were to be affixed to our moccasins in order to cross the Verkhoyansk mountains in safety. But the method did not strike me at the time as practical, and I afterwards had even less respect for its inventor.

Lastly provisions had to be purchased. Our original outfit brought from London comprised rations sufficient for six weeks; but this I was determined not to break in upon, unless absolutely necessary, before the Arctic coast was reached. There was hardly any food to be procured between Yakutsk and Verkhoyansk, and, according to Stepan, still less beyond that isolated village. A reindeer-sled was therefore packed to its utmost capacity with black bread, salt fish, various tinned provisions, and a portion of some animal unknown, weighing (in a raw condition) about 100 lbs. I use the term "animal unknown," as, when cooked at the first station, the latter looked and tasted exactly like horse-flesh. I mentioned the fact to Stepan, who was already installed as *chef*, and he informed me that horse was regarded as a great delicacy by the Yakutes, and fetched twice the price of any other meat in their city. "It was bought as beef," added the Cossack, "so that anyhow we have got the best of the bargain." There was nothing, therefore, for it but to fall to with knife and fork, and with as little repulsion as possible, upon the docile friend of man!

We started for the unknown with a caravan of six sleighs in all, of which two were loaded down with food and baggage. The night of our departure, February 21st, was fine, and a crowd assembled in front of our host's house to bid us farewell. But although long and lingering cheers followed us out of the city, I fancy many of these well-wishers regarded us more in the light of harmless lunatics than as pioneers of a great railway which may one day almost encircle the world. Just before our departure (which was preceded by a dinner-party), a picturesque but rather trying ceremony took place. Farewells having been said we retired to don our furs and were entering the sleds when our hostess recalled us from the frosty night air into the drawing-room, where the heat was that of a hothouse. "You must not take your furs off," said our host, as I was divesting myself of a portion of my cumbersome costume, "remain just as you are." And so we returned to the brightly lit apartment, where the guests had assembled, and here, with a solemnity befitting the occasion, they turned toward the sacred "ikon," and knelt and prayed for our safety and success. This is an old and pretty Russian custom now obsolete in Europe. And I was almost ungrateful enough to wish, as I knelt in my heavy furs, streaming with perspiration, that it was no longer practised in Siberia! But the affecting little ceremony was soon over, and after a final adieu to our kind hosts, my caravan slid silently down the snowy, starlit street. An hour later the lights of Yakutsk had faded away on the horizon, and we had bidden farewell to a civilisation which was only regained, six long months later, at the gold-mining city of Nome in Alaska.

CHAPTER V

THE LAND OF DESOLATION

Lieutenant Schwatka, the famous Alaskan explorer, once remarked that a man travelling in the Arctic must depend upon his own judgment, and not upon the advice of others, if he would be successful. The wisdom of his words was proved by our journey from Yakutsk to Verkhoyansk. Every one at the former place, from the Governor downwards, assured me that certain failure and probable disaster must inevitably attend an attempt to reach Verkhoyansk in under six weeks. Fortunately I turned a deaf ear to well-meant, but unwise, counsel, for in less than nine days we had reached the place in question, and had left it again on our way northward in under a fortnight from the time we left Yakutsk. I should add that our rapid rate of speed was entirely due to Stepan, without whose aid we should probably have taken at least three times as long to complete the journey. But the wiliest of Yakute postmasters was no match for our Cossack, whose energetic measures on previous trips had gained him the nickname of *Tchort* (or "the devil") on the Verkhoyansk track. And a devil he was when drivers lagged, or reindeer were not quickly forthcoming at the end of a stage!

There are two routes from Yakutsk to Sredni-Kolymsk, near the Arctic Ocean, which was now our objective point. These cannot be called roads, or even tracks, for beyond Verkhoyansk (which is only one-third of the distance) the traveller must depend almost entirely upon his compass and the stars. The oldest route to the Kolyma is now very seldom used, although Von Wrangell travelled over it in the early part of the nineteenth century. On this occasion the Russian explorer avoided Verkhoyansk, and, proceeding some distance south of the route we selected, passed through the ruined, and now deserted, town of Zashiversk. By Stepan's advice we chose the Verkhoyansk route, as being the one best known to the Cossack, for it is the one by which political exiles invariably travel. Politicals, Cossacks, and natives alone visit these desolate northern wastes, unless it be a special mission like ours or that of Dr. Herz. The

Governor of Yakutsk had held his post for nearly twenty years, and yet had never summoned the courage to visit even Verkhoyansk. Nor could any of his officials advise me, from personal experience, which road to select, although their remarks on the subject recalled the darkie's advice to the cyclist as to the best of two pathways across a swamp: "Whichebber one you travels, Boss, I guess you'll be d——d sorry you didn't take de udder!"

Horses were used for the first three stages out of Yakutsk, along a narrow track through the forests, vaguely indicated by blazed trees. It was anything but pleasant travelling, for our light *nartas* were specially adapted to the smooth, level stride of the reindeer, and the ponies whisked them about like match-boxes, occasionally dashing them with unpleasant force against a tree-trunk. It was, therefore, a relief to reach Hatutatskaya on the second day, and to find there thirty or forty sturdy reindeer tethered around the station. The method of harnessing this animal is peculiar. Each sled is drawn by four deer, two abreast. In front of the four wheeler is a kind of miniature sled, or platform on runners, on which the driver sits to control the two leaders in front of him. There are no reins, the entire team being managed by a thong attached to the off-leader, and the traces are secured by a loop round the neck, and inside the outer leg of each deer. The latter carried no bells, and although it may sound childish to say so, we missed their music terribly at first. The driver is armed with a long pole, which, however, he seldom uses, for, if the Yakute has a virtue, it is kindness to animals. A plaintive cry, which sounds like *"yahee,"* is uttered to urge on a team, and it generally has the desired effect, for the Siberian reindeer is the gamest animal in the world. I have seen them working incessantly day after day, growing weaker hour by hour, and yet bravely struggling on until the poor little beasts would fall to the ground from sheer exhaustion, never to rise again. We lost many during the long and trying journey to the Arctic, and I shall always recall their deaths with a keen pang of remorse. For their gentle, docile nature made it the more pitiable to see them perish, as we looked helplessly on, unable to alleviate their agony, yet conscious that it was for our sake they had suffered and died.

From Paris to New York by Land

The distance from Yakutsk to Verkhoyansk is 934 versts, or about 625 English miles. Most of the way lies through a densely wooded region and across deep swamps, almost impassable in summer. About half-way the Verkhoyansk range is crossed, and here vegetation ceases and the country becomes wild in the extreme. Forests of pine, larch, and cedar disappear, to give place to rugged peaks and bleak, desolate valleys, strewn with huge boulders, and slippery with frozen streams, which retard progress, for a reindeer on ice is like a cat on walnut-shells. The *stancias*, as the deer-stations are called, are here from forty to sixty versts apart. There are no towns in this region, or even villages in our sense of the word, for a couple of dilapidated huts generally constitute the latter in the eyes of the Yakute. As for the *stancias* they were beyond description. I had imagined that nothing could be worse than a Lena post-house, but the latter were luxurious compared to the native *yurta*, which is merely a log-hut plastered with mud. You enter a low, narrow aperture, the door of which is thickly padded with felt, and find yourself in a low dark room considerably below the surrounding ground, with a floor of beaten mud, slippery with the filth of years, and windows of ice. The walls are of mud-plastered logs, also the ceiling, which would seriously inconvenience a six-foot man. As soon as the eye grows accustomed to the gloom you find that a rough wooden bench surrounds the apartment, and that one portion of it is strewn with wet and filthy straw. This is for the guests. When it was occupied we slept on the floor, and there was little difference, except that cattle also shared the *stancia*, and were apt to walk over us during the night. A fire of pine-logs was kept blazing on the clay hearth night and day, and the heat was sometimes so overpowering that we suffered almost as much from it as from the deadly cold outside. But the stench was even worse to endure, especially when cooking operations were in progress, for the Yakute will not look at fresh pure meat. He prefers it in a condition that would repel a civilised dog, and the odour that used to emanate from a mass of putrid deer-meat, or, worse still, tainted fish, simmering on the embers, is better left to the imagination. At first we suffered severely from nausea in these unsavoury shelters, and there were other reasons for this which cannot here be explained. Suffice it to say that it was a constant source of wonder to me that even this degraded race of beings could live amidst such bestial surroundings and yet survive. Vermin had up till now been a trifling inconvenience, but thousands on the Lena were here succeeded by myriads of the foe, and, for a time, our health suffered from the incessant irritation, which caused us many days of misery and nights of unrest. Stepan told me that in summer the *stancias* were unapproachable, and this I could well believe seeing that we were often driven out of them during dry and intense cold. But in the open season only Cossacks attempt to travel through with the mail to Verkhoyansk, once each way. The journey, which is made on horseback, is a perilous one, owing to unfordable rivers and dangerous swamps, and the mail carriers are occasionally drowned, or lost in the marshy deserts, where they perish of starvation. Stepan had once made the summer trip, and sincerely hoped he might never have to repeat the experiment.

Travellers on this road are luckily rare, so that the post-houses seldom contained any guests besides ourselves. The *stancias* were crowded enough as it was with the Yakute postmaster and his generally numerous and disgusting family, several deer-drivers, and perhaps two or three cows crowded into a space of about thirty feet square. We travelled throughout the twenty-four hours, and only stopped at these places sufficiently long to thaw out some food and swallow a meal. The *stancias* were too far apart to work on a schedule, and we generally left one rest-house with very vague notions as to when we should see the next. On one occasion we were compelled to lay-to in a storm for eighteen hours (although the *stancia* was only a couple of miles away), and to subsist during that time on chocolate and black bread, frozen to the consistency of iron.[26] But luckily the weather was, on the whole, favourable. Most of the nights were clear, and at first there was a bright moon, which was also an advantage, although at times our way lay through forests so deep and dark that it became necessary to use lights. We left Paris supplied with an elaborate electric outfit, which now, and in after-days, would have been a godsend, but the lamps and cumbersome batteries had to be abandoned with our other stores at Moscow. Probably the cold would have rendered the wires useless, at any rate I consoled myself by thinking so.

[26] On such occasions Christy's "Kola Chocolate" is invaluable.

Two days' hard travelling brought us to Tandinskaya. This is the best *stancia* on the road, and we therefore seized the opportunity to make a good, substantial meal and snatch a few hours' sleep before proceeding to the next rest-house, which was nearly a hundred miles distant. At Tandinskaya we changed teams, successfully resenting the extortionate charges made by the postmaster. All the *stancias* on this road are leased by the Government to Yakute peasants, who are legally entitled to receive three kopeks a verst for every pair of deer. This sum includes post-house accommodation, such as it is; but as we always added a rouble or two for the use of these filthy hovels, Stepan was the more incensed at this postmaster's rascality. The latter claimed payment for about fifty versts more than we had actually covered, so Stepan averred, although the distances north of Yakutsk are very vague, and the Cossack was probably wrong. It was amusing to compare the mileage as given in the only post-book of this road (compiled in the reign of the Empress Catherine) with the real distances, which were invariably twice as long. The officials of those days probably reflected that, if three kopeks must be paid for a verst, the latter had better be a long one. And the Yakute, knowing no better, suffered in silence.

On leaving Tandinskaya, we travelled some miles along the river Aldan, a tributary of the Lena, which is dangerous in winter on account of numerous overflows. Our drivers, therefore, proceeded with caution, walking some distance ahead of the sleds, and frequently sounding the ice with their long poles. It was bitterly cold, for a breeze was blowing in our faces, and the deer, as usual, slipped and slithered in all directions, continually upsetting the sleds. This became such a common occurrence that, after a couple of days, we took it as a matter of course, and I would often awaken from a nap inside the hood to find myself proceeding face downwards, the sled having overturned. But the driver would merely halt the team and replace the *narta*, with its helpless inmate, on its runners, with the indifference of a child playing with a toy horse and cart. Luckily the deer never attempted to bolt on these occasions, but waited patiently until their burthen was placed "right side up."

To-day the wind became more boisterous, and the cold consequently more piercing every mile we travelled. We had left Tandinskaya about ten at night, and towards morning Stepan calculated that we had covered twenty miles in seven hours. The stars had now disappeared, and snow was falling fast, also the wind had risen to a gale, which percolated the felt hoods and furs like a stream of iced water. At daybreak the weather turned to a blizzard, which raged for twenty-four hours and nearly buried us in snow; but when the storm lulled a bit we struggled painfully on for about fifteen miles, and hailed the sight of a *povarnia* with delight, for it meant, at any rate, shelter and a fire. *Povarnias* are merely mud-huts erected at intervals along the track, when the *stancias* are long distances apart. They are dark, uninhabited hovels, generally half full of snow, and open to the winds, and yet these crazy shelters have saved many a traveller from death by cold and exposure on this lonely road. A *povarnia* contains no furniture whatever; merely a clay hearth and some firewood which previous travellers have left there, perhaps weeks before. For on leaving these places every one is expected to cut fuel ready for those who come after. Sanga-Ali was the *povarnia* we had now reached, and it was almost blocked by snow which had drifted in through the open doorway. But we set to with a will, and were soon crouching over a good fire on which a pot of deer-meat was fragrantly simmering. Here we remained until early next morning, taking it in turns to pile on fresh logs, for when the flame waned for an instant the cold became so intense that to sleep in it without a fire might have had unpleasant results.

Sordonnakia, the second *povarnia*, was reached after a journey of nine hours, by which time the weather had again become still and clear. Fortunately, bright calm days prevailed south of Verkhoyansk, although in mid-winter these are the realms of eternal darkness. But in our case spring was approaching, and on fine mornings I could throw open my *narta* and bask in warm sunshine while contemplating a sky of sapphire and smoking a cigar—one of the last, alas! I was likely to enjoy on this side of America. On such days the pure frosty air would exhilarate like champagne, and there was only one drawback to perfect enjoyment: the body would be baked on one side by the scorching rays, and frozen in the shade on the other. Another inconvenience was hunger, for there was never more than one square meal in the twenty-four hours, and often not that, and nothing resists cold like a well-lined stomach. Our sufferings were undoubtedly great from Yakutsk to the Arctic Ocean, but they were greatly alleviated by the fact that it was generally possible, even in the coldest weather, to enjoy a cigarette under cover of the hood. A pipe was, of course, out of the question, for the temperature (even under the felt covering) was never over 10° below zero, which would have instantly blocked the stem with frozen nicotine. But a Russian *papirosh* could always be enjoyed in peace, if not comfort, out of the wind, and I have derived relief through many an hour of misery through their soothing influence.

A brief halt only was made at Sordonnakia, for the *povarnia* had been left in such a disgusting state by its last occupants that we were compelled to eat in our sleds. The fifty versts between this place and the *stancia* of Beté-Kul were rapidly accomplished, and during this stage we came in sight of the Verkhoyansk range, a chain of precipitous mountains which would form one of the chief stumbling-blocks to the construction of the proposed All-World Railway. If the Paris-New York line is ever laid it will probably not run through Verkhoyansk. The direction would rather be east direct from Yakutsk to the Okhotsk Sea although that is also mountainous enough. Nearing Beté-Kul the landscape became yet wilder and more desolate, and we travelled along valleys of deep snow and across dark, lonely gorges, the depths of which even a brilliant sunshine could not penetrate. What this region may be like in summer-time I know not, but in winter the surface of the moon itself could scarcely present a more silent, spectral appearance.

At Beté-Kul we were kept some time waiting for reindeer, which had to be brought in from a considerable distance. Deer generally take some finding, as they stray sometimes fifteen or twenty miles from a *stancia* in search of moss, but, in our case, long delays had been avoided by the Cossack who preceded us. The *stancia* at Beté-Kul was kept by a more prosperous-looking Yakute than usual, and his wife was attired in bright silks and wore a profusion of massive gold jewellery. The Yakutes are expert goldsmiths, but chiefly excel in the manufacture of arms, especially a kind of *yataghan*, or huge dagger, which is stuck into the waistband. Yakute steel is much more flexible than Russian, although I have seen a knife made out of the former sever a copper coin as neatly as though it were a meat-lozenge.

We shared the postmaster's meal at Beté-Kul, and were introduced to a peculiar dish, which deserves mention as showing the extraordinary digestive powers of these people. It was a kind of jelly extracted from reindeer-horns and flavoured with the bark of the pine tree, which is scraped into a fine powder for the purpose. I was fated to subsist in after days on disgusting diet of the most varied description, but to this day the recollection of that Beté-Kul jelly produces a faint feeling of nausea, although I can recall other ghoulish repasts of raw seal-meat with comparative equanimity. Pure melted butter formed the second course of this Yakute *déjeuner*, each guest being expected to finish a large bowl. Stepan, however, alone partook of this tempting dish, but he merely sipped it, while our host and his wife drained the hot, oily mess as though it had been cold water. But Yakutes will consume any quantity of butter in this condition. Dobell, the explorer, says that a moderate Yakute butter-drinker will consume from twenty to thirty pounds at a sitting. The same traveller adds that "at other times these natives drink butter as a medicine, and declare it excellent for carrying away the bile." This was written nearly one hundred years ago, and it is curious to note that the most modern European treatment for gall-stones should now be olive oil, given in large quantities, presumably to produce a similar effect to that obtained by the butter of the Yakute. By the time this weird meal was over the deer had arrived, and I declined our host's offer of a pipe of Circassian tobacco, which would probably have finished me off completely. Both sexes here smoke a tiny Chinese pipe, with bronze bowl and wooden stem, which half a dozen whiffs suffice to finish. The stem is made to open so that the nicotine may be collected, mixed with wood shavings, and smoked again.

We left Beté-Kul at four in the morning, intending, if possible, to cross the mountains during the day, but the pass had lately been blocked with snow and the natives reported it in a terrible condition. But time would admit of no delay and I resolved to make the attempt at all hazards. Anna-sook, a miserable little *povarnia* near the foot of the mountain, was reached after a journey of five hours. The hut was, as usual, full of drifted snow, which we had to remove before breakfasting in an atmosphere of 12° below zero, upon which a roaring fire made no appreciable impression. Oddly enough, in this deserted shanty we came upon the sole sign of life which we had encountered (outside of the *stancias*) all the way from Yakutsk. This was a tiny field-mouse, which had survived the Arctic winter, curled up in a little mound of earth in a corner of this cold, dark shanty. The poor little half-frozen thing could scarcely move, but we gathered some fir-boughs and made it a nest, and left with it a goodly supply of biscuit-crumbs, which it devoured with avidity and a grateful look in its beady black eyes.

Starting at midday we commenced the ascent of the mountain, which is crossed by probably the most remarkable pass in the world. From a distance it looked as though a perpendicular wall of ice, some hundreds of feet in height, must be scaled in order to gain the summit. Before ascending, the iron horse shoes brought from Yakutsk were fastened to our moccasins, ostensibly to afford secure foothold, but I discarded these awkward appendages after they had given me five or six bad falls, and my companions did likewise. About two hours of severe work, increased by deep snow and the rarefied atmosphere, brought us to the summit, the reindeer and sleds ascending by a longer but much less precipitous route. During the ascent there were places where a slip must have meant a dangerous, if not fatal, fall, for midway up a precipice of over a thousand feet was crossed by a slippery ledge of ice about three feet in width. Looking down on the northward side, a frozen snow-slope, about a mile in length, was so steep, that it seemed impossible to descend it without personal injury. We awaited the sleds for nearly three hours on the summit, almost perished with cold in a temperature of nearly 45° below zero, accompanied by a strong breeze which resembled one described by a friend of the writer, a Chantilly trainer, as a lazy wind, viz., one that prefers to go straight through the body instead of the longest way round. To descend, the deer were fastened behind the sleds, which we all held back as much as possible as they dashed down the incline. But nearing the valley the pace increased until all control was lost, and we landed in a deep snow-drift half-way down, men, deer, and sleds being muddled up in inextricable confusion. I remember thinking at the time what a fortune such a snow-slide would make for its proprietor at Earl's Court. Imagine an "ice chute" more than a mile in length. To stand upright was even now, half-way down the mountain, out of the question, so the rest of the perilous descent was ignominiously accomplished on all-fours. We reached the valley in safety, followed by the sleds, which were now restrained only by drivers and deer. From below they looked like flies crawling down a white wall. At this point the Verkhoyansk mountains are about 4500 ft. above the level of the sea.

Leaving the mountains we were soon lost in the forests again, and from here to Kangerak, the first station on the northern side of the range, the journey is one of wondrous beauty, for the country strikingly resembles Swiss Alpine scenery. In cloudless weather we glided swiftly and silently under arches of pine-boughs sparkling with hoar-frost, now skirting a dizzy precipice, now crossing a deep, dark gorge, rare rifts in the woods disclosing glimpses of snowy crag and summit glittering against a sky of cloudless blue. The sunny pastures and tinkling cow-bells of lovely Switzerland were wanting, but I can never forget the impressive grandeur of those desolate peaks, nor the weird, unearthly stillness of the lonely, pine-clad valleys at their feet.

We passed a comfortable night at Kangerak, for the long, fatiguing day had rendered us oblivious to the attacks of the vermin with which the *stancia* swarmed. My ears had been badly frost-bitten crossing the pass and caused me great pain, but I slept soundly, and so did my companions who had escaped scot-free. Only one circumstance marred my satisfaction at having successfully negotiated the pass; three of our deer had perished from exhaustion. From Kangerak we travelled some distance along the river Yana, which scatters itself into a series of lakes on either side of the main stream. There are dangerous overflows here, and twice we narrowly escaped a ducking, or perhaps a worse fate, although I fancy the river at this point is very shallow. Nevertheless I heard afterwards at Verkhoyansk that whole caravans, travellers, drivers and deer have occasionally been fatally submerged here, or frozen to death after their immersion. Our deer, as usual, fell about on the ice in all directions, and one, breaking its leg, had to be destroyed. The stage was a hard one, so much so that we halted at a *povarnia* (Mollahoi) for the night. Towards morning I was awakened by the stifling heat and a disgusting odour due to the fact that our drivers had discovered a dead horse in the neighbourhood and were cooking and discussing its remains. Stepan opined that the animal had expired some weeks previously, and I could well believe it. A couple of hours before reaching Mollahoi, Harding caught sight of some ptarmigan within a few yards of the track. I mention the fact as this was the only game we came across throughout the whole of the journey of nearly three months from Yakutsk to the Arctic Ocean.

When the *stancia* of Siremskaya was reached on February 27, I realised with intense satisfaction that the journey, at any rate as far as Verkhoyansk, was practically over. For if this portion of the voyage had been successfully overcome in so short a time why should not the remainder as far as Sredni-Kolymsk be accomplished with equal facility?

And so we travelled on from Siremskaya with renewed hopes and in the best of spirits, although nearing Verkhoyansk the cold became intense—strong gales and heavy snowstorms prevailed—and we all suffered severely. Indeed once Clinchamp was carried out of his sled and into the *povarnia*, a journey of twenty consecutive hours having temporarily deprived him of the use of his limbs. The thermometer had marked 40° below zero even inside my closely covered sled, and one of my feet was also badly frozen, owing, however, to my carelessness in neglecting to change my foot-gear the previous night, for if this is not done the perspiration formed during the day congeals, during sleep, into solid ice. Harding escaped any ill effects, but in truth, although I have said little about physical sufferings, most of that journey was terrible work. I got into a way at last of classifying the various stages of frigidity on departure from a *stancia*, and this was their order: (1) the warm; (2) the chilly; and (3) the glacial. The first stage of comparative comfort was due to the effect of a fire and warm food and generally lasted for two or three hours. In stage No. 2, one gradually commenced to feel chilly with shivers down the back and a sensation of numbness in the extremities. No. 3 stage was one of rapidly increasing cold, until the face was covered by a thin mask of ice formed by the breath during the short intervals of sleep, or rather stupor. The awakening was the most painful part of it all, and when the time came to stagger into some filthy *stancia*, I would have often preferred to sleep on in the sled, although such an imprudence might have entailed the loss of a limb.

At last one bright morning in dazzling sunshine we reached Verkhoyansk, having made the journey from Yakutsk in eight days, a record trip under any circumstances, especially so under the adverse conditions under which we had travelled. I had looked forward to this place as a haven of warmth and rest, and perhaps of safety from the perilous blizzards that of late had obstructed our progress, but the sight of that desolate village, with its solitary row of filthy hovels, inspired such feelings of aversion and depression that my one object was to leave the place as soon as possible, even for the unknown perils and privations which might lie beyond it. It was absolutely necessary, however, to obtain fresh reindeer here, and a stay of at least a couple of days was compulsory. What we saw, therefore, and did in Verkhoyansk will be described in the following chapter.

CHAPTER VI

VERKHOYANSK

Loyal Russians call Verkhoyansk the heart of Siberia. Political exiles have another name for the place also commencing with the letter H, which I leave to the reader's imagination. Suffice it to say that it applies to a locality where the climate is presumably warmer than here. Anyway the simile is probably incorrect, as there are many worse places of banishment than Verkhoyansk, although, indeed, the latter is bad enough. For if prosperous villages near the borders of Europe impress the untrammelled Briton with a sense of unbearable loneliness, conceive the feelings of a Russian exile upon first beholding the squalid Arctic home and repulsive natives amongst whom he is destined, perhaps, to end his days. Forty or fifty mud-plastered log huts in various stages of decay and half buried in snow-drifts over which ice windows peer mournfully, a wooden church pushed by time and climate out of the perpendicular, with broken spire and golden crosses mouldering with rust—on the one hand, a dismal plain of snow fringed on the horizon by a dark pine forest; on the other, the frozen river Yana, across which an icy breeze moans mournfully—such is Verkhoyansk as we saw it on the morning of February 28, 1902. I thought that a more gloomy, God-forsaken spot than this could not exist on the face of the earth. But I had not seen Sredni-Kolymsk. And yet, if we were here forty-eight hours and it seemed a lifetime, what must an enforced sojourn of five or six years mean to the unhappy exiles, some of whom had been here for a quarter of a century. Let the reader imagine, if possible, the blank despair of existence under such conditions; day after day, year after year, nothing to do or look at of interest, tortured by heat and mosquitoes in summer, perished by cold and hunger in the dark, cruel winter, and cut off as completely as a corpse from all that makes life worth living. An exile here told me that the church was his only link with humanity, for it recalled other sacred buildings in which loved ones were worshipping, far away in the busy world of freedom. One could imagine a man entirely losing his identity after a few years here and forgetting that he was ever a human being. In truth Yakutsk was bad enough; but Yakutsk, compared to Verkhoyansk, is a little Paris. And yet, I repeat, this is by no means the worst place of banishment in North-Eastern Siberia.

The *ispravnik* received us in the official grey and scarlet, reminding me that even in this remote corner of the Empire a traveller is well within reach of Petersburg and the secret police. But we found in Monsieur Katcherofsky a gentleman and not a jailer, like too many of his class, whose kindness and hospitality to the miserable survivors of the Arctic exploring ship *Jeannette*, some years ago, was suitably rewarded by the President of the United States.[27] Katcherofsky's invaluable services for twenty years past might also have met, by now, with some substantial recognition at the hands of the Russian Government, for a more honest, conscientious and universally popular official is not to be found throughout the dominions of the Tsar.

[27] The U.S. Arctic exploring steamer *Jeannette* was crushed in the ice and sank on June 12, 1881, in the Arctic Ocean, some hundreds of miles N.-E. of the mouth of the Lena river. Captain de Long and his party, in three ship's boats, made their way over and through the ice towards the Lena delta, but one of the boats (under Lieut. Chipp) foundered with all hands. Another one, commanded by Chief Engineer (now Admiral) Melville, reached the Siberian coast and found the natives and salvation, but Captain de Long and his crew landed on the Lena delta, and being unable to find a settlement or procure food, his entire party, consisting of twelve persons, perished, after horrible sufferings, of exposure and starvation. The bodies were eventually found by Melville, and conveyed to America for interment.

The *ispravnik's* house, or rather hut, was no better, within or without, than others in Verkhoyansk, which consists of one street, or rather straggling avenue of mud hovels with ice windows and the usual low entrance guarded by a felt-covered door. The entire population does not exceed four hundred souls, of whom, perhaps, half were Yakutes and the remainder officials, Russian settlers and political exiles. Talking of exiles, I have found that, as a rule, very erroneous impressions exist in England as to the conditions under which they are sent to Siberia, a country which has often been greatly maligned by the English Press. For this great prison-land is not always one of dungeons and lifelong incarceration. The latter certainly awaits the active revolutionist, but, on the other hand, an erring journalist may, for an "imprudent" paragraph, be sent to vegetate for only a couple of months within sight of the Urals. As Gilbert's "Mikado" would say, "the punishment fits the crime." And in the towns of Western Siberia I have frequently met men originally banished for a short term who, rather than return to Russia, have elected to remain in a land where living is cheaper, and money more easily gained than at home. Olenin, of Yakutsk, was a case in point.

The exile of State offenders to Siberia is generally carried out by what is called the "Administrative Process," or, in other words, by a secret tribunal composed of civil and military members. There are no Press reports of the trial, which is held strictly *in camera*, and, as a rule, a political "suspect" vanishes as completely from the face of the earth as a pebble cast into the sea. Usually the blow falls unexpectedly. A man may be seated quietly at home with his family, in his office, or at some place of public entertainment when the fatal touch on the shoulder summonses him away, perhaps for ever. The sentence once passed, there is no appeal to a higher court, nor can a prisoner hold any communication whatever with the outer world. An exile's relatives, therefore, when ignorant of his fate, frequently ascribe his absence to voluntary motives, and years sometimes elapse before the truth is known. In some cases it never reaches his family, and the harassing thought that he is, perhaps, regarded by the latter as a heartless deserter has driven many a victim of the "Administrative Process" to self-destruction.

A term of imprisonment varying from six months to two years in a European fortress invariably precedes a term of exile, and this rule applies to both sexes. There are hundreds of towns and villages throughout Siberia where men and women are domiciled for various periods of their existence, but as we are now dealing only with the remoter settlements within the Arctic Circle we will follow the footsteps of a political exile deported to, say, Verkhoyansk. From the forwarding prison at Moscow to the city of Irkutsk in Eastern Siberia, politicals not sent by rail travel with a criminal gang, wear prison dress, and live practically the same as ordinary convicts. At night time, however, in the *étapes*[28] a separate cell is set apart for their use. On arrival at Irkutsk prison-dress is discarded, and an exile may wear his own clothes, although he remains under lock and key and in close charge of the Cossack who is responsible for his safe delivery. In summer-time the two-thousand-miles' journey to the first stage northwards, Yakutsk, is made by river-steamer, but during the winter months this weary journey must be accomplished in uncovered sleighs, and is one of great severity and privation, especially for women. At Yakutsk reindeer-sledge conveys the ill-assorted pair ever northwards for another six hundred miles to Verkhoyansk. The reader has seen the difficulties which we experienced crossing the mountains, where delicate women on their way to exile are compelled to clamber unassisted over giddy places that would try the nerves of an experienced mountaineer. I should add that women never travel alone with a Cossack, but are always accompanied on the journey by another exile, either a man or one of their own sex. In the former case, an acquaintance is occasionally made which ends in a life-long *liaison*, if not marriage. Every year from three to six "politicals" arrive in each of the settlements north of Yakutsk.

[28] Rest-houses for convict gangs along the great post-road.

An empty hut was set apart for our use: a tumble-down *yurta* of mud with the usual ice-windows, which necessitated the use of candles even on the brightest day. But it contained two rooms and a kitchen, and was weather-proof, so we lived in comparative luxury. Meals were provided for us at Katcherofsky's hospitable board, and on the evening of our arrival we sat down to a supper to which the kind-hearted old *ispravnik* had invited several "politicals." And here, for the second time, I witnessed the incongruous sight of a Chief of Police amicably hobnobbing with the exiles in his custody. And when one of the latter remarked at table, "I can always feel cheerful in Katcherofsky's house, *even in Verkhoyansk*," I could well believe that our genial and good-natured host was looked upon more in the light of a friend than a guardian by both men and women of the free command. It was a strange but enjoyable evening, and the *menu* of delicious *sterlet* brought from the Lena, roast venison, and ice-cream, accompanied by a very fair champagne, was hardly one which you would expect to find in these frozen wastes. Coffee and *nalivka*, a liquor made of the wild raspberries which grow freely around here, concluded the last decent repast we were likely to enjoy for some months to come. Only one displeasing memory do I retain of that otherwise pleasant supper-party: I smoked my last cigar!

There were under a dozen exiles in all here, of whom two were women. One of the latter was my neighbour at supper;—Madame Abramovitch, a fragile little woman, whom delicate features and dark, expressive eyes would have rendered beautiful, had not years of mental and physical suffering aged and hardened the almost girlish face. Abramovitch, her husband, a tall, fine-looking man of Jewish type, was only thirty-two years old, but his life since the age of twenty-one had been passed in captivity either in Russian prisons or as an exile in Siberia. Abramovitch and his wife were shortly to be released, and it was pathetic to hear them babble like children about their approaching freedom, and of how they would revel in the sight of Warsaw, and enjoy its restaurants and theatres, and even a ride in the electric cars! I visited them next day in their dark and miserable home, which, however, was scrupulously clean, and we drank tea and discussed people and events in distant Europe far into the night. And Madame sang Polish love-songs in a sweet, pathetic voice, and I recounted one or two American yarns in Yankee vernacular which excited inordinate gaiety, so easily amused were these poor souls with minds dulled by long years of lethargy and despair. And I wondered, as I glanced around the squalid room, how many years had elapsed since its mud-walls had last echoed to the sounds of genuine laughter!

Abramovitch and his wife spoke French fluently, the former also English. But two-thirds of the political exiles I met throughout the journey spoke two, and sometimes three, languages besides their own, while German was universal. In most cases the exiles had taught themselves, often under the most adverse conditions, in the gloomy cell of some Polish fortress or the damp and twilit casemates of SS. Peter and Paul. Most exiles make it a rule on their banishment to take up some subject, history, chemistry, natural science, &c., otherwise insanity would be far more prevalent amongst them than it is. At Verkhoyansk books are occasionally obtainable, but further north their scarcity formed a serious drawback to study and mental recreation. Even at Verkhoyansk the censure on literature is very strict, and works on social science and kindred subjects are strictly tabooed by the authorities. On the other hand almost any kind of novel in any language may be read, so long as it does not refer in any way to the Russian Government and its methods. At the time of our visit "Quo Vadis" was on everybody's lips, and the solitary copy had been read and re-read into rags, although it had only been a month in the settlement. Dickens, Thackeray, Zola, and Anthony Hope were favourite authors, but whole pages were missing from most of the volumes in the tiny library, and the books were otherwise mutilated, not by carelessness or ill usage, but by incessant use.

I closely questioned Abramovitch as to the conditions of life at Verkhoyansk and he said that so far as the treatment of the exiles was concerned there was nothing to complain of, but the miserable pittance allowed by the Government for the lodging and maintenance of each exile was, he justly averred, totally inadequate where even the common necessaries of life cost fabulous prices. Apparently this allowance varies in the various districts; thus, at Verkhoyansk it is eighteen roubles, at Viluisk, south of Yakutsk, only twelve! Fortunately, deer-meat is fairly cheap here, but all other provisions are outrageously dear. Flour, for instance, costs twenty-five kopeks or about 6*d*. per pound, milk (in a frozen condition) five kopeks or about 3*d*. per pound, but the latter is bought from the Yakutes, and is generally in a filthy and undrinkable condition. Tea and sugar are so dear that the former is boiled over and over again, but Abramovitch said that he suffered more from the loss of light than anything else, for candles (or rather tallow dips) cost a rouble a pound. My friend was therefore reduced to the dim light shed by the flickering logs of his fire throughout the dreary winter, when daylight disappears for two months. And even in summer time there is no way of eking out the slender sum allowed for existence, which must suffice for lodging and clothes as well as food. Poultry does not exist, the Yana yields few fish, and the soil stubbornly refuses to produce vegetables even of the hardiest kind. By dint of ceaseless care Katcherofsky had contrived to grow a few watery potatoes, which were served at table with as much ostentation as early strawberries or asparagus in England; but the experiment was not a success. The *ispravnik* had also tried cabbages, with a similar result. This seems strange, seeing that Yakutsk, only six hundred miles further south, is a fertile land of plenty, but an exile told me that even in midsummer the forests around Verkhoyansk appear withered and grey, the very grass seems colourless, and the daisies and violets scentless immortelles. This sterility of nature seems to be confined to a radius of about twenty miles of Verkhoyansk, for beyond this arid circle trees flourish, grass grows freely as far as the timber line, while beyond it the *tundra*, from May until August, is gaily carpeted with wild flowers.

Verkhoyansk is not unhealthy. The worst season of the year is in autumn, when dense mists from the river Yana often shroud the place for days together. Bronchitis and rheumatism are then very prevalent, also a kind of epidemic catarrh, which, however, was not confined to the fall of the year, but was raging at the time of our visit. Of this fact we had unpleasant proof, as a couple of days after leaving the place the whole expedition (except Stepan) were attacked with this troublesome complaint, which, in my case, was only cured on arrival in America. I fancy this disease was closely allied to that which attacked Admiral Von Wrangell's party early in the nineteenth century.[29] But all things considered, summer is the most trying season here, not only on account of the heat, which is far greater than that of Yakutsk, but of the mosquitoes, which make their appearance before the snow is off the ground and do not disappear until late in the fall. The exiles said that they were often deprived of sleep for nights together on account of these pests, which swarm in and out of doors, and inflict a nasty poisonous bite. Children had died from the fever produced from the irritation and consequent sleeplessness. This, and continual (and therefore distressing) daylight, made the advent of winter, even with all its cold and darkness, a welcome one. For this season also brings another blessing to these poor outcasts, news from home, which reaches here once a month by reindeer-sledge, whereas in summer a mail is only once despatched from Yakutsk, and frequently fails to arrive at its destination.[30]

[29] In 1820 Von Wrangell wrote: "During my stay in Verkhoyansk a kind of epidemic catarrhal fever prevailed throughout the district; the symptoms were violent depression of the chest, noise in the ears, headache, etc.... A Cossack whom I had previously sent forward with my papers died of the epidemic; every one was more or less ill."

[30] The telegraph wire ceases at Yakutsk.

In addition to his literary pursuits Mr. Abramovitch had kept a record of the temperature during his term of exile, and the result of his careful observations for a period of twelve years was as follows: Mean temperature for the whole year, 4° below zero Fahrenheit. In hard winters the thermometer was frequently 75° below zero, and once touched the almost incredible point of 81° below zero. During our stay only 65° below zero was registered, but at the first *stancia*, two hundred miles north of Verkhoyansk, we experienced 78° below zero, a cold so intense that the breath froze as it left our lips and fell in a white powder to the ground. And yet, I can assure the reader that I have suffered more from cold in Piccadilly on a damp, chilly November day than in the coldest weather in this part of Siberia. For the atmosphere here is generally dry and does not permeate the frame like that of our sea-girt, foggy island. Also, during extreme cold there is never any wind, and this is fortunate, for although 60° or 70° below zero are quite bearable in stillness, 30° or 40° higher, accompanied by only a moderate gale, would probably kill every living thing before it. A few weeks later, when we reached the Arctic Ocean, the approach of a gale was always preceded by a rising thermometer, and clear, cold weather by a fall of the same.

At Verkhoyansk, as at Yakutsk, nothing met me but difficulties, and the *ispravnik* implored me to abandon the journey. Sredni-Kolymsk, he said, was twelve hundred miles away, and with weak reindeer it might take us a couple of months to reach the Tsar's remotest settlement. This would bring us into early May, and about the first week in June the thaw comes, and travelling is impossible. And even at Sredni-Kolymsk another two thousand miles of wild and desolate country, almost bereft of inhabitants, would lie between us and

Bering Straits. Not only Katcherofsky but the exiles begged me to abandon the journey, if not for my own sake, for that of my companions. It was unfair, they urged, to drive men to almost certain death. Altogether I don't think I shall ever forget the hours of anxiety I passed at Verkhoyansk. Should we advance or should we retreat was a question which I alone had the power to decide, and one which Providence eventually settled for me with the happiest results. Nevertheless, even in the dark days which followed, when lost in the blinding blizzards of Tchaun Bay, or exposed to the drunken fury of the Tchuktchis on Bering Straits, I have seldom passed a more unpleasant and harassing period of my existence than those two days under the care of Ivan Katcherofsky, Chief of Police of Verkhoyansk, North-Eastern Siberia.

But notwithstanding adverse pressure on all sides I resolved to burn my boats, and push on, although well aware that, Verkhoyansk once left behind us, there would be no retreat. And it is only fair to add that my companions were just as keen on an advance as their leader. The *ispravnik*, seeing that further argument was useless, shrugged his shoulders and solely occupied himself with cramming the sledges full of interesting looking baskets and bottles. And on the bright sunlit morning of March 2 we left Verkhoyansk, our departure being witnessed by our kindly old host and all the exiles. Our course this time was in a north-easterly direction towards the shores of the frozen sea. Before the start a pathetic little incident occurred which is indelibly photographed on my memory. My small supply of reading matter comprised a *"Daily Mail* Year Book," and although very loth to part with this I had not the heart to take it away from a young exile who had become engrossed in its contents. For the work contained matters of interest which are usually blacked out by the censor. "I shall learn it all off, Mr. de Windt," said the poor fellow, as the Chief of Police for a moment looked away, and I handed him the tiny encyclopædia. "When we meet again I shall know it all by heart!" But twelve long years must elapse before my unhappy friend bids farewell to Verkhoyansk! Nevertheless, the almost childish delight with which the trifling gift was received would have been cheaply bought at the price of a valuable library.

THE CHIEF OF POLICE, VERKHOYANSK.

CHAPTER VII

THROUGH DARKEST SIBERIA

Let the reader picture the distance, say, from London to Moscow as one vast undulating plateau of alternate layers of ice and snow, and he has before him the region we traversed between the so-called towns of Verkhoyansk and Sredni-Kolymsk. Twelve hundred miles may not seem very far to the railway passenger, but it becomes a different proposition when the traveller has to contend against intense cold, scanty shelter, and last, but not least, sick reindeer. For the first seven or eight hundred versts we passed through dense forests, which gradually dwindled away to sparse and stunted shrubs until the timber line was crossed and vegetation finally disappeared. The so-called *stancias*, filthier, if possible, than those south of Verkhoyansk, were now never less than two hundred miles apart. There were also *povarnias* every eighty miles or so, but these were often mere shapeless heaps of timber rotting in the snow. Throughout the whole distance there was no track of any kind and the sledges were steered like ships at sea, our course being shaped by compass and an occasional rest-house or *povarnia*, and these were easily passed unnoticed on a dark night, or after a heavy snow-fall had concealed their low log walls.

> "League on league on league of desolation,
> Mile on mile on mile without a change"

aptly describes the long, dreary expanse that stretches from the Yana River to the Polar Sea, for I doubt if there is a more gloomy, desolate region on the face of this earth. So sparsely is it peopled that even a small town can moulder away here into non-existence and no one be the wiser for years after its disappearance. The authenticity of the following anecdote is vouched for by Mr. George Kennan, the American traveller, who quotes from Russian official statistics.[31]

[31] "Siberia and the Exile System," by George Kennan.

"In the year 1879 there was living in the city of Pultava a poor apothecary named Schiller, who was banished as a political offender to the village of Varnavin, in the Province of Kostroma. Schiller, finding a forced residence in a village to be irksome and tedious, and having no confidence in petitions, changed his location without asking leave of anybody, or in other words ran away. About this time the Tsar issued a command directing that all exiles found absent from their places of banishment without leave should be sent to the East Siberian Province of Yakutsk. When, therefore, Schiller was rearrested in a part of the Empire where he had no right to be, he was banished to Irkutsk, and the Governor-General of Eastern Siberia was requested to put him under police surveillance in some part of the territory named in the Imperial command. Governor-General Anuchin, who had then recently come to Irkutsk, and who had not had time apparently to familiarise himself with the vast region entrusted to his care, directed that Schiller be sent to the district town of Zashiversk, which was (supposed to be) situated on the River Indigirka, a few miles south of the Arctic Circle. A century, or a century and a half, ago Zashiversk was a town of considerable importance, but for some reason it lost its pre-eminence as a fur-trading centre, fell gradually into decay, and finally ceased to exist. Its location was still marked by two concentric circles on all the maps, its name continued to appear regularly in the annals of the Governor-General's Office, and I have no doubt that a coterie of 'Tchinovniks'[32] in Irkutsk were dividing and pocketing every year the money appropriated for repairs to its public buildings; but, as a matter of fact, it had not contained a building or an inhabitant for more than half a century, and forest trees were growing on the mound that marked its site. Poor Schiller, after being carried three or four times up and down the Rivers Lena and Indigirka in a vain search for a non-existent Arctic town, was finally brought back to Yakutsk, and a report was made to the Governor-General that Zashiversk had ceased to exist! The Governor-General therefore ordered that the prisoner be taken to Sredni-Kolymsk, another 'town' of forty-five houses, situated on the River Kolyma north of the Arctic Circle, 3700 miles from Irkutsk and 7500 miles from the capital of the Empire. When, after more than a year, the unfortunate druggist reached the last outpost of Russian power in North-Eastern Asia, and was set at liberty, he made his way to the little log church, entered the belfry, and proceeded to jangle the church bells in a sort of wild, erratic chime. When the people of the town ran to the belfry in alarm and inquired what was the matter, Schiller replied, with dignity, that he wished the whole population to know that 'by the Grace of God, Herman Schiller, after long and perilous wanderings, had reached, in safety, the town of Sredni-Kolymsk!' Months of fatigue, privation and loneliness had probably deprived the poor fellow of his reason, a not unusual occurrence in this isolated portion of the great Russian Empire. But the local police reported to the Governor-General that the exile Schiller was disorderly and turbulent, and that he had caused a public scandal before he had been in Sredni-Kolymsk twenty-four hours, and upon receipt of this information the Governor-General endorsed an order to remove the offender to some place at least twelve versts distant from the town. His idea was probably to have Schiller sent to some small suburban village in the general neighbourhood of Sredni-Kolymsk. Unfortunately there was no suburban village within a hundred miles in any direction, and the local authorities, not knowing what else to do, carried the wretched druggist about twelve versts out into the primæval wilderness, erected a log cabin for him, and left him there. What eventually became of him I don't know."[33]

[32] Petty officials.

[33] No wonder Zashiversk figures to this day on most English maps, when it is shown on an official map of the Russian General Staff published as late as 1883!

The first stage out from Verkhoyansk, one of a hundred and fifty versts, was rapidly accomplished in less than twenty-four hours. This was wonderful travelling, but the snow was in perfect condition, indeed as hard and slippery as ice, for at the first *stancia* the cold was greater than any we experienced throughout the whole journey from France to America, the thermometer registering 78° below zero (Fahr.). We remained here for some hours waiting for reindeer, but the heat and stench of the rest-house produced such nausea that more than once during the night I was compelled to don my furs and brave a temperature that rendered even inhalation painful, and instantly congealed the breath into a mass of ice. To make matters worse, the hut was crowded with Yakutes of loathsome exterior and habits, and a couple of cows and some calves also occupied the foul den, which, of course, swarmed with vermin. And so did we, after passing the night here, to such an extent as to cause actual pain for some days afterwards whenever we left the outer air for a warmer temperature. Oddly enough, these rest-houses were usually crowded with people, who presumably never left them, for in the open we never encountered a solitary human being, nor indeed a single animal or bird, with the exception of a dead ermine which had been caught in a trap and which our Yakute drivers, with characteristic greed, promptly took from the snare and pocketed. Talking of ermine, the district of Sredni-Kolymsk has always been famous as a fruitful breeding-place of this pretty little creature, and they used to be obtainable there at an absurdly low price, from sixpence to a shilling apiece. A friend had therefore commissioned me to procure him as many skins as we could conveniently carry, intending to make a mantle for as many halfpence as the garment would have cost him pounds in England. But we found that ermine had become almost as costly in Sredni-Kolymsk as in Regent Street. The price formerly paid for a score would now barely purchase one, for the Yakutsk agents of London furriers had stripped the district to provide furs for the robes to be worn at the Coronation of his Majesty the King of England. Far-reaching indeed are the requirements of royalty!

It was impossible to procure food of an eatable kind here, or indeed at any other *stancia* throughout this part of the journey. The *ispravnik* at Verkhoyansk had assured me that deer-meat would always be forthcoming; and so it was, in a putrid condition which rendered it quite uneatable. There was nothing else obtainable but frozen milk (generally black with smoke and filth), so we were compelled to subsist solely on the meat from Yakutsk, so long as it lasted, and on "Carnyl,"[34] a kind of palatable pemmican brought from England and intended only for use on the Coast. And we afterwards nearly perished from starvation in consequence of this premature indulgence in our "emergency rations."

[34] "Carnyl" (invented by Dr. Yorke-Davies) is a patent food I can heartily recommend to Arctic explorers, as it is not only sustaining but very palatable.

Shortly after leaving Aditscha, we crossed the river of that name, which flows into the Yana below Verkhoyansk. The former stream is noted for its abundance of fish, which, in summer time, is salted and exported in large quantities to the various settlements throughout the district. Travelling steadily for forty-five versts we crossed the Tabalak mountains (or rather hills), and from here under fifteen versts brought us to Tostach, where the accommodation was a shade less atrocious than at Aditscha, and where we again had to pass the night to await a relay. Stepan tried the effect of threats, and then of kicks, but even the latter failed to arouse the postmaster to any great extent, for the Yakutes add laziness to their other numerous vices, which include an arrant cowardice. Treat one of these people with kindness and he will insult you; thrash him soundly, and he will fawn at your feet. This constant delay in the arrival of the deer now began to cause me some anxiety, for Stepan said that he had frequently had to wait three or four days for these animals at a *stancia*.

Tostach was only outwardly cleaner than Aditscha, for when the inmates of the *stancia* had retired to rest, the warmth and firelit silence brought out such overwhelming legions of vermin that I rose and, lighting a candle, proceeded to beguile the hours until the dawn with a "Whitaker's Almanack," which, with a Shakespeare and "Pickwick," now composed our library. And here an incident occurred which might well have startled a person with weak nerves, for the most practical being scarcely cares to be suddenly confronted, at dead of night, with a ghostly apparition unpleasantly suggestive of graveyards. On this occasion the spectre might have dropped from the clouds, for I looked up from my book for an instant, and noiselessly as a shadow it appeared before me, a shapeless thing in rags with a pale and gibbering face framed in tangled grey locks. A tinkling sound accompanied every movement of the creature, and I then saw that the figure was adorned from head to heel with scraps of iron, copper coins, rusty nails, and other rubbish, including a couple of sardine-tins which reassured me as to the material nature of the unwelcome visitor. When, however, the intruder showed signs of friendliness and nearer approach, I aroused Stepan, who sprang to his feet, and, with one heave of his mighty shoulders, sent the intruder flying into the darker recesses of the *stancia*. "It's only a

Shaman," muttered the Cossack with a yawn, as he rolled back into the dirty straw, and I then regretted that I had not more closely examined this High Priest of, perhaps, the weirdest faith in existence, for an hour afterwards, when the rekindled fire had once more rendered objects clearly visible, the "Shaman" had left the hut as silently and mysteriously as he had entered it.

Shamanism is strictly prohibited by the Russian Government, although many Yakutes practise its rites in secret, and the Tunguses[35] know no other faith. Only few Europeans have beheld the weird ceremonies performed by these people, generally at night in the depths of the forest or out on the lonely "Tundra," far from the eye of officialdom. The most lucid description of Shamanism which I have been able to obtain is that given by Mr. J. Stadling, the Swedish explorer, who led a few years ago an expedition through Northern Siberia in search of Monsieur André. Mr. Stadling writes: "The Universe, according to the Shamans, consists of a number of layers, or strata, which are separated from each other by some kind of intermediate space or matter. Seven upper layers constitute the kingdom of light, and seven or more lower layers the kingdom of darkness. Between these upper or lower layers, the surface of the earth, the habitation of mankind, is situated, whence mankind is exposed to the influence both of the upper and the lower world—*i.e.*, the powers of light and of darkness. All the good divinities, spirits and genii, which create, preserve and support the weak children of men, have their abode in the upper layers, in the world of light. In the layers of the lower world the evil divinities and Spirits lurk, always seeking to harm and destroy mankind. In the highest layers (the 'Seventh Heaven'), the Great Tangara, or 'Ai-Toion,' as he is called in Northern Siberia, is enthroned in eternal light. He is perfect and good, or rather is exalted above both good and evil, and seems to meddle very little with the affairs of the Universe, caring neither for sacrifices nor prayers. In the fifth or ninth layer of the lower world, the fearful Erlik-Khan, the Prince of Darkness, sits on a black throne, surrounded by a court of evil spirits and genii. The intermediate layers are the abode of divinities and spirits of different degrees of light and darkness; most of them are the spirits of deceased men. All spirits exert influence on the destiny of man for good or evil; the children of men are unable to soften or to subdue these spiritual beings, whence the necessity of Shamans or Priests, who alone possess power over the spiritual world."[36]

A VISITOR.

[35] The Tunguses number about 12,000 to 15,000, and inhabit the region lying to the north-west and north-east of Yakutsk.

[36] "Through Siberia," by J. Stadling. London, 1901.

I met some years ago at Tomsk, in Western Siberia, a fur-trader who had once secretly witnessed a Shaman ceremony, which he thus described to me: "Half a dozen worshippers were gathered in a clearing in a lonely part of the forest and I came on them by accident, but concealed myself behind some dense undergrowth. In a circle of flaming logs I saw the Shaman, clad in pure white and looking considerably cleaner than I had previously thought possible. Round his neck was a circular brass plate signifying the sun, and all over his body were suspended bits of metal, small bells, and copper coins, which jingled with every movement. The ceremony seemed to consist of circling round without cessation for nearly an hour, at the end of which time the Shaman commenced to howl and foam at the mouth, to the great excitement of his audience. The gyrations gradually increased in rapidity, until at last the Priest fell heavily to the ground, face downwards, apparently in a fit. The meeting then dispersed and I made my escape as quickly and as silently as possible, for had I been discovered my life would not have been worth a moment's purchase."

The museum at Yakutsk contains some interesting relics pertaining to Shamanism, amongst others some articles found near the Lena, in the tomb probably of an important personage, for the grave contained valuable jewellery, arms and personal effects. I observed that everything, from garments down to a brass tobacco-box, had been punctured with some sharp instrument, and Mr. Olenin explained that all articles buried with persons of the Shaman faith are thus pierced, generally with a dagger, in order to "kill" them before interment. About twenty miles north-east of Tostach we came across the tomb of a Shaman which, judging by its appearance, had been there about a century, and the shell with the remains had long since disappeared.

The deer were a long time coming at Tostach; one of our drivers accounted for the delay by the fact that wolves had been unusually troublesome this year, and when Stepan suggested that the wolves were two-legged ones, did not appear to relish the joke. For the man was a Tunguse, a race noted for its predatory instincts and partiality for deer-meat. Reindeer in these parts cost only from twelve to fifteen roubles apiece, but farther north they fetch forty to fifty roubles each, and the loss of many is a serious one.

We managed to get away from Tostach that afternoon (March 5) in a dense snowstorm, although on the preceding day the sun had blazed so fiercely into the sleds that we could almost have dispensed with furs. The weather, however, was mostly bright and clear all the way from the Lena to the coast, which was fortunate, for with sunshine and blue sky we could generally afford to laugh at cold and hunger, while on dull, grey days the spirits sank to zero, crushed by a sense of intolerable loneliness, engendered by our dismal surroundings and the daily increasing distance from home. The stage from Tostach was perhaps the hardest one south of the Arctic, for we travelled steadily for twelve hours with a head-wind and driving snow which rendered progress slow and laborious. Finally, reaching the *povarnia* of Kürtas[37] in a miserable condition, with frost-bitten faces and soaking furs, we scraped away the snow inside the crazy shelter and kindled a fire, for no food had passed our lips for sixteen hours. But time progressed, and there were no signs of the provision-sled which, as usual, brought up the rear of the caravan. Ignorance was bliss on this occasion, for the knowledge that the vehicle in question was at that moment firmly fixed in a drift ten miles away, with one of its team lying dead from exhaustion, would not have improved matters. When our provisions reached Kürtas, we had fasted for twenty-four hours, which, in North-Eastern Siberia, becomes an inconvenience less cheerfully endured than in a temperate climate. Beyond Kürtas the track was almost overgrown, and our *narta* covers were almost torn to pieces by branches on either side of it. There were places where we had literally to force our way through the woods, and how the drivers held their course remains a mystery. Nearing the Tashayaktak[38] mountain, however, we travelled along the Dogdo River for some distance; but here, although the road was clear, constant overflows compelled us to travel along the centre of the stream, which is about ten times the width of the Thames at Gravesend. Here the sleds occasionally skated over perilously thin ice, and as night was falling I was glad to reach *terra firma*. The

Tashayaktak range is at this point nowhere less than three thousand feet in height, and I was anticipating a second clamber over their snowy peaks when Stepan informed me that the crossing could be easily negotiated by a pass scarcely five hundred feet high. Fortunately the wind had now dropped, for during gales the snow is piled up in huge drifts along this narrow pass, and only the previous year two Yakutes had been snowed up to perish of cold and starvation. However, we crossed the range without much difficulty, although boulders and frozen cataracts made it hard work for the deer, and another one fell here to mark our weary track across Siberia. And we lost yet another of the poor little beasts, which broke its leg in the gnarled roots of a tree, before reaching the *povarnia* of Siss, a hundred and thirty versts from Tostach. Here both men and beasts were exhausted, and I resolved to halt for twelve hours and recuperate.

[37] When the letter "u" is surmounted by two dots it is pronounced like that in "Curtain."

[38] The names of places between Verkhoyansk and Sredni-Kolymsk were furnished by Stepan Rastorguyeff.

The *povarnia* of Siss was more comfortable than usual, which means that its accommodation was about on a par with an English cow-shed. But we obtained a good night's rest, notwithstanding icy draughts and melted snow. The latter was perhaps the chief drawback at these places, for we generally awoke to find ourselves lying inch-deep in watery slush occasioned by the warmth of the fire. At Siss the weather cleared, and we set out next day with renewed spirits, which the deer seemed to share, for they, too, had revelled in moss, which was plentiful around the *povarnia*, while, as a rule, they had to roam for several miles in search of it. Siberian reindeer seem to have an insatiable appetite; whenever we halted on the road (often several times within the hour) every team would set to work pawing up the snow in search of food, with such engrossed energy that it took some time to set them going again. And yet these gentle, patient beasts would labour along for hours, girth-deep in heavy snow, their flanks going like steam-engines, and never dream of stopping to take a rest unless ordered to do so.

From Paris to New York by Land

It would weary the reader to enumerate in detail the events of the next few days. Suffice it to say that half a dozen *povarnias* were passed before we reached Ebelach, a so-called village consisting of three mud-huts. Ebelach is more than seven hundred versts from Verkhoyansk, and we accomplished the journey in under a week. Only one place, the *povarnia* of Tiriak-Hureya, is deserving of mention, for two reasons: the first being that it exactly resembled the valley of Chamonix, looking down it from Mont Blanc towards the Aiguilles. I shall never forget the glorious sunset I witnessed here, nor the hopeless feeling of nostalgia instilled by the contemplation of those leagues of forest and snowy peaks, the latter gradually merging in the dusk from a delicate rose colour to bluish grey. Only the preceding summer I had stood on the principal "place" of the little Swiss town and witnessed almost exactly the same landscape, and the contrast only rendered our present surroundings the more lonesome and desolate. No wonder the Swiss are a homesick race, or that Napoleon, on his distant campaigns, prohibited, from fear of desertion, the playing of their national airs. Smoky cities could be recalled, even in this land of desolation, without yearning or regret, but I could never think of the sunlit Alps or leafy boulevards without an irresistible longing to throw reputation to the winds and return to them forthwith!

The other circumstance connected with Tiriak-Hureya is that the *povarnia*, measuring exactly sixteen feet by fourteen feet, was already tenanted by a venerable gentleman of ragged and unsavoury exterior, his Yakute wife, or female companion, three children, and a baby with a mysterious skin disease. We numbered sixteen in all, including drivers, and that night is vividly engraven on my memory. It was impossible to move hand or foot without touching some foul personality, and five hours elapsed before Stepan was able to reach the fire and cook some food. But notwithstanding his unspeakably repulsive exterior the aged stranger excited my curiosity, for his careworn features and sunken eyes suggested a past life of more than ordinary interest. He was an exile, one of the few who have lived to retrace their steps along this "Via Dolorosa." I addressed the poor old fellow, who told us that he had once spoken French fluently, but could now only recall a few words, and these he unconsciously interlarded with Yakute. Captain — —, once in the

Polish Army, had been deported to Sredni-Kolymsk after the insurrection of 1863, and had passed the rest of his life in that gloomy settlement. He was now returning to Warsaw to end his days, but death was plainly written on the pinched, pallid face and weary eyes, and I doubt whether the poor soul ever lived to reach the home he had yearned for through so many hopeless years.

Nearing Ebelach the forest became so dense that we travelled almost in darkness, even at midday. Snow had fallen heavily here, and the drifts lay deep, while the trees on every side were weighted down to the earth with a soft, white mantle, that here and there assumed the weirdest resemblance to the shapes of birds and animals. I have never seen this freak of nature elsewhere, although it is mentioned by ancient explorers as occurring in the forests of Kamtchatka. And as we advanced northward optical delusions became constantly visible. At times a snow hillock of perhaps fifty feet high would appear a short distance away to be a mountain of considerable altitude; at others the process would be reversed and the actual mountain would be dwarfed into a molehill. These phenomena were probably due to rarefied atmosphere, and they were most frequent on the Arctic sea-board.

A number of small lakes were crossed between the last *povarnia* and Ebelach. There must have been quite a dozen of these covering a distance of twenty miles, and fortunately the ice was well covered with snow or it must have considerably impeded the deer. These lakes vary in size, ranging from about one to four miles in diameter, and are apparently very shallow, for reeds were visible everywhere sprouting through the ice. Swamps would, perhaps, better describe these shoaly sheets of water, which in summer so swarm with mosquitoes that deer and even the natives sometimes die from their attacks.

Ebelach was reached on March 9, and as the *stancia* here was a fairly clean one, I decided, although reindeer were in readiness, to halt for twenty-four hours. For even one short week of this kind of work had left its mark on us, and the catarrh, from which we now all suffered, did not improve the situation. When I look back upon the daily, almost hourly, fatigues and privations of that journey from the Lena

River to Bering Straits, I sometimes marvel that we ever came through it at all; and yet this part of the voyage was a mere picnic compared to the subsequent trip along the Arctic coast. And indeed this was bad enough, for in addition to physical hardships there were hundreds of minor discomforts, a description of which would need a separate chapter. Vermin and bodily filth were our chief annoyances, but there were other minor miseries almost as bad as these. One was the wet inside the sleds at night. You lay down to sleep, and in a short time your breath had formed a layer of ice over the face, and the former melting in the warmer region of the neck gradually trickled down under your furs, until by morning every stitch of underclothing was saturated. On very cold nights the eyelids would be frozen firmly together during sleep, and one would have to stagger blindly into a *stancia* or *povarnia* before they could be opened. Again, on starting from a *stancia* at sunset, the hood of the sled is closed down on its helpless occupant, who must remain in this ambulant ice-box for an indefinite period, until it is re-opened from the outside, for no amount of shouting would ever attract the attention of the driver. The midnight hours were the worst, when we lay awake wondering how long it would be before the last remnant of life was frozen out of us. Two or three times during the night there would be a halt, and I would start up and listen intently in the darkness to the low sound of voices and the quick nervous stamp of the reindeer seeking for moss. Then came an interval of suspense. Was it a *povarnia*, or must I endure more hours of agony? But a lurch and a heave onward of the sled was only too often the unwelcome reply. At last the joyous moment would arrive when I could distinguish those ever-pleasant sounds, the creaking of a door followed by the crackling of sticks. A *povarnia* at last! But even then it was generally necessary to yell and hammer at the sides of your box of torture for half an hour or so, the drivers having fled to the cosy fireside intent upon warming themselves, and oblivious of every one else. No wonder that after a night of this description we often regarded even a filthy *povarnia* as little less luxurious than a Carlton Hotel.

The cold was so great that I had not slept for thirty-six hours before reaching Ebelach, but we soon made up for it here, where everything was fairly clean and even the ice windows were adjusted with more than usual nicety. Glazing is cheap in these parts. When the ponds are frozen to a depth of six or eight inches blocks of ice are cut out and laid on the roof of the hut out of reach of the dogs. If a new window is required the old melted pane is removed, and a fresh block of ice is fitted on the outside with wet snow, which serves as putty and shortly freezes. At night-time boards are placed indoors against the windows to protect them from the heat of the fire, but the cold in these regions is so intense that one ice window will generally last throughout the winter. The light filters only very dimly through this poor substitute for glass, which is almost opaque. By the way, here as in every other *stancia* a wooden calendar of native construction was suspended over the doorway. Some superstition is probably attached to the possession of these, for although I frequently tried to purchase one at a fancy price the owners would never sell this primitive timekeeper which was generally warped and worm-eaten with age. I never saw a new one.

After a square sleep of twelve hours we awoke to find the inmates of the *stancia* discussing a dish of fine perch caught from the adjacent lake. They had simply thawed the fish out and were devouring it in a raw state, but we managed to secure a portion of the welcome food, which, when properly cooked, was delicious, and a welcome change from *Carnyl* and the beef (or horse) from Yakutsk, which had lasted us until now. Every lake in this region teems with fish, which are never salted here for export, but only used for local consumption.

The postmaster's family was a large and thriving one. I noticed that the politeness of these natives increased as we proceeded northward, and that at the same time their mental capacity diminished. For instance, two of the people at Ebelach were hopeless idiots and I was prepared for the terrible percentage of insane persons which I afterwards found amongst the exiles of Sredni-Kolymsk by the large number of Yakutes of feeble intellect whom we encountered at the rest-houses beyond Verkhoyansk. Nearly every one contained one or more unmistakable lunatics, and it afterwards struck me that in a land where even the natives go mad from sheer despondency of life, it is no wonder that men and women of culture and refinement are driven to suicide from the constant dread of insanity. Idiocy, however, is more frequent amongst the natives, and in one *povarnia* we found a poor half-witted wretch who had taken up his quarters there driven away from the nearest *stancia* by the cruelty of its inmates. This poor imbecile had laid in a store of putrid fish and seemed quite resigned to his surroundings, but we persuaded him to return to his home with us. This was an exceptional case, for the Yakutes are generally kind and indulgent towards mental sufferers, their kindness perhaps arising to a certain extent from fear, for in these parts mad people are credited with occult powers which enable them to take summary vengeance on their enemies.

Leaving Ebelach the lakes became so numerous that the country may also be described as one vast sheet of water with intervals of land. We must have crossed over a hundred lakes of various sizes between the *stancia* of Khatignak and Sredni-Kolymsk, a distance of about five hundred versts. The majority were carpeted with snow, and afforded good going; but smooth black ice formed the surface of others, swept by the wind, and these worked sad havoc amongst our deer, of which four, with broken legs, had to be destroyed. Nearing Khatignak we crossed the Indigirka[39] river, which rises in the Stanovoi range and flows through many hundred miles of desolation to the Arctic Ocean. The country here is more hilly, but sparse forests of stunted bushes and withered looking pine-trees were now the sole vegetation, and these were often replaced by long stretches of snowy plain. A long stage of seventy-five versts without a break brought us to Khatignak, where another reindeer dropped dead from exhaustion before the door of the *stancia*.

[39] The now obsolete town of Zashiversk was situated on the right bank of this river.

Some miles beyond Khatignak another chain of mountains was crossed, although downs would more aptly describe the Alazenski range. But the snow lay deep and we were compelled to make the ascent on foot, a hard walk of five hours in heavy furs under a blazing sun. On the summit is a wooden cross marking the boundary between the Kolyma and Verkhoyansk districts. The cross was hung with all kinds of rubbish, copper coins, scraps of iron, and shreds of coloured cloth suspended by horse-hair, which had been placed there by Yakute travellers to propitiate the gods and ensure a prosperous journey. The cross, as a Christian symbol, did not seem to occur to the worshippers of the Shaman faith, who had left these offerings. We slept on the northern side of the mountain at a *povarnia* renowned even amongst the natives for its revolting accommodation. In the Yakute language "Siss-Ana" signifies literally "one hundred doors," and the name was given to this sieve-like structure on account of the numberless and icy draughts which assail its occupants. The place is said to be accursed, and I could well believe it, for although a roaring fire blazed throughout the night, the walls and ceiling were thickly coated with rime in the morning, and towards midnight a bottle of "Harvey's Sauce" exploded like a dynamite shell, not ten feet from the hearth! The condiment was far too precious to waste, so it was afterwards carried in a tin drinking-cup, in a frozen state, and not poured out, but bitten off, at meals!

Between Siss-Ana and the *stancia* of Malofskaya the country becomes much wilder, and forests dwindle away as we near the timber line. Occasionally not a tree would be visible from sled to horizon, only a level plain of snow, which under the influence of wind, sunshine and passing clouds would present as many moods and aspects as the sea. On one day it would appear as smooth and unbroken as a village pond, on another the white expanse would be broken by ripples, solid wavelets stirred up by a light breeze, while after a storm, billows and rollers in the shape of great drifts and hillocks would obstruct our progress. As we neared the frozen ocean many storms were encountered, and approaching Sredni-Kolymsk these occurred almost daily as furious blizzards. On such occasions we always lay to, for it was impossible to travel against the overwhelming force of the wind. Frequently these tempests occurred in otherwise fine weather, and on such days the snow did not fall but was whirled up from the ground in dense clouds, and during the lulls, a momentary glance of sunshine and blue sky had a strange effect. And, as we gradually crept further and further north, a sense of unspeakable loneliness seemed to increase with every mile we covered. Let the reader try and realise that during the journey from Verkhoyansk of over one thousand miles, we had seen perhaps fifty human beings and—a dead ermine! When at Irkutsk I spoke of journeying to Sredni-Kolymsk I was regarded as a lunatic by the majority of my hearers. Yakutsk was their end of the world! And now that cold, monotony and silence were gradually telling upon the brain and nerves, I sometimes questioned, in moments of despondency, whether my Irkutsk friends were not right when they exclaimed: "You are mad to go there." There were compensations, notwithstanding, for a lover of Nature—the sapphire skies and dazzling sunshine, the marvellous sunsets under which the snowy desert would flash like a kaleidoscope of delicate colours, and last, but not least, the glorious starlit nights, when the little Pleiades would seem to glitter so near that you had but to reach out a hand and pick them out of the inky sky.

On March 14 a large caravan hove in sight, composed of perhaps a score of horse-sleds, which, as we neared it, halted, and a European emerged from the leading sled to greet us. This bearded giant in tattered furs proved to be the Russian naturalist, Yokelson, returning to Europe after a two years' exploration in North-Eastern Siberia— principally in the neighbourhood of Kamtchatka and the Okhotsk Sea. From Gijiga, Yokelson had struck in a north-westerly direction to Sredni-Kolymsk, and was bringing home a valuable collection for the society which had employed him in the United States. The Russian could only give us the worst of news from the Kolyma, where my expedition was expected by the *ispravnik*, although the latter had assured Yokelson that our projected journey to Bering Straits was out of the question. A famine was still raging, there were very few dogs, and those half starved and useless, and neither this official nor any one else in the place knew anything about the country east of Sredni-Kolymsk. Three years previously a Russian missionary had started with a driver on a dog-sled to travel from the Kolyma along the coast to the nearest Tchuktchi settlement, about 600 miles away, and the pair had never been heard of since. This was the cheerful information which, happily, the Russian traveller imparted to me in strict privacy.

Shortly after leaving Yokelson we crossed the Utchingoikel, or "Beautiful Lake," so called from its picturesque surroundings in summer time. At Andylach horses were harnessed to the sleds and we used no more deer, there being no moss between here and Sredni-Kolymsk. The change was not a desirable one, for the Yakute horse is a terrible animal. "Generally he won't move until your sled is upset, and then he runs away and it's impossible to stop him." So wrote Mr. Gilder, the American explorer, and his experience was ours. But Gilder was compelled to ride several stages and thus graphically describes his sufferings: "The Yakute horse can scarcely be called a horse, he is a domesticated wild animal. A coat or two was placed under the wooden saddle, so that the writer was perched high in the air like on a camel. The stirrups were of wood, and it was an art to mount, for they depended immediately from the pommel. When you mounted ten to one that you fell in front of the pommel, and as you could not get back over a pommel ten inches high you slid over the horse's head to the ground and tried again. Yakute horses are docile, provokingly so, for they have not enough animation to be wicked. The favourite gait is a walk so slow and deliberate that you lose all patience, and, if possible, raise a trot which is like nothing known to the outside world; your horse rises in the air and straightens out his legs and then comes down upon the end which has the foot on it, the recoil bouncing you high up from your seat just in time to meet the saddle as it is coming up for the next step. It's like constant bucking, and yet you don't go four miles an hour!"

I could sympathise with the writer of the above, for during the first day's work with these brutes I was upset five times, and felt towards evening like an invalid after a hard day with hounds.

Crossing lake after lake (this is a Siberian Finland) with intervals of forest and barren plain, we reached the last *stancia* of any size, Ultin. This is about two hundred miles from Sredni-Kolymsk, and the rest-house showed signs of approaching civilisation, or rather Russian humanity. For the floor was actually clean, there was a table and two chairs, and a cheap oleograph of his Majesty the Emperor pinned to the plank wall. The place seemed palatial after the miserable shelters we had shared, and I seized the opportunity of a wash in warm water before confronting the authorities at Sredni-Kolymsk.

On March 17 Atetzia was reached. This is, indeed, a land of contradictions, for, although only ten miles from Sredni-Kolymsk, the *povarnia* here was the filthiest we entered throughout the journey from Verkhoyansk. It contained two occupants, an old and ragged

Yakute woman and a dead deer in an advanced state of decomposition. The former lay upon the mud floor groaning and apparently in great pain, with one arm around the neck of the putrid carcase beside her, and I inferred that she had been poisoned by partaking of the disgusting remains, probably in a raw condition, for there were no signs of a fire. But the medicine-chest alleviated her sufferings, and we left the poor wretch full of gratitude and in comparative comfort. The same afternoon we reached our destination, having accomplished the journey from Verkhoyansk in eighteen days, although four months had been freely predicted as its probable duration!

CHAPTER VIII

AN ARCTIC INFERNO

NOTE.—The information contained in the following chapter was chiefly obtained from Government officials stationed at Sredni-Kolymsk, the facts being afterwards verified, or otherwise, by political exiles at the same place by my request.

We reached Sredni-Kolymsk early in March on a glorious day, one of those peculiar to the Arctic regions, when the pure, crisp air exhilarates like champagne, and nature sparkles like a diamond in the sunshine. But as we neared it, the sight of that dismal drab settlement seemed to darken the smiling landscape like a coffin which has been carried by mistake into a brilliant ball-room. I once thought the acme of desolation had been reached at Verkhoyansk, but to drive into this place was like entering a cemetery. Imagine a double row of squalid log-huts, with windows of ice, some of which, detached by the warm spring sunshine, have fallen to the ground. This is the main "street," at one extremity of which stands a wooden church in the last stage of decay, at the other the house of the Chief of Police, the only decent building in the place. So low indeed are these in stature that the settlement is concealed, two or three hundred yards away, by the stunted trees around it. Only the rickety spire of a chapel is visible, and this overtops the neighbouring dwellings by only a few feet. Picture perhaps a score of other huts as squalid as the rest scattered around an area of half a mile, and you have before you the last "civilised" outpost in Northern Siberia. All around it a desolate plain, fringed by grey-green Arctic vegetation and bisected by the frozen river Kolyma; over all the silence of the grave. Such is Sredni-Kolymsk, as it appeared to me even in that brilliant sunshine—the most gloomy, God-forsaken spot on the face of this earth.

At first sight the place looked like an encampment deserted by trappers, or some village decimated by deadly sickness; anything but the abode of human beings. For a while our arrival attracted no attention, but presently skin-clad forms emerged here and there from the miserable huts, and haggard faces nodded a cheerless welcome as we drove past them towards the police office. Here a dwelling was assigned to us, and we took up our residence in quarters colder and filthier than any we had occupied since leaving Verkhoyansk. And yet our lodgings were preferable to many of those occupied by the exiles.

During our visit Sredni-Kólymsk had a population of about three hundred souls, of whom only fourteen were political offenders. The remainder were officials, criminal colonists, and natives of the Yakute, Lamute, or Tunguse races. The Cossacks here subsist chiefly by trapping and fishing, but are also nominally employed as guards—a useless precaution, as starvation would inevitably follow an attempt to escape. The criminal colonists are allotted a plot of ground in this district after a term of penal servitude, and I have never beheld, even in Sakhalin, such a band of murderous-looking ruffians as were assembled here. They were a constant terror to the exiles, and even officials rarely ventured out after dark.

The police officials here were sour, stern-visaged individuals, and our welcome was as frigid as it had been warm at Verkhoyansk. The Chief of Police had recently met his death under tragic circumstances, which I shall presently describe, and I was received by the acting *ispravnik*, whose grim manners and appearance were in unpleasant contrast to those of our kind old friend Katcherofsky. Although this natural prison had no bolts and bars or other evidences of a penal system, the very air seemed tainted with mystery and oppression, and the melancholy row of huts to scrawl the word "captivity" across the desolate landscape. Even the *ispravnik's* room, with its heavy black furniture and sombre draperies, was suggestive of the Inquisition, and I searched instinctively around me for the rack and thumbscrews. How many a poor wretch had stood in this gloomy apartment waiting patiently, after months of unspeakable suffering, for some filthy hovel wherein to lay his head. It seemed to me that crape and fetters would more fittingly have adorned those whitewashed walls than a sacred *Ikon* encrusted with jewels, and heavily gilt oil-paintings of their Imperial Majesties! A couple of tables littered with papers occupied the centre of the room, and at one of these sat the *ispravnik*, a wooden-faced peremptory person in dark green tunic and gold shoulder straps. A couple of clerks, also in uniform, were busily engaged at the other desk, sorting the mail which our Cossack had brought, and in expectation of which a group of poorly clad, shivering exiles were already waiting in the piercing cold outside. But when we left this place ten days later not a single letter had reached its destination, although the post-bag contained over a hundred addressed to the various politicals.

Even the Governor-General's all-powerful document produced little effect here, for the *ispravnik* appeared to regard himself as beyond the reach of even the Tsar's Viceroy, which, indeed, from an inaccessible point of view, he undoubtedly was. "You cannot possibly go," was the curt rejoinder to my request for dogs and drivers to convey us to the Bering Straits. "In the first place, a famine is raging here and you will be unable to procure provisions. Stepan tells me that you have barely enough food with you to last for two weeks, and it would take you at least twice that time to reach the nearest Tchuktchi settlement, which we know to be beyond Tchaun Bay, six hundred miles away. A year ago two of our people tried to reach it, and perished, although they left here well supplied with dogs and provisions. For all I know the *Kor* (which has decimated this district) may have killed off the coast natives or driven them into the interior of the country, and then where would you be, even supposing you reached Tchaun Bay, with no shelter, no food, and another month at least through an icy waste to Bering Straits. As for dogs, most of ours have perished from the scarcity of fish caught last summer; I don't think there are thirty sound dogs in the place, and you would need at least three times that number. Reindeer, even if we could get them, are out of the question, for there is not an ounce of moss on the coast. But even with dogs forthcoming I doubt whether you would find drivers to accompany you, for all our people are in deadly terror of the Tchuktchis. No, no! Take my advice and give up this mad project even if you have to remain here throughout the summer. It will at any rate be better than leaving your bones on the shores of the Arctic Ocean."

My experience of Russian *ispravniks* is varied and extensive, and I therefore realised that argument was useless with this adamantine official, whose petty tyranny was evidently not confined to his dealing with his exiles. I therefore returned to our cheerless quarters in anything but a pleasant frame of mind, and almost convinced that our overland expedition was now finally wrecked. The outlook was not a cheerful one, for the homeward journey would in itself be miserable enough, without the addition of floods and a possible detention through a sultry, mosquito-infested summer at Verkhoyansk. It has seldom been my lot to pass such a depressing evening as that which followed my interview with the *ispravnik*, but the prospect of an entire summer's imprisonment in Arctic wilds affected us far less than the failure of the expedition. Harding probably echoed the feelings of all when he exclaimed with a gesture of despair: "When we set out on this job the devil must have taken the tickets!"

Stepan alone was silent and taciturn. When I awoke next morning at daybreak he had disappeared, presumably to procure reindeer for the return journey. But the season was now so far advanced that the *ispravnik* called during the day to beg me not to risk a spring journey to Yakutsk. It was far better, he averred, to remain here and travel back in safety and comparative comfort in the late fall. It would even be preferable to attempt the summer journey down the Kolyma River and over the Stanovoi Mountains to Ola on the Okhotsk Sea. The trip had certainly never been made, but then no more had our projected one to America, and how infinitely preferable to arrive at Ola, where we might only have to wait a few days for a steamer, than to start off on a wild goose chase to Bering Straits which we should probably never reach at all. "Besides," continued the *ispravnik*, "the Ola trip would be so easy by comparison with the other. No drivers and dog-sleds to be procured, merely a flat-bottomed boat which could be put together in a few days." From my friend's eagerness to avoid trouble of any kind I now strongly suspected that laziness was the chief cause of our present dilemma, although this official's demeanour was so much more conciliatory than on the previous day, that I fancied that a night's reflection had revealed the unpleasant results that might follow my unfavourable report of his conduct at Irkutsk. Although we sat for hours that day consuming tea and innumerable cigarettes, I was no nearer the solution of the problem at sunset than at dawn. And had I but known it, all the time I was vainly urging this stolid boor to reconsider his decision, help was arriving from a totally unexpected quarter. I discussed a cheerless and silent meal with my companions, and we were turning in that night when Stepan strolled in, cool and imperturbable as usual. He even divested himself of furs and helped himself to food before making an announcement which sent the blood tingling through my veins with excitement and renewed hope.

"I have got the dogs," said the Cossack quietly, with his mouth full of fish and black bread. "Sixty-four of them; we can go on now!" The news seemed too good to be true, until Stepan explained that he had travelled thirty miles down the river that day to obtain the animals from a friend. The dogs were poor, weakly brutes, and the price asked an exorbitant one, but I would gladly have paid it thrice over, or pushed on towards our goal, if need be, with a team of tortoises. Even now I anticipated some difficulty with the *ispravnik*, and was relieved when, the next morning, he consented without demur to our departure. Indeed, I rather fancy he was grateful to the Cossack for ridding him so easily of his troublesome guests. The indefatigable Stepan had also procured three drivers, so that I had no further anxiety on that score. But several days must elapse before sufficiently strong sleds for our purpose could be constructed. I therefore resolved to utilise the time by making the acquaintance of the exiles and studying the conditions of their existence in this out-of-the-way corner of creation. This was at first no easy matter, for if the officials here were suspicious the politicals were a thousand times more so, of one who had invariably written in favour of Russian prisons. Most of these "politicals" were familiar with Mr. Kennan's indictment and my subsequent defence of the Russian exile system, but the fact that my party was the first to visit this place for a period of over thirty years imbued an investigation of its penal system with such intense interest that, notwithstanding many rebuffs, I finally gained the confidence of all those who had been banished to this Arctic inferno. And the information which I now place before the reader is the more valuable in that it was derived, in the first place, from an official source.

I should perhaps state that my experience of Russian prisons dates from the year 1890. Mr. Kennan's report on the conditions of the penal establishments throughout Siberia was then arousing indignation throughout civilised Europe, and his heart-rending accounts of the sufferings endured by political and criminal offenders obviously called for some sort of an explanation from the Tsar's Government. A mere official denial of the charges would have been useless; a disinterested person was needed to report upon the prisons and *étapes* which had been described as hells upon earth, and to either confirm or gainsay the statements made by the American traveller. The evidence of a Russian subject would, for obvious reasons, have met with incredulity, and it came to pass, therefore, that through the agency of Madame de Novikoff, herself a prison Directress, I was selected for a task, which although extremely interesting, subjected me to much unfavourable criticism on my return to England. Some yellow journals even went so far as to suggest that I had received payment from the Russian Government for "whitewashing" its penal system, but I fancy the following pages should conclusively disprove the existence of any monetary transactions, past or present, between the Tsar's officials and myself, to say nothing of the fact that my favourable account of the prisons of Western Siberia has been endorsed by such reliable and well-known English travellers as Dr. Lansdell and Mr. J. Y. Simpson. In fairness, however, to Mr. Kennan, I should state that my inspection of the Tomsk forwarding prison and similar establishments was made fully five years after his visit.

In 1894 I again proceeded to Siberia (under similar conditions) to report upon the penal settlement on the Island of Sakhalin, the political prison of Akatui, and the mines, where only convict labour is employed, of Eastern Siberia. On this occasion I travelled from Japan to the Island of Sakhalin on board a Russian convict ship, a voyage which convinced me that the Russian criminal convict is as humanely treated and well cared for at sea as he is on land, which says a great deal. I have always maintained that were I sentenced to a term of penal servitude I would infinitely sooner serve it in (some parts of) Siberia than in England. It is not now my intention, however, to deal with the criminal question, but to describe, as accurately as I can, the life led by a handful of political exiles.

There are now only two prisons throughout the Russian Empire where political prisoners are actually incarcerated,[40] one is the fortress of Schlüsselburg on Lake Ladoga within a short journey of St. Petersburg, the other the prison of Akatui, in the trans-Baikal province, about three hundred miles east of Irkutsk. Schlüsselburg I have never visited, but I inspected the prison of Akatui, and conversed freely with the politicals within its walls. The majority were men of education, but dangerous conspirators, condemned to long terms of penal servitude. The strictest prison discipline, the wearing of fetters, hard labour in the silver mines, and association at night in public cells with the vilest criminals was the lot of those whom I saw at Akatui, and yet I doubt if any of these men would willingly have changed places with their exiled comrades "domiciled" in comparative liberty at Sredni-Kolymsk. For the stupendous distance of the latter place from civilisation surrounds it with even more gloom and mystery than the Russian Bastille on Lake Ladoga, which is the most dreaded prison of all.

[40] Political prisoners are no longer confined in the fortress of SS. Peter and Paul. Short terms of imprisonment previous to banishment to Siberia are served in the citadels of Warsaw and other cities, but Schlüsselburg and Akatui are the only establishments now used as political prisons in the real sense of the word.

At the time of our visit, the exiles here numbered twelve men and two women, only two of whom had been banished for actual crime. One of these was Madame Akimova, who was found with explosives concealed about her person at the coronation of Nicholas II., and the other, Zimmermann, convicted of complicity in the destruction of the public workshops at Lodz by dynamite a few years ago. With these two exceptions the Sredni-Kolymsk exiles were absolutely guiltless of active participation in the revolutionary movement, indeed, most of them appeared to be quiet, intelligent men, of moderate political views who would probably have contributed to the welfare and prosperity of any country but their own. Only one or two openly professed what may be called anarchistic views, and these were young students, recent arrivals, who looked more like robbing an orchard than threatening a throne. So far as I could see, however, most of these so-called political offenders had been consigned to this living tomb merely for openly expressing opinions in favour of a constitution and freedom of speech. And strange as it may seem, some of them were occasionally almost cheerful under circumstances that would utterly annihilate the health and spirits of an average Englishman. But even European Russia is an unutterably dreary land in a stranger's eyes, which perhaps accounts for this remarkable fact.

The most pitiable characteristic about Sredni-Kolymsk is perhaps the morbid influence of the place and its surroundings on the mental powers. The first thing noticeable amongst those who had passed some years here was the utter vacancy of mind, even of men who in Europe had shone in the various professions. Amongst them was a well-known Polish author,[41] who, upon his arrival here, only three years ago, set to work upon an historical novel to lighten the leaden hours of exile. But it must be more than disheartening to realise that your work, however good it may be, will never reach the printer's hands. In six months the book was thrown aside in disgust, and in less than a year afterwards the writer's mind had become so unhinged by the maddening monotony of life, that he would, in civilisation, have been placed under restraint. I met also a once famous professor of anatomy (who had been here for seven years), and who, although completely indifferent to the latest discoveries of surgical science, displayed an eager interest as to what was going on at the Paris music-halls. Indeed, I can safely state that, with three exceptions, there was not a perfectly sane man or woman amongst all the exiles I saw here.

[41] I was requested to suppress the name.

"A couple of years usually makes them shaky," said an official, "and the strongest-minded generally become childish when they have been here for five or six."

"But why is it?" I asked.

My friend walked to the window and pointed to the mournful street, the dismal hovels, and frozen river darkening in the dusk.

"That," he said, "and the awful silence. Day after day, year after year, not a sound. I have stood in that street at mid-day and heard a watch tick in my pocket. Think of it, Mr. de Windt. I myself arrived here only a few months ago, but even I shall soon have to get away for a change, or — —" and he tapped his forehead significantly.

The insanity which I found so prevalent amongst the exiles here is no doubt largely due to physical privation. When a man is banished for political reasons to Siberia, his property is confiscated to the uttermost farthing by the Russian Government, which provides a fixed monthly allowance for his maintenance in exile. At Sredni-Kolymsk it is nineteen roubles a month, or about £1 16s., an absurdly inadequate allowance in a place where the necessaries of life are always at famine prices. During our stay here flour was selling at a rouble a pound, and an abominable kind of brick tea at two roubles a pound, while candles, sugar, and salt cost exactly five times as much as at Yakutsk, where European prices are already trebled. The price of deer-meat was, therefore, prohibitive, and the exiles were living throughout the winter upon fish caught the preceding summer, unsalted, and therefore quite unfit for human consumption. And this at mid-day was their sole nourishment, breakfast and supper consisting of one glass of weak tea and a small piece of gritty black bread! Sugar was such a luxury that a lump was held in the teeth while the liquid was swallowed, one piece thus serving for several days in succession. Were a house and clothing provided, even the miserable pittance provided by the Government might suffice to keep body and soul together, but this is not the case. Some of the exiles were accordingly occupying almost roofless sheds that had been vacated by the Yakutes, while many were so poorly clad that in winter time they were unable to leave their miserable huts.

The house occupied by Monsieur Strajevsky, a Polish gentleman, whose personality I shall always recall with sincere regard and sympathy, will serve as a type of the better class of dwelling occupied by these exiles. It consisted of a low, mud-plastered log hut about 6 ft. in height, 14 ft. by 10 ft. was the measurement of the one room it contained, with a floor of beaten earth, glistening with the filth of years. A yellow light filtered dimly, even on the brightest day, through the slab of ice which formed the solitary window, but it revealed only too clearly the dirt and squalor of the room. Some planks on trestles formed my friend's sleeping-place, and more planks strewn with books and writing materials, his table. An old kerosene tin was the only chair, and as I seated myself my friend went to the mud hearth and kindled a few sticks, which burned brightly for a few moments and then flickered out. He then left the hut, climbed on to the roof, and closed the chimney with a bundle of rags. This is the Yakute mode of warming an apartment, and it is practised for economy, for Sredni-Kolymsk is near the tree line, and firewood, like everything else, is an expensive article. Even timber is so costly here that towards sunset every inhabitant of Sredni-Kolymsk fired up preparatory to blocking up his chimney for the night. The outlook from our hut was at this hour a weird and unique one, as an avenue of fires rose from the mud hovels and ascended in sheets of flame to the starlit sky. But this illumination was stifled in a few seconds by dense clouds of smoke. This method of obtaining warmth is scarcely a success, for I sat during my visit to Strajevsky in an atmosphere minus 47° Fahrenheit by my thermometer. And in this miserable den my Polish friend, once a prosperous barrister in Warsaw, had passed eight of the best years of his life, and is still, if alive, dragging out a hopeless existence.

In summer time life here is perhaps less intolerable than during the winter, for the Kolyma River teems with fish, and edible berries are obtainable in the woods. Geese, duck, and other wild fowl are plentiful in the spring, and as fire-arms are not prohibited, game at this season is a welcome addition to a generally naked larder. Manual labour, too, is procurable, and an exile may earn a few roubles by fishing, trapping, wood-cutting, &c.; but the dark winter months must be passed in a condition of inactive despair. During the winter season there are two mails from Russia brought by the Cossacks in charge of the yearly consignment of exiles, but in spring, summer, and early autumn Sredni-Kolymsk is as completely cut off from the outer world, as a desert island in mid-ocean, by swamps and thousands of shallow lakes which extend landwards on every side for hundreds of miles. A reindeer-sled skims easily over their frozen surface, but in the open season a traveller sinks knee-deep at every step into the wet spongy ground.

Summer here is no glad season of sunshine and flowers, only a few brief weeks of damp and cloudy weather, for even on fine days the sun looms through a curtain of mist. Rainy weather prevails, and the leaky huts are often flooded for days together by an incessant downfall. Swarms of mosquitoes and sand flies are added to other miseries, for there is no protection against these pests by night or day, save by means of *dimokuris*, a bundle of leaves, moss, and damp pine logs which is ignited near a hut and envelops it in a perpetual cloud of pungent and stifling smoke. At this season of the year there is much sickness, especially a kind of low fever produced by the *miasma* from the surrounding marshes. Epidemics are frequent, and during our stay smallpox was raging, but chiefly amongst the native population. Leprosy is as prevalent here as in Central Asia, but Russians suffer chiefly from bronchitis and diphtheria, which never fail to make their appearance with the return of spring. Every one suffers continually from catarrh, irrespective of age or race, indeed we all had it ourselves. And yet in this hotbed of pestilence there is no Government infirmary, nor is any provision whatever made for the sick. Mr. Miskievitch (a young medical student and himself an exile) was attending the community, but a total lack of medical and surgical appliances rendered his case a hopeless one. I inquired for the old hospital and was shown a barn-like construction partly open to the winds and occupied by a family of filthy but thriving Yakutes. The new infirmary for which a large sum of money was subscribed in St. Petersburg ten years ago adjoined the older building, but the former was still in its initial stage of foundations and four corner posts, where it will probably reign, the silent witness of a late *ispravnik's* reign and rascality.

But there exists a mental disease far more dreaded than any bodily affliction, or than even death itself, by this little colony of martyrs. This is a form of hysteria chiefly prevalent amongst women, but common to all, officials, exiles, and natives alike, who reside for any length of time in this hell upon earth.[42] The attack is usually unexpected; a person hitherto calm and collected will suddenly commence to shout, sing, and dance at the most inopportune moment, and from that time the mind of the patient becomes permanently deranged. A curious phase of this disease is the irresistible impulse to mimic the voice and actions of others. Thus I witnessed a painful scene one night in the home of an exile who had assembled some comrades to meet me, and, in the street one day, a peasant woman, born and bred here, seized my arm and repeated, with weird accuracy, a sentence in French which I was addressing to de Clinchamp. This strange affliction is apparently unknown in other Arctic settlements. It is probably due to gloomy surroundings and the eternal silence which enfolds this region. The malady would seem to be essentially local, for the daughter of a Sredni-Kolymsk official who was attacked, immediately recovered on her removal to Yakutsk. On the other hand, sufferers compelled to remain here generally become, after a few years, hopelessly insane. In the opinion of Dr. Miskievitch the affliction is largely due to a total inertia of the reasoning faculties, which after a time becomes a positive torture to the educated mind.

[42] The Russian explorer, Von Wrangell, mentions an apparently similar mental disease as existing in these regions in 1820. He writes: "There is here, indeed (Sredni-Kolymsk), as in all Northern Siberia, that singular malady called *mirak*, which, according to the universal superstition of the people, proceeds from the ghost of a much-dreaded sorceress, which is supposed to enter into and torment the patient. The *mirak* appears to me to be only an extreme degree of hysteria; the persons attacked are chiefly women."—"Siberia and the Polar Sea," by Von Wrangell, 1829.

This evil could undoubtedly be remedied. For instance, were mental work of any kind, even unremunerative, provided by the Government it would be eagerly welcomed by every exile with whom I conversed, but the authorities seem to consider apathy of the mind as essential a punishment as privation of the body. Some years ago the exiles here were permitted to instruct young children of the Free Community, and their life was thus rendered infinitely less unbearable than before, but shortly afterwards, and for no apparent reason, an order was issued from St. Petersburg to cancel this "privilege."

I found, oddly enough, an almost total lack of resentment amongst the victims consigned here by an infamous travesty of justice. Madame Akimova, for instance, a plain but homely-looking person, seemed devoted to the care of her miserable little household to the exclusion of all mundane matters. I sometimes wondered, as I sat in her hut, and watched the pale, patient little woman clad in rusty black ceaselessly striving to make his home less wretched for her husband, whether this could really be Theisa Akimova, the famous Nihilist, whose name had one time, and not so very long ago, electrified Europe. We often spoke of Paris, which Akimova knew well, but she evinced little or no interest in the political questions of the day, and I never once heard her murmur a word of complaint. Nevertheless she is here for life. Zimmermann was another example of mute resignation, but I fancy that in his case years of exile had somewhat dulled the edge of a once powerful intellect. Strajevsky, Miskievitch, and the others were enduring a life of captivity and suffering for offences which, in any country but Russia, would scarcely have subjected them to a fine, and yet they never in my hearing showed vindictiveness towards those who had sent them into exile. And it is a significant fact that, although the higher officials of State were sometimes execrated, I never once heard a member of the Imperial family spoken of with the slightest animosity, or even disrespect. A reason for this is perhaps to be found in the following incident: Upon one occasion I expressed my surprise to an exile that his Majesty the Tsar, a ruler renowned for his humanity and tolerance, should sanction the existence of such a place of exile as Sredni-Kolymsk.

"The Emperor!" was the answer with a bitter laugh; "you may be quite sure that the Emperor does not know what goes on, or we should not be here for a day longer."

Although the expedition remained here for only ten days, it seemed, on the day of our departure, as though as many months had elapsed since our arrival. Each day seemed an eternity, for my visit to the huts of the exiles always took place, for obvious reasons, after dark. During the hours of daylight there was absolutely nothing to do but to stare moodily out of the window at the wintry scene as cheerless as a lunar landscape. Outdoor exercise is undesirable in a place where you cannot walk three hundred yards in any direction without floundering into a snow-drift up to your waist. So during the interminable afternoons I usually found my way to the tiny hut known as the Library. It contained seven or eight hundred books on dull and dreary subjects which, however, had been read and reread

From Paris to New York by Land

until most of the volumes were torn and coverless. Amongst the numerous photographs of exiles past and present that were nailed to the log wall one object daily excited my curiosity. This was a funeral wreath composed of faded wild flowers secured by a black silk ribbon, and bearing the golden inscription "Auf Wiedersehen" in German characters. One evening at the house of an official I happened to mention this withered garland, and learned that it had been laid upon the coffin of a young exile by his comrades only a few weeks previously. The sad circumstances under which this youth met his death, and the startling *dénouement* which followed the latter, form one of the darkest tragedies that has occurred of recent years in the annals of Siberian exile. I give the story word for word as it was related to me by the successor of the infamous Ivanoff who figures in the tale.

In the winter of 1900 there came to Sredni-Kolymsk one Serge Kaleshnikoff, who, previous to his preliminary detention at the prison of Kharkoff, had held a commission in the Russian Volunteer Fleet. For alleged complicity with a revolutionary society known as the "Will of the People"[43] Kaleshnikoff was sentenced to imprisonment for twelve months in a European fortress, and subsequent banishment for eight years to Siberia.

[43] Russian: *Narodna-Volya*.

Kaleshnikoff was a young man of about twenty-three years of age, whose sympathetic nature and attractive manners soon rendered him a universal favourite. Even the officials regarded him more as a friend than a prisoner — with one exception. This was Ivanoff, the Chief of Police, whose marked aversion to the young sailor was noticeable from the first day the latter set foot in the settlement. But as Ivanoff was an ignorant and surly boor, disliked even by his colleagues, Kaleshnikoff endured his petty persecutions with comparative equanimity.

One day during the summer of 1901, while fishing from a canoe on the Kolyma, Kaleshnikoff espied the barge of Ivanoff returning from Nijni-Kolymsk, a settlement about three hundred miles down the river. The exile, who was expecting a letter from a fellow "political" domiciled at the latter place, paddled out into mid-stream and boarded the barge, leaving his canoe to trail astern. Ivanoff, who met him at the gangway, had been drinking heavily, as was his wont. His only answer to Kaleshnikoff's polite inquiry was an oath, and a shameful epithet, to which the other naturally replied with some warmth. An angry discussion followed, with the result that the Chief of Police, now livid with rage, summoned the guard. By Ivanoff's orders Kaleshnikoff was then bound hand and foot, flogged with rope's ends into a state of insensibility, and flung, bruised and bleeding, into his boat. The latter was then cast adrift, and the police barge proceeded on her way up the river.

The incident occurred some miles below Sredni-Kolymsk. The next evening, as Madame Boreisha and M. Ergin (both exiles, and the latter an intimate friend of Kaleshnikoff) were strolling by the riverside, they met the latter, who, weakened by exhaustion and loss of blood, had taken more than twenty-four hours to return to the settlement. Ergin, shocked by his friend's wild and blood-stained appearance, pressed him for an explanation, but Kaleshnikoff, with a vacant stare, waved him aside, and with a despairing gesture disappeared into his hut, only a few yards distant. A few minutes later a pistol-shot was heard, and Ergin, instinctively fearing the worst, rushed to his friend's assistance, only to find that the latter had taken his life. Beside the dead man was a sheet of paper bearing the words, hastily scrawled in pencil: "Farewell! I go to a happier land."[44]

[44] I was told that the majority of the suicides amongst the exiles here occur towards the end of their term of banishment, a fact which seemed incredible until I learned that sentences are frequently prolonged for an indefinite period, just at the time when the exile is expecting release. The suspense and uncertainty attending the last months of captivity are thus a frequent cause of self-destruction, especially amongst women and the younger men.

An inquiry followed, and Ivanoff was placed under temporary arrest. Unfortunately for the Chief of Police, this order did not entail confinement to the house, or he might have escaped the tragic fate which overtook him on the afternoon of the very day that his victim was laid to rest in a lonely grave in the suicides' graveyard[45] on the banks of the river. As luck would have it, the hated official was lounging outside his doorway, smoking a cigarette, as Ergin, a gun on his shoulder, strolled homeward from the marshes. The latter asserts that the act was unpremeditated, for at the time his thoughts were far away. But Ergin adds: "The sudden appearance of that evil face and the recollection of its owner's foul and inhuman cruelty suddenly inspired me with uncontrollable fury, and I raised my fowling-piece and shot the man dead, just as he had divined my purpose and turned to rush indoors." Ergin has ere this been tried for murder at Yakutsk, but I was assured that he would be acquitted, for Ivanoff's conduct would in any case have met with severe punishment at the hands of the authorities in St. Petersburg. Physical brutality is, as regards Russian political exiles, a thing of the past, and an official guilty of it now lays himself open to instant dismissal, or even to a term of imprisonment.

[45] Only suicides are buried in this plot of ground, which contains over a score of graves.

Such is a plain and unvarnished account of the penal settlement of Sredni-Kolymsk, an accursed spot which should assuredly and without delay be erased from the face of civilisation. The above tragedy is but one of many that have occurred of recent years, and although space will not admit of my giving the details of others, I can vouch for the fact that since the year 1898 no fewer than three cases of suicide and four of insanity have occurred here amongst about a score of exiles. And yet every winter more miserable hovels are prepared for the reception of comrades; every year Sredni-Kolymsk enfolds fresh victims in her deadly embrace. "You will tell them in England of our life," said one, his eyes dim with tears, as I entered the dog-sled which was to bear me through weeks of desolation to the Bering Straits. And the promise then made in that lifeless, forsaken corner of the earth, where, as the exiles say, "God is high and the Tsar is far away," I have now faithfully kept. For the first time in thirty years I am able to give an "unofficial" account of the life of these unfortunates, and to deliver to the world their piteous appeal for deliverance. May it be that these pages have not been written in vain, that the clemency of a wise and merciful Ruler may yet be extended towards the unfortunate outcasts in that

Siberian hell of famine, pestilence, and darkness, scarcely less terrible in its ghastly loneliness than those frozen realms of eternal silence which enshrine the mystery of the world.

CHAPTER IX

THE LOWER KOLYMA RIVER

"Why don't you try to escape," I once asked an exile at Sredni-Koylmsk, "and make your way across Bering Straits to America?" For I was aware that, once in the United States, a Russian "political" is safe from the clutch of the bear.[46]

[46] A political exile escaping to the United States can become (in ten years) an American citizen.

"You do not know the coast," was the reply, "or you would not ask me the question." My friend was right. A month later I should certainly not have done so.

Indeed, had I been aware, at this stage of the journey, of the formidable array of obstacles barring the way to the north-easternmost extremity of Asia, I might perhaps even now have hesitated before embarking upon what eventually proved to be the most severe and distressing of all my experiences of travel. It does not look much on the map, that strip of coast-line which extends from the Kolyma River to Bering Straits (especially when viewed from the depths of a cosy armchair); and yet I don't think there is a mile throughout its length which is not associated in my mind with some harassing anxiety, peril or privation.

Provisions of all kinds had become so scarce that a special permit from the *ispravnik* was necessary in order to enable us to purchase even a pound of flour. Luckily a relief convoy had arrived from Yakutsk during the week preceding our departure or a total lack of food must have brought the expedition to a final standstill. However, after endless difficulties and a lavish expenditure of rouble-notes, I managed to procure provisions enough to last us on short rations, with the addition of our own remaining stores, for about three weeks. I also secured a cask of *vodka* (or rather pure alcohol) to trade with the Tchuktchis, for a sum which, in England, would have stocked a moderate-sized cellar. Within three weeks I hoped to reach the first native settlement, said to be six hundred miles distant. Should we fail to do so starvation seemed unpleasantly probable, or death from exposure, our sole shelter being a flimsy canvas tent more suitable for a Thames picnic than an Arctic clime. And so we set out from Sredni-Kolymsk with seven men, five sleds and sixty-four dogs. One of the sleds was loaded down with provisions, our precious cask of *vodka*, and sundry deal cases containing clasp-knives, cheap revolvers, glass beads, wooden pipes, &c., for the natives, who do not use money. A sack of *mahorka* was also taken along for the same purpose. This is a villainous leaf tobacco so rank and sour that it must be soaked in warm water before smoking; and yet, long before we reached the Straits, it became far too precious to waste on the Tchuktchis! Another sled was packed with dog-food, consisting of inferior salt-fish, which we were also compelled to share with the teams before Tchaun Bay was reached. My greatest anxiety, next to the food supply, was regarding fuel. Every drop of oil had been exhausted some days before reaching Sredni-Kolymsk, where no more was procurable, so that artificial heat, that essential of Arctic travel, would have to be entirely derived from the sodden drift-wood occasionally found on the shores of the Polar Sea. I did not care to think much about what would happen if this commodity failed us for any length of time. All things considered, it is no exaggeration to say that my expedition was about as suitably equipped for the work before it as a man who, in England, goes out duck shooting in the depth of winter in a silk night-shirt!

Here, as at Verkhoyansk, our departure was witnessed by officials, exiles and natives. Even the politicals took an active interest in this hitherto unattempted journey, although perhaps this was partly due to the fact that certain sealed missives, destined for Europe, were snugly concealed about my person. Poor Strajevsky, whom I had learned to regard more as a friend than as an acquaintance, made a sketch of our departure which he promised to forward to me, but of course the drawing never reached its destination. Where is now, I often wonder, the unfortunate artist? He had lived for some time at Montrouge, in Paris, in order to study the French language, but I was unable to trace any of the friends there to whom he sent messages announcing his terrible fate.

From Sredni-Kolymsk, which we left on March 22, our way lay along the Kolyma River[47] to Nijni-Kolymsk,[48] an almost deserted collection of log huts surrounding a ruined wooden chapel. Our sleds were now lightly built, uncovered contrivances to carry two men, about a dozen dogs being harnessed to each. With a good team one may cover a long distance during the day over level ground, but our poor half-starved brutes travelled so slowly that my heart sank when I thought of the distance before them. Throughout that dismal time America used to seem as unattainable as the North Pole itself! I now directed that the sleds should travel in a certain order. Mine was the leading *narta*, and Nos. 2, 3 and 4 were occupied by de Clinchamp, Harding and Stepan respectively. Numbers 4 and 5 were provision-sleds which should have headed, not brought up the rear of the caravan, although I did not discover this mistake, which nearly cost us dearly, until after the passage across Tchaun Bay.

[47] The River Kolyma, like the Indigirka, has its source in the Stanovoi Mountains.

[48] "Sredni" signifies "Middle," and "Nijni" "Lower" Kolymsk, according to their situations on the Kolyma River.

Harding and Stepan each drove a sled, the three other drivers being half-breed Kolyma-Russians, of whom two were of the usual stolid, sulky type. The third, who accompanied me, was a character. A squat little bundle of furs, with beady black eyes twinkling slyly from a face to which incessant cold and bad brandy had imparted the hues of a brilliant sunset. Local rumour gave Mikouline forty years, but he might have been any age, certainly an octogenarian in such primitive vices as were feasible within the restricted area of his Arctic home. Mikouline had once travelled some distance down the coast, and was therefore installed as guide. He and the other drivers agreed to accompany us as far as the first Tchuktchi settlement, where I hoped to procure assistance and transport from the natives. And at first I believed in my driver, for he was a cheery, genial little fellow, so invariably facetious that I often suspected his concealment of a reserve stock of *vodka*. And although Mikouline's casual methods concerning time and distance were occasionally disquieting, he was a past master in the art of driving dogs, which is not always an easy one. The rudiments of the craft are soon picked up, but, as I afterwards found to my cost, a team will discover a change of driver the moment the latter opens his mouth, and become accordingly unmanageable. Illustrations of dog-sleds in the Arctic generally depict the animals as bounding merrily away at full speed, to be restrained or urged on at the will of their driver, but this is a pure fallacy, for a sled-dog's gallop is like a donkey's, short and sweet. The average gait is a shuffling trot, covering from five to seven miles an hour over easy ground; and even then desperate fights frequently necessitate a stoppage and readjustment of the traces. There are no reins, the dogs being fastened two abreast on either side of a long rope. To start off you seize the sled with both hands, give it a violent wrench to one side, and cry "Petak!" when the team starts off (or should start off) at full gallop, and you jump up and gain your seat as best you may. To stop, you jab an iron brake into the snow or ice and call out "Tar!" But the management of this brake needs some skill, and with unruly dogs an inexperienced driver is often landed on his back in the snow, while the sled proceeds alone upon its wild career. Laplanders and the Eskimo have each their method of dog driving, but the above was that practised by ourselves and by the Tchuktchis on the Siberian coast.

The journey of three hundred miles to Nijni-Kolymsk was accomplished in five days, and it was pleasant enough, for every night was passed in the hut of some fisherman or trapper who regaled us with tea and frozen fish. The Kolyma settler is generally a half-breed; an uncouth but hospitable being who leads a queer existence. During the short summer his days are passed on the river in canoes, fishing and trapping, but in winter furs are donned and dog-sled and rifle become a means of livelihood. Fish is the staple article of food, and when the summer catch has been a poor one a winter famine is the invariable result, and this is what had marred our progress. Nevertheless, a famine here is generally due to laziness, for the river teems with fish of all kinds, sturgeon and salmon-trout predominating, and there is also the *tchir*, a local delicacy. The busiest fishing season is in the early autumn, when herrings ascend the river in such shoals that forty or fifty thousand are frequently taken in a couple of days with a single net. Our dogs were fed on this fish, which appeared to be much larger than the

European species. In the spring-time the Kolyma settler can revel in game, for swans, geese, duck and snipe abound, although weapons here are very primitive and the muzzle-loader prevails. Elk and Polar bear are occasionally shot in the winter, but the former have become scarce, and the latter only frequent the sea-coast.

Every hut, or even shed, we passed on the Kolyma had a name, which duly appears on the table of distances in the Appendix, but there are only two so-called villages between Middle and Lower Kolymsk, Silgisit and Krest, making the stages of the journey 90, 180, and 240 miles respectively. A little drive like the final stage of, say, London to Durham with such short rests would probably knock up an English horse, but even our weakly teams were fit to continue after twenty-four hours at Lower Kolymsk. Krest, so named from a large wooden cross which stands amidst a few log huts, was reached on March 24, and here we were hospitably entertained by the inhabitants, who all appeared to live in one house, the interior of which was cosy enough; and I here noticed for the first time that the windows were made, not of ice, but of fish skin. The other huts were deserted, for Krest is a fishing village only fully populated in summer-time. There seemed to be a fair lot of cattle and horses about the inhabited dwelling, where we shared the usual evening meal of frozen fish, to which a goodly portion of roast deer had been added in our honour. The meat would have been excellent had it not reeked of wild thyme, a favourite ingredient on the Kolyma, but the frozen berries served with it as a *compôte* were delicious. These were a species of bilberry, but my host informed me that a dozen edible kinds are found within a couple of miles of the village, a kindly provision of nature, as vegetables are here unknown. There were also edible roots, one of which I tasted, but have no desire to repeat the experiment. I was surprised at the sleek appearance of my host's cattle, but he told me that the plains around Krest afforded good, but coarse, pasturage, and sufficient hay to last throughout the winter months.

When we left Krest the night was bitterly cold, but clear and starlit, and that evening is memorable on account of a strange dream which disturbed my slumbers as I lay snugly ensconced in the sleeping-bag which was now my nightly couch. Perhaps the roast deer and bilberries had transported my astral self to the deck of a P. and O. liner at Colombo, where the passengers were warmly congratulating me on a successful voyage across Asia. "You have now only Bering Straits to get over," said one, pledging me in champagne, and the geographical inconsistency did not strike me until a captain in gold lace, with the face of a Yakute, pointed out the little difference of several thousand miles lying between Ceylon and our projected goal. The shock of this discovery awoke me in terror, to shiver until dawn, yet heartily thankful that Colombo and I were still where we should be! Not that a short interval of tropical warmth would have been unwelcome that night, for although the cold was not so severe as it had been inland, I found on halting for breakfast that a mirror in a small bag under my pillow was coated with a thin film of ice.

Grey skies and frequent snow-flurries were experienced as we neared Nijni-Kolymsk, and as each mile was covered the vegetation on either side grew scantier, for even at Srendi-Kolymsk the pine forests had lost their grandeur. Here they dwindled away to scanty fir-trees, stunted larches and grey-green willows drooping in the snow. There is no sadder sight in creation than a sunset in these regions, when the heart seems to sink in sympathy with the dying day, and a dull despair to deaden the mind, as darkness creeps over a frozen world.

On the morning of Friday, March 28, we reached Nijni-Kolymsk, about thirty log huts in various stages of decay. This settlement, which was founded by Cossacks about the middle of the seventeenth century, is surrounded by low scrub, and, as at Sredni-Kolymsk, the buildings left standing are so low that they are invisible from the level of the river, which is here about two miles wide. The surroundings, however, are more picturesque than those of Middle Kolymsk, for a picturesque chain of mountains breaks the horizon to the eastward, although the remainder of the landscape consists of level and marshy tundra. In the reign of the Empress Catherine Nijni-Kolymsk contained over five hundred sturdy Cossacks and their families; it was peopled at the time of our visit by about fifty poor souls, whose gaunt and spectral appearance told of a constant struggle against cold, hunger and darkness. Nijni-Kolymsk had once apparently boasted of a main street, but the wooden huts had fallen bodily, one by one, till many now formed mere heaps of mud and timber; those still erect being prevented from utter collapse by wooden beams propped against them.

We found the entire community, consisting of half-breeds, Yakutes and Tunguses, gathered outside the hut of the only Russian in the place, one Jacob Yartsegg, who was banished here for life for smuggling rifles for revolutionary purposes into Russia. Yartsegg, a tall elderly man in ragged deerskins, informed me that the village possessed no *ispravnik* but himself, at which I could scarcely restrain a smile. There was something so "Gilbertian" in the idea of a prisoner acting as his own jailer! This man spoke a little English and apologised for the damp and darkness of the only hut he had to offer us. And in truth it was a piteous hovel half filled with snow, which was soon melted by the heat of our fire, rendering the floor, as usual, a sea of mud. There was not a mouthful of food to spare in the place, and we ate from our own stores. Yartsegg's dwelling was shared by a miserable creature who had lost a hand and leg in a blizzard the previous year. The wounds, with no treatment, had not even yet healed, and it made me shudder to think of the agony the poor fellow must have endured, with cold and hunger to add to his misery. But although the sufferer was a young man, now maimed for life, he never complained save when pain in the festering limbs became excruciating. Under such conditions a European would probably have succumbed in a few weeks, but Arctic Siberia must be visited to thoroughly realise the meaning of the words "suffering" and "patience."

The cold is not generally so severe at Nijni-Kolymsk as at the settlement up river (Yartsegg's record showed 42° F. as the minimum temperature of the month of March), but the climate here is less endurable on account of violent snowstorms which occasionally occur even in summer, and dense fogs which, during spring and autumn, continually sweep in from the Polar Sea. The sun remains above the horizon for fifty-two days, and the rest of the year varies from twilit nights in June to almost complete darkness in midwinter. The village was certainly not an attractive one, and as its occupants evinced a decided tendency to encroach on our provisions I resolved to remain in it only a couple of days. But here occurred the first of a series of *contretemps* which dogged my footsteps throughout the coast journey, for the drivers now refused to carry out their contract, urging that even if a Tchuktchi settlement were safely reached the natives there would certainly murder us.[49] Here was an apparently insurmountable difficulty, for Mikouline, who acted as spokesman, simply snapped his fingers at Yartsegg's authority. Threats were therefore useless, and kindness equally futile where this little scoundrel was concerned. In *vodka* lay my sole hope of victory, and the "exile-jailer" luckily possessed a limited store, some of which I purchased, and set to work to subjugate the unruly Mikouline by the aid of alcohol; an immoral proceeding no doubt, but no other course was open. For I knew that my driver's example would at once be followed by the others who, like sheep, blindly followed him in everything. It would weary the reader to describe my hopes and fears during the ten interminable days and nights that the war was waged. But he will appreciate what they meant to the writer from the fact that every day, even every hour, was now of utmost importance, owing to the late season and probable break up of the sea-ice at no distant date. Also we were rapidly consuming the provisions which were to form our sole subsistence in the desolate Arctic. It therefore became necessary to place each man on half rations, consisting of two frozen fish, one pound of black bread and a quarter of a pound of *Carnyl* per diem. My triumph over Mikouline cost me several gallons of *vodka*, to say nothing of hours of disgust and annoyance passed in close companionship with the now maudlin, now abusive, little half-breed. To make matters worse, the weather during that wasted fortnight was still, clear, and perfect for travelling, and the very morning of our departure it broke up with a gale and blinding snowstorm which occasioned another irksome delay down river. Just as we were starting, the now sober Mikouline again showed symptoms of weakening, until I plied him with bumpers of *vodka*. So long as "the spirit moved him" my driver was all right; but alas! the *Vodka* would not last for ever, and where should we be then?

[49] The Kolyma Russians have apparently always held this tribe in great awe, for as far back as 1820 Von Wrangell wrote: "Our sled-drivers were certainly not free from the deeply-rooted fear of these

people (the Tchuktchis), generally entertained by the inhabitants of Kolymsk."

Yartsegg begged me to visit some of his relatives in New York and acquaint them of his existence, but although furnished with their address I could never trace these people, and the exile talked so wildly at times that my failure to execute the commission was perhaps due to his impaired mind and memory. But half-witted and almost repulsive as this poor fellow had become, it went to my heart to leave him in that God-forsaken settlement, when on the morning of April 2nd we again set out, in the teeth of a biting north-easter, for the shores of the Arctic Ocean.

CHAPTER X

A CRUEL COAST

A few miles below Nijni-Kolymsk vegetation entirely disappears, and in winter nothing is visible on all sides but vast and dreary plains of snow-covered tundra. The first night was passed in a tiny log hut belonging to a trapper and bearing the name, like any town or village, of Tchorniusova. It was pleasant to reach even this rude shelter, the last but one to separate us from the homeless immensity of the Arctic, for the strong breeze of the morning increased by sunset to a northerly gale which the dogs would not face. Towards midnight two Yukagirs (a small tribe inhabiting the country due east of the Kolyma) arrived in a dog-sled and begged for shelter, having with difficulty reached the hut after several hours of battling against a furious *poorga* which had succeeded a change of wind to a westerly quarter. A *poorga* is a kind of Arctic typhoon justly dreaded on this coast, for its fury is only equalled by the suddenness with which it overtakes the traveller. During these tempests (which sometimes last two or three days) the snow is whirled up in such dense clouds that objects a few yards away become invisible, and it is impossible to make headway, for the dogs, instinctively aware of peril, generally lie down and howl, regardless of the severest punishment. The trapper here told me that on one occasion he observed, after one of these storms, an unusual mound of snow near his dwelling, and extricated from it the frozen remains of a Yukagir driver and five dogs. The former had lain down to die within fifty yards of shelter and salvation.

The weather improved towards daybreak and enabled us to make an early start. A hard day's travelling followed, for the wind had cleared the river of snow, and we sledded over slippery black ice, which would have made a schoolboy's mouth water, but sadly impeded the dogs. Nearing the ocean the Kolyma widens by several miles, and here we made our first acquaintance with the ice-hummocks or "torosses" formed by the breakers of the Polar Sea. Towards sunset a black speck was sighted on the snowy waste, and two hours later we reached Sukharno, the Tsar's remotest outpost on the shores of the Arctic Ocean, about eight thousand miles from Petersburg. Here there was a single hut, so low in stature and buried in the drifts that we had to crawl into it through a tunnel of snow. The occupant was an aged Cossack who lived amid surroundings that would have revolted an English pig, but we often recalled even this dark, fetid den as a palace of luxury in the gloomy days to come.

We were awakened the following morning by the roaring of the wind, for another *poorga* had swooped down during the night, which kept us prisoners here for the three following days. It was madness to think of starting in such weather, and there was nothing for it but to wait for a lull, alternately smoking, sleeping, and cursing Mikouline, the cause of the delay. Fortunately the hut was weatherproof, and but for perpetual anxiety I could almost have enjoyed the rest and warmth out of reach of the icy blast. But who could sit down in peace or sleep for more than five consecutive minutes when tortured by the thought that the *poorga* might rage for an indefinite period and that the journey to Tchaun Bay must occupy at least three weeks, while our stock of food was slowly but surely diminishing? Even the scanty allowance I had fixed upon for each man was doled out by Harding reluctantly, and with a doubtful glance, as much as to say, "Will it last?" a question which for the past week had dinned itself into my brain several thousand times within the twenty-four hours. Here again Mikouline showed signs of mutiny, and I was compelled to broach our store of *vodka* to keep him up to the mark, which I did so successfully that my driver started from Sukharno in an advanced state of intoxication, after a bout of fisticuffs with his aged host. But the little scoundrel would certainly not have started in a sober condition.

We left Sukharno on the morning of April 6, in a strong north-westerly gale accompanied by driving snow, but later in the day the sky brightened and we forged ahead as rapidly as rough sea ice would permit. Soon it became much colder, a favourable sign, for here a falling thermometer invariably precedes clear, still weather. But it seemed ages before we lost sight of Sukharno, and while it was still in sight I often glanced back for a last look at that lonely snow-covered hut, for it was our last link with civilisation, indeed with humanity. This is, however, not strictly correct, for later in the day we passed the wooden beacon erected by the Russian explorer Lieutenant Laptief in the year 1739. The tower, which stands on a prominent cliff, is still in a remarkable state of preservation and is visible for a great distance around. And talking of Laptief reminds me of other travellers who have explored these frozen wastes. I had before leaving Europe ransacked the book-stores of London and Paris, but had failed to obtain any practical knowledge of the country which we were about to traverse. Nordenskjold's "North-East Passage, or the Voyage of the *Vega*," was invariably produced by every bookseller I questioned, but as the Swedish explorers never left their ship, this work, as a guide, was quite useless to me. So far, therefore, as finding the Tchuktchis was concerned I was much in the position of a wild Patagonian who, set down at Piccadilly Circus, is told to make his way unassisted to the Mansion House. For although Mikouline affected a knowledge of the coast, I doubt if he knew much more than I did. My literary researches showed me that the journey we were undertaking had only twice been performed by Europeans, or rather Americans (in a reverse direction) about twenty years ago. This was when the U.S. surveying ship *Rodgers* was destroyed by fire in the ice of Bering Straits, and Captain Berry (her commander) and Mr. W. Gilder (correspondent of the *New York Herald*) started off in midwinter to report her loss, travelling through Siberia to Europe, which was reached, after many stirring adventures, in safety.

The works of the earlier explorers afforded me almost as little assistance as the "Voyage of the *Vega*." In a volume, however, written by the famous Russian explorer Admiral Von Wrangell, I gleaned that, "The first attempt to navigate the Polar Ocean to the east of the Kolyma was made in 1646 by a company of fur hunters under the guidance of Issai Ignatiew. The sea was covered with thick drift-ice, nevertheless the travellers found a narrow passage, through which they advanced for two days, when they ran into a bay surrounded by rocks and obtained by barter some walrus teeth from the Tchuktchis dwelling there. Their ignorance of the language of the natives and the warlike disposition of the latter made it appear prudent not to venture further, and Ignatiew returned to the Kolyma. From his imperfect report it is difficult to judge how far his voyage extended. From the time expended, however, it is probable that he reached Tchaun Bay."

The subsequent expedition and fate of the Russian explorer Schalarof are thus chronicled by the same author:

"The ice in the Kolyma did not break up in 1762 until July 21, when Schalarof put to sea and steered for a whole week on a N.-E. and N.-E.-by-¼-E. course. On August 19 the ship was completely beset by large fields of ice. In this dangerous situation, rendered more alarming by a dense fog which concealed the shore, they continued until the 23rd, when they found means to work themselves out of the ice and to gain open water again. They tacked for some time among the fields of ice, in the hope of making and doubling Cape Shelagskoi; but being detained by ice and contrary winds, the advanced season at length obliged Schalarof to seek for a convenient wintering place. This he hoped to find in an inlet on the west side of the cape which led into Tchaun Bay, first visited and surveyed by him. On the 25th he passed between the mainland and the island of Arautan. On the 26th he struck upon a sand-bank, from which it cost the crew much labour to get afloat again. Schalarof went on shore, but finding neither trees nor drift-wood, was obliged to sail further, in search of some place provided with this indispensable requisite. He shaped his course along the southern shore of the bay, as far as the island of Sabadei. Finally, he resolved to return to the Kolyma, which he entered on September 12, and reoccupied his quarters of the preceding winter."

"On the return of spring, Schalarof desired to put to sea again, in the hope of effecting his favourite object, the doubling of Cape Shelagskoi; but his crew, weary of the hardships and privations they had endured, mutinied, and left him. This forced him to return to the Lena. He then went to Moscow, and having obtained some pecuniary assistance from the Government, undertook, in 1764, another voyage to Cape Shelagskoi, *from which he never returned*."

"For a long time none but vague rumours circulated respecting his fate. I was so fortunate in 1823 as to discover the spot, about seventy miles from Cape Shelagskoi, where Schalarof and his companions landed, after they had seen their vessel destroyed by the ice. Here, in a black wilderness, struggling against want and misery, he ended his active life; but a late posterity renders this well-deserved tribute of acknowledgment to the rare disinterested spirit of enterprise by which he was animated."

"On Schalarof's chart, the coast from the Yana to Cape Shelagskoi is laid down with an accuracy that does honour to its author. He was the first navigator that examined Tchaun Bay, and since his time no fresh soundings have been taken there."

Apparently the Russian explorer Laptief only once made an attempt to travel by land from the Kolyma to Bering Sea, but this was by an entirely different route to ours.

"Considering it impossible to effect by sea the task assigned him by surveying the Anadyr River,[50] Laptief resolved on an undertaking attended by equal danger and difficulty, namely, to proceed overland with his whole crew, crossing the mountains, and traversing the country of the hostile Tchuktchis. With this view he left Nijni-Kolymsk on October 27th, 1741, and directed his course towards the Anadyr, with forty-five *nartas* drawn by dogs. On November 4th he arrived at Lobasnoie, on the Greater Anui. As that river forms the boundary of the country inhabited by the wandering Tchuktchis, Laptief deemed it prudent, during his passage through what might in some measure be considered an enemy's territory, to observe the utmost caution, and to subject his men to a strict military discipline. They ascended the Greater Anui, crossed the chain of mountains Yablonoi Khrebét, and reached the Anadyr Ostrog on November 17th *without having seen a single Tchuktchi on the way*."

[50] Which in those days was supposed to fall into the Polar Sea.

Concerning another expedition Von Wrangell writes: "The Geodets undertook a third excursion over the ice in 1771. Starting from the Kolyma they arrived on the last of the Bear Islands on March 9th. There they remained six days on account of bad weather, and then started for Tchaun Bay. Three days they continued in a due east direction, and having gone forty-eight versts, turned off to the Baranov rocks, from which they were fifty versts distant, and where they arrived on the 18th. Having rested there and killed a white bear, they continued their journey along the coast in an easterly direction, but on the 28th, their provisions running short, they were forced to return. On April 6th they arrived again at Nijni-Kolymsk, after driving about 433 versts."

All this was not very encouraging, especially the fact, recorded by Von Wrangell, that a traveller named Hedenstrom once made an attempt to reach Shelagskoi about the same time of year as ourselves, but "found the ice already so thin that he was obliged to renounce the plan. He even found it difficult to retrace his own track to the Kolyma, where, however, he arrived in safety and spent the following summer."

This was the sole information which I was able to extract from a score of volumes dealing with Arctic exploration, and, briefly, it came to this: Von Wrangell had once travelled in winter, with dogs, from Nijni-Kolymsk to Koliutchin Bay (about two-thirds of the distance to Bering Straits). Berry and Gilder had traversed the entire distance, from the Straits to the Kolyma River, under similar conditions; and why, therefore, should we not do likewise? There was a "but," however, and a formidable one. These three travellers had made the coast journey in the depth of winter (with a good three months of solid ice before them), while we were about to attempt it in the declining spring.

On the first day, when travelling about two miles out to sea not far from the mouth of the Kolyma River, Harding, with an exclamation of surprise, drew my attention to a group of men apparently gathered together on the brink of a cliff. But a moment's reflection showed me that, viewed from this distance, these figures, if human beings, must have been giants of fifty feet high. The resemblance, however, was so startling that we steered inshore for a closer inspection, and my glasses then revealed the rocky pinnacles which nature has so weirdly fashioned in the shape of man. The effect in this desolate and ice-bound wilderness was uncanny in the extreme. Von Wrangell noticed these pillars in 1820, and measuring one found it forty-three feet in height. He describes it as "something like the body of a man, with a sort of cap or turban on his head, and without arms or legs," but to us they appeared much more lifelike.

We made good headway during the greater part of the first day in clear and cloudless weather, but towards evening the sky became overcast and a rapidly rising wind brought down another shrieking *poorga*, which compelled us to encamp in haste under the lee of a rocky cliff, luckily at hand when the storm burst upon us. At this time a breastplate of solid ice was formed by driving snow on our deerskins, and an idea of the intense and incessant cold which followed may be gleaned by the fact that this uncomfortable cuirass remained intact until we entered the first Tchuktchi hut nearly three weeks later. But this first *poorga*, although a severe one, was nothing compared to the tempests we afterwards encountered. Nevertheless, our flimsy tent was twice blown down before morning, its re-erection entailing badly frozen hands and faces, for having encamped without finding drift-wood there was no fire and therefore no food. Cold and hunger precluded sleep, and I passed the cold and miserable hours vainly endeavouring to smoke a pipe blocked by frozen nicotine. This may be taken as a fair sample of a night in dirty weather on that cruel coast. At daybreak we commenced another hunt for drift-wood, which was not discovered for several hours, when every one was utterly worn out from the cold and lengthened fast.

Sometimes a *poorga* would rage all day, and in this case progress was out of the question. The solitary meal would then consist of frozen fish or iron-like chunks of *Carnyl* which were held in the mouth until sufficiently soft to be swallowed. There was of course no means of assuaging thirst, from which we at first suffered severely, for the sucking of ice only increases this evil. And want of water affected even the sleds, the runners of which should be sluiced at least once a day, so as to form a thin crust of ice which slides easily over a frozen surface.

On April 7 we reached a landmark for which Mikouline had been searching in some anxiety, the Bolshaya-Reka or Big River. All that day we had been at sea, picking our way through mountainous bergs and hummocks, some quite sixty feet in height, while the sleds continually broke through into crevasses concealed by layers of frozen snow. On the right bank of this river we found a deserted village once occupied by trappers; half a dozen ruined huts surrounding a roofless chapel. The place is known as Bassarika, a corruption of Bolshaya-Reka, and Mikouline had known it ten years ago as the abode of prosperous fur traders. But one hard season every living being perished from smallpox and privation, and the priest alone escaped to carry news of the disaster to Nijni-Kolymsk.[51]

[51] Twenty or thirty years ago there were three or four Russian settlements, and at least as many Tchuktchi villages between the Kolyma River and Tchaun Bay, but there is now not a solitary being on the coast throughout the whole distance of nearly six hundred miles.

Our drivers camped here with reluctance, for the place is said to be haunted, and its silent, spectral appearance certainly suggested an abiding-place of evil spirits. But one of the ruined huts, although pitch dark and partly filled with snow, offered a pleasanter shelter than our draughty tent, and I insisted upon a halt. Drift-wood was plentiful (it always was near the mouth of a river), and a fire was soon kindled, or rather a bad imitation of one, for this fuel only yields a dull, flickering flame. This latter, however, melted the snow sufficiently to convert the floor of our shanty into a miniature lake, and we therefore left it in disgust and adjourned to the deerskin tent shared by Stepan and the drivers, hard snow being a preferable couch to several inches of icy-cold water. This happened to be my birthday, and Harding triumphantly produced a tiny plum pudding, frozen to the consistency of a cannon-ball, which he had brought all the way from England in honour of the occasion. But we decided to defer the feast until we could enjoy it in comparative comfort, perhaps on the shores of Bering Straits—if we ever reached them! My notes between Bassarika and Tchaun Bay are very incomplete, for they were generally made at night, when the temperature inside the tent seemed to paralyse the brain as completely as it numbed the fingers. Oddly enough there is nothing colder than paper, and when the bare hand had rested upon it for a few moments it had to be thrust back into a fur mit to restore circulation.

Imagine a barren, snow-clad Sahara absolutely uninhabited for the first six hundred miles, and then sparsely peopled by the filthiest race in creation, and you may faintly realise the region traversed by my expedition for nearly two months of continuous travel from the last Russian outpost to Bering Straits. Place a piece of coal sprinkled with salt on a white tablecloth, a few inches off it scatter some lump sugar, and it will give you in miniature a very fair presentment of the scenery. The coal is the bleak coast-line continually swept clear of snow by furious gales; the sugar, sea-ice, and the cloth the frozen beach over which we journeyed for over 1600 miles. The dreary outlook never changed; occasionally the cliffs vanished and our way would lie across the tundras—marshy plains—which in summer encircle the Polar Sea with a belt of verdure and wild flowers, but which in winter-time are merged with the frozen ocean in one boundless, bewildering wilderness of white. In hazy weather land and sky formed one impenetrable veil, with no horizon as dividing line, when, even at a short distance away, men and dog-sleds resembled flies crawling up a white curtain. But on clear days, unfortunately rare, the blue sky was Mediterranean, and at such times the bergs out at sea would flash like jewels in the full blaze of the sunshine, while blocks of dark green ice, half buried in snow under shadow of the cliffs, would appear for all the world like *cabochon* emeralds dropped into a mass of whipped cream. But the reverse of this picture was depressing in the extreme. For on cloudy days the snow would assume a dull leaden appearance, and the sea-ice become a slate grey, with dense banks of woolly, white fog encircling the dismal scene. Fair and foul weather in the Arctic reminded me of some beautiful woman, bejewelled and radiant amid lights and laughter, and the same divinity landing dishevelled, pale, and sea-sick from the deck of a Channel steamer.

But we had little time, or indeed inclination, to admire the beauties of nature, which are robbed of half their charms when viewed by the owner of an empty stomach. Did not Dr. Johnson once truthfully remark that, "the finest landscape is spoiled without a good inn in the foreground"? Time also in our case meant not merely money, but life, and we were therefore compelled to push on day after day, week after week, at the highest rate of speed attainable by our miserable teams, which, to do them justice, did their best. The poor beasts seemed to be instinctively aware that our food would only last for a limited period. When the coast was visible we steered by it, travelling from 6 A.M. until we struck drift-wood, the traveller's sole salvation on this coast. Sometimes we found it and sometimes we didn't, in any case it was seldom more than sufficient to boil a kettle, and bodily warmth from a good fire was an unknown luxury. Even a little oil would have been a godsend for heating purposes, but we had used up every drop we possessed before reaching Sredni-Kolymsk, where no more was attainable, and I dared not waste the alcohol brought for the purpose of bartering with the Tchuktchis. I can safely say I have never suffered, physically or mentally, as I did during those first two weeks along the shores of North-Eastern Siberia. We were often compelled to go without food throughout the twenty-four hours, and sometimes for thirty-six, our frozen provisions being uneatable uncooked. At night, after a cheerless meal, we would crawl into sleeping-bags and try to sleep in a temperature varying from 35° to 45° below zero. And sometimes lying sleepless, miserable, and half frozen under that flimsy tent, I resolved to give it all up and make an attempt to return to the Kolyma River, although even retreat would now have been attended with considerable peril. And yet, somehow, morning always found us on the march again eastward. On the beach we got along fairly well, but steep, precipitous cliffs often drove us out to sea, where the sleds had to be pushed and hauled over rough and often mountainous ice, about the toughest work I know of. We then travelled about a mile an hour, and sometimes not that. The end of the day generally found us all cut about, bruised, and bleeding from falls over the glassy ice; and the wounds, although generally trifling, were made doubly painful by frost and the absence of hot water. I enter into these apparently trivial details as at the time they appeared to us of considerable importance, but the reader may think them unnecessary, just as the man who has never had toothache laughs at a sufferer. Toothache, by the way, was another minor evil that greatly increased our sufferings during those dark days of hunger and incessant anxiety.

And yet, if all had gone well, all these troubles—added to intense cold and semi-starvation—would have been bearable; but everything went wrong. First it was the dogs, as famished as ourselves, who dragged their tired limbs more and more heavily towards evening as the weary days crawled on, and every morning I used to look at their gaunt flanks and hungry eyes, and think with despair of the thousand odd miles that lay between us and Bering Straits. Then the Russian drivers, secretly backed by Mikouline, threatened almost daily to desert us and return to the Kolyma. One morning all three burst into my tent and vowed that nothing should induce them to proceed a mile further. Finally, force had to be employed to keep these cowards together, and, luckily, we were well armed, which they were not. But this trouble necessitated a watch by night, as exhausting as it was painful in the pitiless cold. Only ten days out from the Kolyma we were living on a quarter of a pound of *Carnyl* and a little frozen fish a day, a diet that would scarcely satisfy a healthy child. Bread, biscuits, and everything in the shape of flour was finished a week after leaving Kolymsk, but luckily we had plenty of tea and tobacco, which kept life within us to the last.

Then sickness came. Owing to the frequent dearth of fuel our furs and foot-gear were never quite dry, and during sleep our feet were often frozen by the moisture formed during the day. One fireless night De Clinchamp entirely lost the use of his limbs, and a day's delay was the result. Four days later he slipped into a crevasse while after a bear and ruptured himself. This bear, by the way, was the only living thing we saw throughout that journey of nearly six hundred miles to Tchaun Bay. Then I was attacked by snow-blindness, the pain of which must be experienced to be realised. Goggles gave me no relief, and in civilisation the malady would have necessitated medical care and a darkened room. Here it meant pushing on day after day half blinded and in great agony, especially when there was no drift-wood and therefore no hot water to subdue the inflammation. Sleep or rest of any kind was impossible for nearly a week, and for two days my eyes closed up entirely and I lay helpless on a sled, which was upset, on an average, twice every hour on the rough, jagged ice. At last we struck a fair quantity of wood and halted for forty-eight hours, and here I obtained relief with zinc and hot water, while Mikouline proceeded to rub tobacco into his inflamed optics, a favourite cure on the Kolyma, which oddly enough does not always fail. About this time one of the dogs was attacked with rabies, and bit several others before we could shoot it. We lost over a dozen dogs in this way before reaching Bering Straits, this being probably due to the casual manner in which Stepan treated the disease. When one animal had to be destroyed he coolly led it about at the end of a string to find a suitable spot for its execution, and when another went mad, and I was for despatching it, suggested that we could ill spare it from the team for a few days longer! And yet, notwithstanding these hourly difficulties, privations, and hardships, I am proud to say that I never once heard a word of complaint from a single member of my party, although those days of constant toil and suffering in that grave of nature, the Arctic, might well have tried the constitution of a Sandow and the patience of a Job! And I may add that no leader of an expedition could wish for three more courageous and unselfish companions than the Vicomte de Clinchamp, George Harding, and last, but not least, the Cossack Stepan Rastorguyeff, whose invaluable services throughout this journey will, I am informed, be suitably rewarded by the Russian Government.

About one day in four was bright and sunny, and would have been almost pleasant under other circumstances. Even our chicken-hearted drivers would become less gloomy under the genial influence of bright sunshine, and join together in the weird songs of their country until darkness again fell, bringing with it disquieting fears of the murderous Tchuktchi. Most of that memorable journey was made through a constant succession of snowstorms, gales and *poorgas*. We met three of the latter between the Kolyma River and Cape North, the last one striking us on the twentieth day out, as we were crossing Tchaun Bay, on the eastern shores of which I hoped to find a settlement. Although the weather just before had been perfectly clear and calm, in five minutes we were at the mercy of such a tempest that men and dogs were compelled to halt and crouch under the sleds to escape its fury.

During a temporary lull we got under way again, and for seven of the longest hours of my life we floundered on. As even a gentle zephyr up here, blowing against the face, means considerable discomfort, and anything like a gale, acute distress, the reader may imagine what it meant to struggle against a howling *poorga*. During those terrible hours one could only glance hastily to windward, for the hard and frozen snow cut like a whip into cheeks and eyeballs. Every few minutes the weak, half-starved dogs would lie down, and were only urged on by severe punishment which it went to my heart to see inflicted, but to reach land was a question of life or death. Sometimes the coast would loom ahead through the blinding snow, but we had to steer by the compass, which, for some occult reason, was that day useless, for it pointed east and led us due north towards the sea. At last, after a journey from the opposite coast of ten hours, with faces, feet and hands badly frozen, we reached land exhausted, and, for the time being, safe. Some drift-wood and the shelter of a friendly cave were handy, or that night some of us must inevitably have perished. But after a painful struggle up a steep cliff, waist-deep in snow, and a crawl into the cheerless refuge, the cry was raised, "A sled is lost!" and there was nothing for it but to face the *poorga* again in search of the missing *narta* and its driver, one of the Kolyma men. For perhaps an hour every man floundered about the hummocks and crevasses of the bay with a dogged perseverance born of the knowledge that at this time of the year large floes are often detached from the main pack and blown out to sea. But at last even Stepan's pluck and endurance were exhausted (to say nothing of my own), and I blew the whistle for a general retreat to our cavern, only to find the missing sled triced up with the others and its occupant snugly reposing inside the rock. And right glad we were to find not only the man in charge of it but also the missing sled, which had contained the last remnants of our provisions!

That night, after the evening meal, every mouthful of food we had left was two pounds of *Carnyl* and fourteen frozen fish, and this must suffice for nine men and sixty ravenous dogs! Hitherto we had joked about cannibalism. Harding, we had said, as being the stoutest member of the party, was to be sacrificed, and Stepan was to be the executioner. But to-night this well-worn joke fell flat. For we had reached the eastern shores of Tchaun Bay, and this was where we should have found a Tchuktchi village. When the sun rose next morning, however, not a sign of human life was visible. Even Stepan's features assumed a look of blank despair, but the plucky Cossack aroused our miserable drivers as usual with his cruel *nagaika*[52] and compelled them to make a start, although the poor wretches would willingly have resigned themselves to a death which undoubtedly overtook them a few days later.

[52] Cossack whip.

We had lost three dogs during the blizzard on Tchaun Bay, and the rest were so weary and footsore that it seemed little short of brutal to drive them on. But to stop here meant starvation, so we struggled painfully onwards to the eastward, growing weaker and weaker every hour. At times I felt as if I must lie down in the snow and give way to an overpowering feeling of drowsiness, and Harding and De Clinchamp afterwards confessed that they frequently experienced the same feeling. But Stepan, perhaps more inured to hardships than ourselves, was the life and soul of our party during that long, miserable day, and it was chiefly due to his dogged determination (combined with a small slice of luck) that on that very night, when things seemed to be on the very verge of a fatal termination, we came upon signs of human life in the shape of a kayak with a paddle propped against it on the snowy beach. An hour later we sighted our goal—the first Tchuktchi settlement! And the relief with which I beheld those grimy, walrus-hide huts can never be described, for even this foul haven meant salvation from the horrors of a lingering death.

CHAPTER XI

IN THE ARCTIC

Our reception by the Tchuktchis at Cape Shelagskoi[53] was so surly that I began to think there might be some reason for the repeated warnings of our friends on the Kolyma. Two or three woebegone creatures in ragged deerskins, crawled out of the huts and surveyed us with such suspicion and distrust that I verily believe they took us for visitors from the spirit world. As a rule the Tchuktchi costume is becoming, but these people wore shapeless rags, matted with dirt, and their appearance suggested years of inactivity and bodily neglect. I noticed, however with satisfaction that their churlish greeting was not unmingled with fear, although they obstinately refused the food and shelter begged for by means of signs, pointing, at the same time, to a black banner flapping mournfully over the nearest hut. This I knew (from my experiences at Oumwaidjik in 1896) to be the Tchuktchi emblem of death. Our sulky hosts then indicated a dark object some distance away upon the snow, which I sent Stepan to investigate, and the Cossack quickly returned, having found the corpses of several men and women in an advanced stage of decomposition. An infectious disease was apparently raging, for several sufferers lay helpless on the ground of the first hut we entered. I imagine the malady was smallpox, for a lengthened experience of Siberian prisons has made me familiar with the characteristic smell which accompanies the confluent form of this disease. On the other hand, it may have been *kor*, the mysterious epidemic which had lately desolated the Kolyma district, and of which we had heard even as far south as Yakutsk.

[53] Von Wrangell writes that during his coast journey an old Tchuktchi near here told him that he was descended from the Chelagi, or, as they are usually called by the Tchuktchi, the Tchewany, who many years since migrated towards the west and have not since been seen. He adds: "The first of these names has been preserved in Cape Shelagskoi, and the second in that of Tchewan or Tchaun Bay."

But food must be obtained at any cost. To leave this place without an adequate supply would have been sheer madness, especially as we had ascertained from the natives that the next settlement was at least nine "sleeps" (or, in Tchuktchi dialect, days) away. Our own stores had now dwindled down to a few frozen fish, but here, for the first (and by no means the last) time, *vodka* came in useful, for there lives no Tchuktchi who will not sell his soul for alcohol. The fiery spirit procured seal-meat sufficient to last us, with care, for ten days. I can safely say that this is the most disgusting diet in creation, but we devoured it greedily, with keen appetites sharpened by the knowledge that twenty-four hours more would have seen us starving.

There were about thirty people in this place who had escaped the prevailing pestilence, but all showed such a marked aversion to our presence that I sparingly dispensed our *vodka*. A drunken Tchuktchi is a murderous devil, and I had no desire to repeat my experiences amongst these people of 1896, when my life was more than once in jeopardy during their orgies. However, the natives of Erktrik (as this place is called), were so openly hostile that even the usually truculent Mikouline, who once, under the influence of his favourite beverage, had offered to accompany me to a much warmer and remoter place than this, was paralysed with fear. I therefore resolved to push on early the following day (April 22), but that night we were all too exhausted to keep the usual watch, and when we awoke late the next morning our three Kolyma friends had bolted, taking some of our seal-meat with them. There can be no doubt that the fugitives perished trying to reach their home, for panic had deprived them of the reasoning power to steal a sled and dogs, or even a compass, which they might easily have done. The food the poor fellows took was perhaps sufficient for a week's consumption, certainly not for a journey of at least a couple of months on foot. A more vicious and unprincipled scoundrel than Mikouline probably never existed, and yet I missed him sorely afterwards, and would give a good deal, notwithstanding all the trouble he gave me, to know that the little ruffian had reached the Kolyma in safety. But this is, I fear, outside the bounds of possibility. We did not leave the next day, for Erktrik, or rather Cape Shelagskoi, proved a Pandora's box of unpleasant surprises, including another tempest, which, though not so severe as the *poorga* which preceded it, detained us here for forty-eight hours. These were passed in scouring the coast in search of the drivers, but although their footsteps were visible for a couple of miles they ceased abruptly where the runaways had taken to the ice in order to recross Tchaun Bay.

On the morning of April 23 we left Erktrik, now each driving a sled, the fifth team being hitched on to Stepan's *narta*. A dead calm had now succeeded the wind, and we halted at midday for a rest of an hour. There being drift-wood near camp, I decided to eat our daily meal here instead of waiting, as usual, until the evening. And that was one of the pleasantest hours throughout the whole of that distressing journey, for the air was still, and the sun blazed down upon our little tent and filled it with a bright warm light, which, but for the desolate surroundings and unsavoury odour of seal-meat, would have recalled Nice or Monte Carlo. The ice, too, on beard and moustache, and clinking against the drinking-cup, was scarcely suggestive of the Riviera; but, nevertheless, the momentary peace and warmth were little short of luxurious. And the dogs seemed to relish the sun and warmth as much as ourselves, as they lay around, asleep or indulging in the quaint antics which often made me wonder whether they were not in some way distantly allied to the human race. For the Siberian sled-dog is unquestionably the most sagacious animal in existence, and many a time have his comical vagaries lightened my hours of despondency. In appearance the Siberian differs essentially from the Eskimo dog, and is a stronger though smaller animal, seldom of a uniform colour, being generally black and white, black and tan, &c. His eyes are often of a light blue colour from the incessant snow-glare, which has a queer effect, especially, as often happens, when one pupil has retained its original colour. The leader of my team, a lean, grizzled old customer with the muzzle of a wolf, was the quaintest of all. Oddly enough, kicks gained his friendship much more readily than kindness, if the kicker happened to be a favoured acquaintance; if not, trouble was likely to ensue, as De Clinchamp once found to his cost! Towards the other male dogs of my team "Tchort," or the Devil, assumed an air of almost snobbish superiority, but to the females he was affability itself. The reader will scarcely believe that I have seen this weird animal squat gravely in front of one of the opposite sex, extend his right paw and tap her playfully on the jowl, the compliment being returned by an affectionate lick on Tchort's right ear. But this is a fact, and only one of many extraordinary eccentricities which I observed amongst our canine friends while journeying down the coast. Tchort, however, was a sad thief and stole everything he could lay his hands, or rather teeth, upon, from seal-meat to a pair of moccasins. At night, therefore, when other dogs were free to roam about camp, my leader was invariably fastened firmly to a sled, where he usually revenged himself by howling dismally at intervals. But he was a capital leader and as steady as a rock, excepting when the team, at the sight of a distant object on the snow, would give one piercing yelp of joy, and bolt towards it at breakneck speed, utterly regardless of the brake or curses of the driver. I am bound to say that on these occasions Tchort was the most unruly of the lot.

Beyond Erktrik the coast becomes so rocky and precipitous that we travelled chiefly over the sea, and progress was slower than it had been yet on account of the mountainous ice we encountered around the numerous headlands. There was little driving to do, every man having to turn to and haul with the dogs, or lift the sleds bodily across crevasses, or over steep, slippery icebanks. For a week the sky remained unclouded, and the sun beat down so fiercely that during the day our garments were soaked with perspiration, which would freeze to the skin at night and intensify the cold. West of Cape North the coast is of no great height, and although distance and the rarefied atmosphere often made the cliffs appear of formidable dimensions, a nearer approach generally showed that a man could stand on the beach and, metaphorically, shake hands with one on their summits. With plenty of decent food this part of the journey would have been comparatively enjoyable, but as we had only enough seal-meat to last for ten days, and as I feared that the Erktrik natives, wishing to be rid of us, had misinformed me as to the distance away of the next village, I could only issue provisions very sparingly. Luckily my fears were unfounded, for in a week we reached the second settlement, Owarkin, which was more prosperous, and where a goodly supply of food was produced in exchange for half a dozen dogs, some tea and a few articles of barter. The natives here were less unfriendly, but as most of them had never seen a white man we were regarded with great curiosity. All day the tent was packed with eager faces, and at night-time the canvas opening was continually pushed aside, much to our discomfort, for the cold here was very severe. But these people were such a welcome contrast to the sulky, ill-conditioned natives down coast that we gladly suffered this minor discomfort. We remained in this place for one night only, and pushed on with renewed hope, encouraged by the kindly demeanour of the natives, for Cape North. But now the fair weather broke up, and almost daily we had to fight against gales and blizzards, which weakness, caused by filthy diet, almost rendered us incapable of. But we pegged away cheerfully enough, although every one was suffering more or less from troublesome catarrh; De Clinchamp was partially crippled by frost-bite, and snow-blindness caused me incessant pain—agony on sunny days when there was a glare off the ice. To make matters worse, drift-wood was so scarce at this time that a small fire was only attainable every second day. Luckily I had kept a few wax candles, and with the aid of these enough snow was melted to serve as a lotion for De Clinchamp and myself. I was harassed, too, by the thought that at our slow rate of speed Koliutchin Bay (still eight hundred miles away) would probably be found broken up and impassable, in which case the entire summer would have to be passed amongst these treacherous natives. For should the Revenue cutter, which the American Government had kindly undertaken to send to our assistance in June, not find us at East Cape, she would probably sail away again, under the impression that we had returned to the Kolyma. In any case she would scarcely come more than a hundred miles or so west of Bering Straits, and Koliutchin was quite three times that distance. There is probably no region in the world more inaccessible than North-Eastern Siberia, and even had the ill-fated André managed to effect a landing, say between Tchaun Bay and the Kolyma River, he would, unless well supplied with provisions, in my opinion, have perished.

Near Cape Kyber a huge bear and its cub were seen in the ice off the island of Shalarof,[54] about three miles from the coast. De Clinchamp, Stepan and half a dozen dogs at once went in pursuit, less for the sake of sport than of replenishing our larder, but after an exciting chase the brute got away, leaving its cub to be devoured by the dogs before Stepan could secure it, a keen disappointment to us all.[55] We frequently came across tracks after this, but saw no more bears, which from everything but a gastronomical point of view was no loss. For there is no more sport in shooting the polar species than in knocking over a rook or a rabbit.

[54] About three and a half versts north of Cape Kyber there is a rocky island of two and a half versts in circumference, entirely surrounded by hummocks. I gave it the name of Shalarof, after the man whose enterprise, courage, and perseverance, and finally whose death in these regions, have well deserved that his name should be so recorded.—"The Polar Sea," by Von Wrangell.

[55] Von Wrangell writes that dogs have a remarkable aversion to bear's flesh as long as it is warm, but this was not our experience on this occasion.

Finally Areni, a large village near Cape North, was reached, and here we found food in plenty, even some deer-meat, which, although putrid, was most acceptable. The *kor*, or smallpox, had not visited this place, and we saw and heard no more of this dread disease eastward of this. From here on to Cape North villages became more frequent and natives more friendly. In one place the sight of a San Francisco newspaper filled us with joy and a pleasant sense of proximity, although it *was* two years old. We traced it to an American whaler, for the trade of this coast is now no longer in Russian hands, but in those of the whaling fleet from the Golden Gate. At present there is no communication whatsoever between the Tchuktchis and the Kolyma, as we had already found to our cost.

A hard journey of over two days from here, during which scarcity of drift-wood caused us much trouble, brought us to Cape North.[56] Darkness had now almost left us, and on April 28 we travelled nearly throughout the night in a dim daylight, arriving the next morning at a small village of three huts called Yugetamil. "And it's about time," murmured Harding, on hearing the name. But the atrocious pun was justly received in silence. About fifteen miles east of this we sighted mountains, perhaps thirty miles to the southward, known to the Tchuktchis as the Puk-tak range. The highest peak, Mount Uruni, about 3000 feet high, was visible in clear weather.

[56] Concerning this region Von Wrangell wrote: "Drift-wood is scarce along this coast, partly from the consumption by Tchuktchis, and partly from natural causes. The greater part of the drift-wood found between the Shelagskoi and the Bering Straits is probably of American origin, for it consists chiefly of stems of pines and firs. My opinion that the drift-wood on this part of the coast comes from America is confirmed by the assertion of the Tchuktchis that among the trunks of fir they not unfrequently find some that have been felled with stone axes."

Nearing Cape North the ice was so bad that our progress seldom exceeded two miles an hour, but the cliffs here are quite perpendicular, so that it was impossible to travel by land. In places they were covered to a height of forty feet or so by the clear green or blue ice formed by breakers of the preceding year, and the dazzling colours reflected by the sunshine on the glassy surface of the rocks was marvellous to behold. Nearing the cape the ice was piled up so high that I feared at one time we should never succeed in rounding the headland. The sleds were constantly hauled up hummocks sixty to seventy feet high, and much care was needed to prevent them falling headlong from the summits with the dogs. Every one had over a score of bad falls that day, and although no bones were broken I slipped up towards midday and landed heavily on the back of my head with my feet in the air. But for three thick fur caps my skull must have been fractured, and for several minutes I lay unconscious. All that day we toiled along, now scrambling over mountainous "torosses," now wading waist-deep in soft snow, which occasionally gave way to precipitate us into invisible holes. When, late at night, we reached a small village of two huts (name unknown), men and dogs were quite exhausted, and had the tiny settlement been half a mile further we could never have reached it. Here again we disposed of three dogs for more seal-meat, and went on the next morning rejoicing, notwithstanding a stiff gale from the eastward accompanied by snow.

CAPE DESPAIR.

At Cape North the natives were the friendliest we had yet seen, and we actually obtained flour and molasses, priceless luxuries. Pancakes fried in seal oil may not sound appetising, but to us they tasted like the daintiest of *petits fours*. And the welcome news that Koliutchin Bay would remain frozen until late in May enabled me to hope that we might now reach Bering Straits, a contingency which only a few days before had seemed extremely remote. This information was furnished by a Tchuktchi named Yaïgok, whose home was within a few miles of Bering Straits, and who spoke a few words of English picked up from the American whalemen. This man was returning with a sled-load of bearskins and fox furs, to trade to the whaling fleet. He was a fine, strapping fellow, and I gladly accepted his offer to guide us as far as his village, for twelve dogs, some tobacco and a couple of clasp-knives. Several natives here had travelled as far as the Bering Straits, which they called the "Big River," the land beyond it, Alaska, being known as "Nagurok" in the Tchuktchi dialect.

The village at Cape North is known to the natives as Irkaïpien. From a distance the promontory presents almost the appearance of an island, as it is joined to the low land by a landspit hidden in winter by stranded ice. This is probably the point seen in 1777 by Captain Cook, from whom it received its present name, but I rechristened it Cape Despair, on account of the difficulty we experienced in reaching it from the time when it was first sighted. Mentioning the fact to Stepan, I was much entertained by an anecdote related by the Cossack in connection with the names of places. He had once accompanied a German traveller, who was compiling a volume of his experiences, down the Yenisei River in Siberia. On several occasions the tourists' inquiries as to topographical names were met with the reply, "Imia niet," for the country they were travelling was new to Stepan. When, however, the book of travel was published in Berlin, a mountain, two rivers and a village were carefully described under the title of the above two words which in Russian signify: "It has no name!"

I was rather disturbed while at Cape North to hear the name of my old friend Koari of Oumwaidjik continually mentioned by the natives, for although I well knew the old scoundrel's influence extended along the coast in a southerly direction, I was not prepared to find it existing amongst the Tchuktchis of the north-eastern seaboard. One of my chief objects had been to avoid the Oumwaidjik people, and I had therefore planned our route so as to steer north of the place by over two hundred miles. However, nothing was known here of the enmity existing between myself and this old bandit, who, by reason of the punishment inflicted on him on my account by the United States Government, would probably have made things warm for us had he been aware of my proximity, I had hitherto imagined that no land communication existed between Oumwaidjik and the Arctic Coast, and that by the time navigation re-opened we should be far away from the clutches of my old enemy, with whom our guide, Yaïgok, was apparently on intimate terms. I therefore resolved to be careful, the more so that at Natska, a village about ten days east of Cape North, we found a caravan of sixteen dog-sleds, laden down with furs, on the point of departure.

"Where are those people going?" I inquired of Yaïgok, as the team started away across the tundra in a south-easterly direction.

"Over the mountains to Koari!" replied the Tchuktchi, and I prudently refrained from questioning him further.

Another unpleasant incident occurred at Cape North, where a gale and heavy snow detained us for two days. A young native, having imbibed our *vodka*, clamoured loudly for more, and when Stepan refused to produce the drink, drew a knife and made a savage lunge which cut into the Cossack's furs. In an instant the aggressor was on his back in the snow, and foreseeing a row I seized a revolver and shouted to my companions to do likewise. But to my surprise the crowd soundly belaboured their countryman, while Yaïgok apologised on behalf of the chief, for the man's behaviour. Nevertheless, there were dissentient voices and ugly looks, so that I was not altogether sorry to leave Irkaïpien behind us.

We made rapid headway after this, for most of the way lay over tundra as smooth and flat as a billiard-table. Our guide's sled continually left us far behind, for the Tchuktchi's *nartas* are far superior to those made on the Kolyma. Yaïgok's dogs, too, were fresh and hardy, while ours were exhausted by hunger and hardship. Our method of harnessing was also inferior to the Tchuktchi method, which brings the strain on the shoulders instead of the neck. These people, like the Yakutes, are very kind to animals.

I never once saw them strike their dogs, which were urged on by rattling an iron ring fixed for the purpose to the end of the brake. Yaïgok knew every inch of the road and saved many a mile by short cuts taken across land or sea. The cold here was great and drift-wood scarce, but one could be sure now of passing some settlement at least every three or four days, where even a foul glimmer of a seal-oil lamp was better than no fire at all. About this time the sleds gave us much trouble—the rough usage they had undergone necessitating constant repairs, but these were quickly made, for not a scrap of metal enters into the construction of a Kolyma dog-sled; merely wooden pegs and walrus-hide thongs, which are more durable and give more spring and pliancy than iron nails. Three days after leaving Cape North, and in fine weather, Wrangell Land was sighted, or, I should perhaps say, was probably sighted, for at times huge barriers of icebergs can easily be mistaken for a distant island. Yaïgok, however, averred that it was an island, and his judgment was probably correct.

The journey from here eastwards to Bering Straits would under ordinary circumstances of travel have seemed a severe one, for we travelled through head winds and constant snowstorms, which now, with a rising temperature, drenched our furs and made the nights even more miserable than those of intense, but dry, cold. One thing here struck me as curious, every snow-flake was a most perfect five-pointed star, as accurately shaped as though it had passed through a tiny mould. Discomforts, as I have said, continued, not to say hardships, but we had become so inured to the latter that we could now, with well-lined stomachs, afford to despise even blizzards with shelter never more than twenty or thirty miles distant. Our diet was not appetising, consisting as it did for the most part of oily seal and walrus-meat, but drift-wood was now more plentiful, and we could usually reckon on that blessing, a fire at night. There was now little difficulty in finding settlements, one of which was reached on an average every twenty-four hours, but it was necessary to keep a sharp look-out, for the low, mushroom-like huts of the Tchuktchis are invisible a short distance away and are easily passed unnoticed during a fog or in driving snow. Fogs, by the way, were very prevalent as we neared the Straits, and became denser in proportion as the spring advanced.

East of Cape North we had no bother whatever with the natives, who in many places even refused payment for food and assistance. Passing the villages of Wankarem and Onman[57] we reached, on May 10, Koliutchin, a large village situated on an island in the bay of that name. Here we were received with open arms by the chief, who spoke a little English, picked up, like Yaïgok's, from American whalemen at East Cape. Professor Nordenskjold's ship the *Vega* wintered here some years ago, and the natives showed us souvenirs of the Swedish explorer's visit in the shape of clasp-knives and tin tobacco-boxes. The irony of fate and obstinacy of pack-ice are shown by the fact that all on board the *Vega* were expecting an easy passage through Bering Straits to the southward, and yet within twenty-four hours were compelled to remain for another winter securely ice-locked off this dreary settlement.

[57] Our American charts made these villages sixty miles apart, whereas they are not divided by a third of the distance.

Koliutchin Island was called Burney Island by Captain Cook, but Whale Island would be a better name for it than either, for it exactly resembles a narwhal on the surface of the sea. There appeared to be frequent communication with the mainland, for we reached the island (about four miles in circumference and twenty-five miles from the coast) by a well-defined sled-track; perhaps luckily, for the bay was otherwise obstructed by heavy ice. News travels like lightning along this part of the coast, and Kouniang, the chief, and a crowd of natives received us as we landed along the beach. As soon as our tent was pitched, deer-meat (only slightly tainted!), flour and molasses were brought us, also some sticky American sweets, which having reposed for some time in the chief's deerskin *parka*, were covered with hairs. But we were used to this slight inconvenience, for since leaving Yakutsk I had seldom partaken of a meal which was not freely sprinkled with capillary particles, either from our own furs or the surroundings. I verily believe that between Verkhoyansk and East Cape I consumed, in this way, enough hair to stuff a moderately sized pillow!

Kouniang was one of the richest natives on the coast, and his trade with the whale-ships was extensive; he providing the Americans with whalebone, walrus tusks and furs, in exchange for cotton goods, canned provisions and rubbish of all kinds "made in Germany." The chief would take no payment for his hospitality, and this was perhaps fortunate, as I had very little to give him. So many of our dogs had died or been bartered that only thirty-one were now left, and these, with four sleds, about fifteen pounds of Circassian tobacco and under a gallon of *vodka*, represented the entire assets of the expedition. Poverty is a serious crime in a civilised country, but in some savage lands it means absolute starvation, and the problem of tiding over perhaps a couple of months at East Cape without means of paying for food now caused me considerable anxiety. A credit was awaiting me at Nome City in Alaska, but the Tchuktchi scarcely understands banking transactions. Everything depended upon the charity or otherwise of the chief at East Cape; and, as the reader may imagine, I left Koliutchin in a very perplexed state of mind.

Koliutchin Bay was negotiated in beautiful weather, much to my relief, for I had experienced misgivings after our terrible experiences in Tchaun Bay. But a blue sky and perfect stillness enabled our now exhausted dogs to carry us across in under seven hours, and I was glad to reach the eastern shore, for great lakes of open water on every side showed that we were not a day too soon. The sun had now become so powerful that most of our travelling was done by night, for during the daytime the ice was often inch-deep in water, and the runners were imbedded in the soft and yielding snow. The coast from here on to Bering Straits is said to be rich in minerals; but although coal was frequently seen cropping out from the cliffs and mica is plentiful, we saw no gold, and only heard on one occasion of the precious metal. This was at Inchaun, about a day's journey from East Cape, where one Jim, an English-speaking Tchuktchi informed me that he knew of "a mountain of gold" about ten miles away. The lad offered to walk to the place (now almost inaccessible on account of melting snow), and to bring me specimens of the ore, which I agreed to, undertaking to repay him with one of our much-battered sleds on arrival at East Cape. The next day Jim returned with several attractive bits of rock, which, however, when tested by an expert at Nome City, were found to be absolutely worthless. I had heard of this mountain of gold in London, where I believe it once figured in an alluring prospectus! Jim, I fancy, was a bit of a humbug, who had served on a whaler and was therefore not wholly unacquainted with iron pyrites. Indeed this was the most intelligent Tchuktchi I ever met, although his language would have startled an English bargee. The white man he regarded with extreme contempt, alluding to us indiscriminately as "disfellah" as he sat in our tent, calmly sharing (without invitation) any repast that was going on, and occasionally pausing to exclaim, between the mouthfuls, "By G—! you come a long way!"

At Inchaun, Yaïgok left us, and we proceeded alone and rapidly along the now level beach and rolling tundra. The comparative ease and comfort with which we accomplished the last three hundred miles of the coast journey was due to the fact that the natives are in yearly touch with the American whaling fleet, and are therefore generally well provided with the necessaries of life. On May 19 we reached East Cape, the north-easternmost point of Asia, after a voyage of nearly two months from Sredni-Kolymsk. At this point the expedition had accomplished rather more than half the entire journey, and had travelled, from Paris, a distance of about 11,263 English miles.

CHAPTER XII

AMONG THE TCHUKTCHIS

The wintry aspect of nature around Bering Straits seemed to predict a late summer, and it looked as though months must elapse before the Revenue cutter courteously placed at my disposal by the United States Government could break through the ice and reach us. My original idea was to try and cross over the frozen Straits to Cape Prince of Wales, in Alaska, a feat never yet attempted by a white man, but I found on arrival at East Cape that the passage is never essayed by the Tchuktchis, and only very rarely by the Eskimo. During the past decade perhaps a dozen of the latter have started from the American side, but only a third of the number have landed in Siberia, the remainder having either returned or perished. The distance from shore to shore at the nearest point is about forty miles, the two Diomede Islands and Fairway Rock being situated about half-way across. Bering Straits are never completely closed, for even in midwinter floes are ever on the move, which, with broad and shifting "leads" of open water, render a trip on foot extremely hazardous. Our subsequent experience on nearly seven miles of drifting ice, across which we were compelled to walk in order to land on American soil, inspired me with no desire to repeat the experiment.

East Cape, Bering Straits, practically "the end of the end of the world," is about the last place where you would expect to find a white man, especially in springtime, which, in this far North, answers to the depth of winter in England. When we arrived there, East Cape had been cut off by ice from the world ever since the previous summer, which rendered the presence of "Billy," as the natives called him, the more remarkable. At first I mistook the man for a Tchuktchi, for he had adopted native costume, and a hard winter passed amongst these people, combined with a painful skin disease, had reduced him to a skeleton. The poor fellow had suffered severely, mentally and physically, and could only crawl about the

From Paris to New York by Land

settlement with difficulty, and yet, when news first reached the cape of our approach, he had set out to walk along the coast and meet us, and was brought back from the first village, fifteen miles away, more dead than alive. Billy was a young man, about twenty-five years old, whose hardships had given him a middle-aged appearance. He belonged to the American middle class and was apparently well educated, and, as I suppress his name, there can be no harm in giving his history.

A year before we found him, Billy had left his home in San Francisco to ship as ordinary seaman on board a whaler. But a rough life and stormy weather soon cured him of a love for the sea, and while his ship was lying at Nome City he escaped, intending to try his luck at the diggings. A report, however, had just reached Nome that tons of gold were lying only waiting to be picked up on the coast of Siberia, and the adventurous Billy, dazzled by dreams of wealth, determined to sink his small capital in the purchase of a boat in which to sail away to the Russian "El Dorado." Having stocked his craft with provisions, Billy started alone from Nome, and after many hair-breadth escapes from shipwreck in the Straits, managed to reach East Cape. This was early in the month of August, when an American Revenue cutter is generally cruising about, and the Californian was delighted with his kindly reception from the Tchuktchis, ignoring that the latter are not so pleasantly disposed when alone in their glory and fortified by a frozen sea. For nearly a month Billy remained at East Cape, prospecting every day, and working like a galley slave in the marshy "tundras" swarming with mosquitoes, only to return, every night, to his walrus-hide hut with growing despair. For although the streams teemed with fish, not a glimmer of gold rewarded his labours. Time crept away and the coming winter had shown her teeth with a cutting blizzard, while ice was forming around the coast, when one gloomy October day the Revenue cutter anchored, for the last time that season, off the settlement. And Billy regarded her hopelessly, knowing that desertion from his ship had rendered him an outlaw. To board the *Bear* would mean irons and imprisonment, and the deserter dared not face an ordeal which, a few months later, he would gladly have undergone to escape from

Siberia. Billy watched the Government vessel sink below the horizon with some uneasiness, for his sole property now consisted of the furs he stood up in. His boat, clothes and even mining tools had all been bartered for food, and the discomfited prospector was now living practically on the charity of his savage hosts. The reflection, therefore, that nine long months must be passed in this Arctic prison was not a pleasant one, especially as the natives had already indulged in one of the "drink orgies" which were afterwards resumed at intervals throughout that terrible winter.

How the man survived is a mystery—treated as a rule like a slave, clothed in ragged furs, nourished on disgusting food, and ever at the beck and call of every man, woman and child in the settlement. Christmas-time found Billy suffering severely from scurvy, and covered from head to foot with painful boils. Throughout this period, however, he received every attention and care from the women, who, however, without medical appliances, could do little to alleviate his sufferings. Billy said that at times these strange people showed a consideration and kindness only surpassed on other occasions by their brutality and oppression. One day gifts of food and furs would be showered upon the white man, and nothing be too good for him; on the next he would be cursed and reviled, if not actually ill-treated by all. On drink-nights Billy concealed himself, even preferring to sleep in the snow rather than brave the drunken fury of the revellers, which, as the reader will presently see, was one of my greatest anxieties during our sojourn on these barren shores. All things considered, our arrival on the scene was a godsend to this poor castaway, who averred that another month of solitude would assuredly have driven him out of his mind. But our presence worked a marvellous difference in a short space of time, and Billy visibly gained in health and strength as the days went on, chiefly on account of congenial companionship; for we were almost as badly off, in material comforts, as our poor friend himself.

East Cape consists of a few walrus-hide huts which cling like limpets to the face of a cliff overhanging the Straits. In anything like windy weather you can't go out without danger of being blown bodily into the sea. Also, on the occasion of my last overland trip, I had been warned by the officers of the *Bear* against dangerous natives here, so I resolved to move on to Whalen, a village a few miles west of East Cape on the Arctic Ocean, to await the arrival of the *Thetis*.[58]

[58] The name Whalen should probably be written as it is pronounced—Oo-aylin, but I have adopted the mode of spelling in use amongst the whaling fraternity.

Whalen consists of about thirty *yarats* (as a Tchuktchi dwelling is called) and about three hundred inhabitants. The village stands on a sandy beach only a few yards from the sea, but when we arrived here the entire country was knee-deep in partly melted snow, which rendered locomotion very wet and unpleasant. Here we were kindly received, indeed rather too kindly, for our presence was the signal for a feast, and in a few hours every man in the settlement was mad with drink. Fortunately the chief remained sober and we hid in his hut until the orgie was over. But all that night men were rushing about the village, firing off Winchesters, and vowing to kill us, although that morning when sober they had been quite friendly. We did not pass a very pleasant night, but the next day all was quiet, and remained so until the appearance of a whaler again demoralised the settlement. When a Tchuktchi gets drunk, his first impulse is to get a rifle and shoot. He prefers a white man to practise upon, but if there are none handy he will kill anybody, even his mother, without compunction, and be very sorry for it when he is sober, which unfortunately does not mend matters. Many whalemen have been slain on this coast during the past ten years, and during the few weeks we were at Whalen two natives were killed, also a German trader on the Diomede Islands in Bering Straits. But as the latter individual had set up a primitive still and announced his intention of flooding the coast with "tanglefoot,"[59] his own poison was probably seized by the islanders, who, when intoxicated, murdered its manufacturer.

[59] A slang term for whisky on the Alaskan coast.

Teneskin, the chief of Whalen, was, luckily for ourselves, a very different type of man to the ruffian Koari; and his stalwart sons,

From Paris to New York by Land

Yemanko and Mooflowi, who were, like their father, teetotalers, became our powerful allies when the demon of drink was rampant. Yemanko, the elder, spoke English fairly well, and the comparative comfort in which we lived here was chiefly due to his intelligence, for he managed to persuade his father that my cheques, or rather receipts for food, would be honoured by the commander of the *Thetis* on her arrival. This was our only way out of a tight corner, and I awaited the chief's verdict with intense anxiety, for should his decision be unfavourable starvation stared us in the face, and the worst kind of starvation, in the midst of plenty. For Billy told me that Teneskin received a yearly consignment of goods, in exchange for native produce, from the whalers, and that a shed adjoining his hut was packed from floor to ceiling with canned provisions, groceries and other luxuries. To my great relief the conclave, which lasted for several hours, terminated satisfactorily, and it was agreed that every article furnished by Teneskin should on her arrival be doubly repaid from the store-room of the Revenue cutter. And notwithstanding some anxious qualms as to subsequent repayment which occasionally assailed our host, this plan worked well, for while here we never once suffered from actual hunger. Stepan alone was disgusted with the preliminary discussion regarding the food supply. These Tchuktchis were subjects of the Tsar, he urged, and should therefore be compelled to furnish goods free of cost to the illustrious travellers under His Majesty's protection. The Cossack even donned his uniform cap with the gold double eagle in order to impress the natives with a sense of our official importance. But although the head-dress was at once removed by irreverent hands and passed round with some amusement, I regret to say that its effect (from an awe-inspiring point of view) was a total failure.

As a matter of fact the Tchuktchis know nothing whatever about Russia, and even the Great White Tsar has less influence here than a skipper of the grimiest Yankee whaler. For the latter is the unfailing source, every summer, of the vile concoction known as whisky, for which a Tchuktchi will barter his existence, to say nothing of whalebone and walrus tusks. Indeed, were it not for the whalers these people would undoubtedly perish, for although a Russian gunboat generally visits them once during the summer, it is more with the object of seizing anything her commander can lay his hands upon than of affording assistance. The "Stars and Stripes" are therefore the only colours with which the coast Tchuktchis are familiar, and I had therefore brought an American flag as well as our now tattered Union Jack, which proved a wise precaution. The British ensign they had never seen before.

There are perhaps twelve thousand Tchuktchis in all, the race consisting of two tribes: the coast Tchuktchis, inhabiting the shore from Tchaun Bay to the mouth of the Anadyr River; and the land Tchuktchis, who are more or less nomads, roaming amongst the plains and mountains of the interior with herds of reindeer, which form their sole means of existence, while their brethren of the coast are entirely dependent upon the sea for a living. Although nominally Russian subjects, these people are the freest subjects in the world, paying no taxes and framing their own laws, which is perhaps only just seeing that they have never been really conquered by Russia. Samoyedes, Buriates and Yakutes have all gone down before the iron heel of the Cossack, but for two centuries the Tchuktchi has stood his ground, and with cold and desolation for allies, has invariably routed all invaders.[60] Thus, to this day, these people are respected, if not feared, by their Russian neighbours, and although several attempts have been made in St. Petersburg to establish a *yassak*[61] amongst them, no official has yet penetrated far enough into the Tchuktchi country to collect it. Although Russia is their common foe, the land and sea Tchuktchis are staunch friends, for each tribe is more or less dependent on the other; the coast Tchuktchis furnishing whalebone, walrus tusks, hides, seal-meat and oil to the landsmen, and receiving deer-meat for food, and skins for clothing, in return.

[60] "These people for many years resisted every attempt made by the Russians either to subdue them or to pass through their country. Of a force numbering two hundred armed men who were sent into their territory, rather for the purpose of scientific exploration than with any views of conquest, not a soul returned, nor has their fate ever been ascertained." — "Frozen Asia," by Professor Eden.

[61] The fur-tax formerly paid to the Crown by the Yakutes and other Siberian races.

It is a far cry from Bering Straits to Borneo, and I was therefore surprised to find many points of resemblance between the coast Tchuktchis and the Dyaks of that tropical island, with whom I became well acquainted some years ago while in the service of Raja Brooke. The Tchuktchi is perhaps physically stronger than the Dyak—unquestionably he is, by nature, a greater drunkard—but otherwise these races might pass for each other so far as features, complexion and characteristics are concerned. And although I have heard men assert that the Tchuktchis originally migrated to Asia from the American continent, my own experience leads me to doubt that this fact, the more so that there is not an atom of resemblance (save perhaps in a partiality for strong drink) between the Eskimo of Alaska and their Siberian neighbours. As a rule the coast native is intelligent, and of strong and graceful build, owing to his life of almost ceaseless activity; out in all weathers, in summer fighting the furious gales of the Arctic in skin boats, in winter tracking the seal, walrus or bear, sometimes for days together, amid the cold, dark silence of the ice. Towards springtime this becomes a dangerous occupation, for floes are often detached without warning and carried away from the main pack into Bering Sea, whence there is generally no return, although marvellous escapes are recorded. Yemanko, the chief's son, had lived for six days floating about on a block of ice, and subsisting upon a seal which he had caught before he was swept into Bering Sea, eventually grounding near East Cape. His only companion was frozen to death.

I was relieved to find that the country between this and Koari's village (about three hundred miles south) was now impassable on account of melting snow, for, if only for the sake of revenge, this wily old thief would probably have set the natives here against us. Communication between the two places had been frequent throughout the winter, and Koari's son, Oyurápok (a deadly enemy of mine), had lately been at Whalen, but had of course ignored my movements.[62] An Oumwaidjik man, however, who accompanied him had remained here on account of sickness. He was almost a lad and therefore knew nothing of Harding and myself, but we were much amused one day to see him proudly produce a many-bladed clasp-knife, *once my property* (!) which Koari had confiscated, with our other goods, in 1896! There seemed to be no love lost between the Whalen and Oumwaidjik people, whom I had found as surly and inhospitable as these were (when sober) friendly and well disposed. It is curious to notice how the various settlements of this coast vary with regard to the reputation of their inhabitants. Thus, although we were generally well treated here, a stay at East Cape would probably have meant serious trouble with the natives, from whom Billy had fled to take refuge at Whalen. But the East Cape people are probably the worst on the coast, although the natives at St. Lawrence Bay are nearly as bad, and those at Oumwaidjik even worse. And yet, unless a drink feast is in progress, a stranger who behaves himself is safe enough in most Tchuktchi villages, so much so that these people are known as *Masinker* (which in their dialect signifies "good") amongst the American whalemen. The odour of a Tchuktchi is indescribable, but so powerful and penetrating as to be noticeable some distance from a settlement, this characteristic smell being caused by a certain emanation of the human body which enters largely into the *Masinker's* daily use. The fluid is employed chiefly for tanning purposes, but it is also used for cleaning food platters, drinking cups and, worst of all, for washing the body, which it is said to protect from cold. Both here and at Oumwaidjik I tried in vain to discover the origin of this disgusting habit, which also prevails to a lesser extent amongst the Alaskan Eskimo. This is only one of the many revolting customs which I unfortunately had an opportunity of studying at close quarters while at Whalen, where I came to the conclusion that the Tchuktchi race must be the filthiest in the world. Were I to describe one-tenth of the repulsive sights which came under my daily notice, the reader would lay down this book in disgust.

[62] See "Through the Gold Fields of Alaska," by Harry de Windt. London: Chatto and Windus.

Furs are worn by the coast Tchuktchis throughout the year, which, as they are seldom removed, did not make them pleasant neighbours in a crowded hut. The men wear a deerskin *parka*, a loose garment reaching a little below the waist and secured by a belt or walrus thong, and hair seal boots and breeches. In rainy weather a very light and transparent yellow waterproof, made of the intestines of the walrus, is worn. Men and boys wear a close-fitting cap covering the ears, like a baby's bonnet, and have the crown and base of the skull partly shaved, which gives them a quaint monastic appearance, while every man carries a long sharp knife in a leather sheath thrust through his belt. The women are undersized creatures, some pretty, but most have hard weather-beaten faces, as they work in the open in all weathers. Many have beautiful teeth, which, however, are soon destroyed by the constant chewing of sealskin to render it pliable for boots and other articles. They wear a kind of deerskin combinations made in one piece and trimmed at the neck and wrists with wolverine, a pair of enormous sealskin moccasins, which gives them an awkward waddling gait, completing their attire. The hair is worn in two long plaits, intertwined with gaudy beads, copper coins and even brass trouser buttons given them by whalemen. Unlike the men, all the women are tattooed — generally in two lines from the top of the brow to the tip of the nose, and six or seven perpendicular lines from the lower lip to the chin. Tattooing here is not a pleasant operation, being performed with a coarse needle and skin thread — the dye (obtained from the soot off a cooking-pot moistened with seal oil) being sewn in with no light hand by one of the older squaws. Teneskin's daughter, Tayunga, was not tattooed, and therefore quite good-looking, but even the prettiest face here is rendered unattractive by the unclean personality and habits of its owner. So filthy are these people that even the *parkas* of both sexes are made so that the hand and arm can be thrust bodily inside the garment, not, as I at first imagined, for the sake of warmth, but to relieve the incessant annoyance caused by parasites. Hours of idleness were often passed by a couple of friends in a reciprocal hunt for vermin.

TENESKIN'S DAUGHTERS.

From Paris to New York by Land

I was naturally anxious to avoid the close companionship with the natives, which residence in a *Yarat* would have entailed. Teneskin's hut was the cleanest in the village, but even this comparatively habitable dwelling would have compared unfavourably with the foulest den in the London slums. The deep, slushy snow made it impossible to fix up a tent, but Teneskin was the proud possessor of a rough wooden hut built from the timbers of the whaler *Japan*, which was wrecked here some years ago, and in this we took up our abode. The building had one drawback; although its walls were stout enough a roof was lacking, and our tent was a poor substitute. However, the place was cleaned out and made fairly cosy with our rugs, furs and four sleds which were used as bunks. Then came a serious difficulty, artificial warmth, which, without a roof, was sorely needed at night. Teneskin's trading goods comprised a small iron cooking stove, which seemed to be the very thing, with plenty of drift-wood about, and which Stepan, with Cossack promptitude, annexed without leave. But an hour later Yemanko rushed into the hut, pale with rage, and without a word seized our treasure and carried it away. Things looked even more ugly when very shortly afterwards the Chief, accompanied by a crowd of natives, entered our dwelling, with Billy as spokesman in their midst. Then amidst frequent interruptions from the Chief the mystery was explained. It appeared that a superstition exists amongst these people that if a cooking place is used by strangers in a hut belonging to the father of a newly born child, the latter dies within a *moon* or month. Teneskin's family had recently received an addition which was the cause of our trouble, but during the height of the argument, Stepan quietly seated himself beside me and whispered the word "Mauser," which reminded me that our host had cast longing eyes on a rifle in my possession. Much as I prized it a fire was essential, and the rifle had to go; which it did without delay, for Teneskin, once possessed of the precious weapon, the baby, to use a sporting expression, was knocked out at a hundred to one! The stove was replaced by willing hands with one proviso: that only the Chief's pots and pans were to be used for the preparation of our food, which proved that a Tchuktchi is not unlike some Christians in the soothing of his conscience.

As the spring wore on, strong gales accompanied by storms of sleet drove us to seek the warmth and filth of Teneskin's residence, which was of walrus hide, about forty feet round and fifteen feet high in the centre. The only aperture for light and air was a low doorway. There was a large outer chamber for fishing and hunting tackle where dogs roamed about, and inside this again a small dark inner room, called the *yaranger*, formed of thick deerskins, where the family ate and slept. In here seal-oil lamps continually burning make it average about 85° throughout the winter. Beyond the tiny doorway there was no ventilation whatsoever, and the heat and stench of the place were beyond description. At night men, women and children stripped naked, and even then the perspiration poured off them. The nights we passed here were indescribable. Suffice it to say that the hours of darkness in the inner chamber of that *yarat* were worthy of Dante's Inferno. And the days were almost as bad, for then the indescribable filth of the dwelling was more clearly revealed. At the daily meal we reclined on the floor, like the Romans in "Quo Vadis," by a long wooden platter, and lumps of seal or walrus meat were thrown at us by the hostess, whose dinner costume generally consisted of a bead necklace. Rotten goose eggs and stale fish roe flavoured with seal oil were favoured delicacies, also a kind of seaweed which is only found in the stomach of the walrus when captured. Luckily a deer was occasionally brought in from inland, and Stepan then regaled us with good strong soup followed by the meat which had made it. Every part of the animal was greedily devoured by the natives, even the bones being crushed and the marrow extracted from them, flavoured with seal oil, and eaten raw. Teneskin, however, had plenty of flour, and this, with desiccated vegetables, was our mainstay during the greater part of the time. As spring advanced, game was added to our bill of fare in the shape of wild duck, which flew in enormous clouds over the settlement. A large lagoon hard by swarmed with them, and one could always bag a couple at least every morning and evening without leaving the hut. But a shooting party was usually made up every day, and we sallied out with the natives, perhaps a score of men and boys, the former armed with Winchesters and the latter with slings, which projected a row of five or six balls cut out of walrus teeth. To shoot a duck on the wing with a bullet is not easy, but the natives seldom returned empty handed;

and many a time I have seen a tiny lad of ten or twelve years old bring down his bird with a sling at twenty or thirty yards. Once I saw Yemanko, with the same weapon, put a stone clean through a biscuit tin at twenty yards range. And one memorable day (for once only) a regal repast was served of three courses consisting of reindeer, wild duck, and Harding's plum pudding, which, notwithstanding its novel experiences, proved delicious. It only had one irreparable fault—there was not enough of it. All things considered, our stay here was by no means the worst part of the journey, for beyond filthy food and surroundings and the deadly monotony of existence, there was little to complain of. Every now and then a drunken orgie would necessitate close concealment, but this was practically the only annoyance to which we were subjected. Once, however, Stepan ventured out during one of these outbursts, and was instantly fired at by a band of ruffians who were reeling about the village. The man who fired the shot was, when sober, one of our best friends, and, luckily for the Cossack, was too far gone to shoot straight. This incident was therefore a comparatively trivial one, although it served to show the unpleasant affinity between a barrel of whisky and bloodshed, and the undesirability of Whalen as a sea-side resort for a longer period than was absolutely necessary. But Teneskin and his sons were always ready to protect us by force if necessary against the aggression of inebriates. Indeed had it not been for these three giants I doubt if the Expedition would have got away from Whalen without personal injury or perhaps loss of life.

Although our host himself did not indulge in alcohol, he was the sole retailer of it to our neighbours. I only once saw the stuff, which was religiously kept hidden save when an orgie had been decided upon and Teneskin, after receiving payment, barricaded himself and prepared for squalls. When we arrived at Whalen, most of the fiery spirit left by the whalers the preceding year was exhausted, and Teneskin was issuing an inferior brand of his own brewing, concocted much in the same way as the "gun-barrel water" of the Eskimo and even more potent, if possible, than San Francisco "Tangle-foot." This is made by mixing together one part each of flour and molasses with four parts of water and then letting the mixture stand for four days in a warm atmosphere until it ferments. The distillery consists of a coal oil tin, an old gun-barrel, and a wooden tub. The mash is put in the coal oil tin, and the gun-barrel, which serves as the coil, leads from this tin through the tub, which is kept filled with cracked ice. A fire is then built under the tin, and as the vapour rises from the heated mess it is condensed in the gun-barrel by the ice in the tub, and the liquor comes out at the end of the gun barrel drop by drop, and is caught in a drinking cup. This process is necessarily slow, and it took a long time to obtain even a half pint of the liquor, but the whisky made up in strength what it lacked in quality, and it did not take much of it to intoxicate, which (from a Tchuktchi standpoint) was the principal object. I am told on reliable authority that, on the Alaskan coast, the Eskimo women join freely in the drunken debauches of the men, but this was certainly not the case amongst the Siberian natives, at any rate those at Whalen. For throughout our stay there I only once saw an intoxicated female. This was the wife of Teneskin, who during an orgie was invariably the only inebriated member of his household. But she certainly made up for the rest of the family!

CHAPTER XIII

AMONG THE TCHUKTCHIS—(*continued*)

The time at Whalen passed with exasperating slowness, especially after the first ten days, when monotony had dulled the edge of success and worn off the novelty of our strange surroundings. On the Lena we had experienced almost perpetual darkness; here we had eternal daylight, which, with absolutely nothing to do or even to think about, was even more trying. Almost our sole occupation was to sit on the beach and gaze blankly at the frozen ocean, which seemed at times as though it would never break up and admit of our release from this natural prison. Every day, however, fresh patches of brown earth appeared through their white and wintry covering, and wild flowers even began to bloom on the hillsides, but the cruel waste of ice still appeared white and unbroken from beach to horizon. One day Harding fashioned a rough set of chessmen out of drift-wood, and this afforded some mental relief, but only for a few days. "Pickwick" had been read into tatters, even our Shakespeare failed us at last, and having parted with the *"Daily Mail* Year Book" at Verkhoyansk, this was our sole library. Sometimes we visited our neighbours, where we were generally kindly received, presents occasionally being made us. One day the Chief's eldest daughter worked and presented me with a pair of deerskin boots with a pretty pattern worked in deerskins of various colours, obtained from dyes of native manufacture. I naturally wondered how these could be extracted from natural products in this barren land of rock, sand and drift-wood, but Billy partly explained the secret of the operation which is, I fancy, peculiar to the coast.[63] The ex-whaleman furnished me with this information during a talk we had over his experiences of the previous winter. From the same source I also gleaned many facts concerning these people, who invariably try to mislead the ingenuous stranger. Billy, however, enjoyed their complete confidence, and had stored up a fund of interesting information, some of which I reproduce for the reader's benefit.

[63] A bright red colour is obtained from a rock found in the interior. Green by boiling the fur in the urine of a dog. I was unable to ascertain how dark blue, the only other dye, is made.

Next to irresponsible and armed drunkards my greatest anxiety at Whalen was caused by the medicine men, of whom there were about a score, and who never lost an opportunity of setting their patients against us. Medicine men are all-powerful here, although their treatment consists solely of spells and incantations. But the unfortunate dupes have a firm belief in these men, who are not only medical advisers, but are consulted on everything pertaining to the affairs of life, from marital differences to the price of whalebone. Billy had at one time aroused the enmity of these impostors, who naturally distrust the influence generally gained by the owner of a modern medicine chest. Our friend had landed in Siberia with a bottle of embrocation and some Cockle's pills, but even this modest pharmacopœia had aroused the bitterest jealousy amongst the doctors at East Cape. But familiarity breeds contempt, and when Billy had gradually been reduced to the social standing of the humblest Tchuktchi the medicine men simply ignored him, and made no objection to his presence at their *séances*, which generally took place in the dark. Occasionally, however, the Shamans officiated in the daylight, when their skill as conjurers would, according to Billy, have eclipsed an Egyptian Hall performance. To swallow several pieces of walrus hide, and afterwards vomit forth a pair of miniature moccasins, would seem a trick beyond the powers of the untutored savage, but the whaleman often saw it accomplished. He also assisted to bind a Shaman hand and foot with walrus thongs, and in less than ten seconds the man had freed himself, although secured by knots which Billy himself could not have unravelled in a week.

My friend is probably the only white man who has ever assisted at a whale dance, which took place in a hut, dimly lit by seal oil lamps and crowded with both sexes in a state of nature, with the exception of their sealskin boots. The performance commenced with music in the shape of singing accompanied by walrus-hide drums, after which a long plank was brought in and suspended on the shoulders of four men. Upon this three women were hoisted astride, and commenced a series of wild contortions, back and forth and from side to side, not unlike the "Dance du ventre." Relays of girls continued this exercise for two or three hours, until all were exhausted, and then flesh of the whale, caught the preceding summer, was handed round by children, and washed down by floods of raw whisky, which brought the entertainment to a close for that night. The following day athletic sports were indulged in by those sufficiently sober, the owner of one hut furnishing the prizes and refreshments. This giver of the feast and his family were distinguished by faces plastered with the red paint already mentioned as being obtained from the mountains of the interior. Wrestling and racing were the chief pastimes, the prizes consisting of a cartridge, a piece of calico, or perhaps a fox skin. The women did not join in these contests, but with them a form of "tossing in a blanket" was gone through. A walrus skin perforated around with holes to give a firmer grip was held by seven or eight stalwart men, and at a given signal a girl lying in the centre was sent flying into the air, she who reached the greatest height receiving the appropriate prize of a needle or thimble. At night the dance was continued, and on this occasion a fire was kindled around which the medicine men seated themselves, mumbling incantations and casting small pieces of deer or walrus meat into the flames as a sacrifice to the evil spirits. The whale entertainment lasted for three nights, but the incidents which occurred upon the last evening are not fit for reproduction here. The whaleman, being more or less of a celebrity, had attracted the bright glances of several Tchuktchi maidens. But even when he found his affinity poor Billy's courtship was of short duration, for his ladylove, when embraced for the first time upon the lips, indignantly thrust him away and screamed for help. According to Tchuktchi customs, she had suffered an irreparable insult, the only recognised mode of kissing here being to rub noses while murmuring "Oo" for an indefinite period. This was Billy's first and last experience of love-making here, although Teneskin would gladly have welcomed a white man as a son-in-law, and without the tiresome preliminaries which generally precede a Tchuktchi marriage. For, on ordinary occasions, a man must first obtain the consent of his *fiancée*, then that of her parents, and when these points are settled he must reside for several months as an inmate of the girl's hut before he becomes her husband. A Tchuktchi may put a wife away on the slightest pretext, but no crime on his part entitles his wife to a divorce. A curious custom here is that of exchanging wives with a friend or acquaintance, who thereupon becomes a brother, even legally, and so far as the disposal of property is concerned.

A Tchuktchi may have as many wives as he pleases or can afford, but married life here is usually a happy one, which is probably due to the fact that a wife is never idle. Not only must she attend to the wants of the household, needlework, cooking, washing, and in winter clearing the roof of the *yarat* of snow, but there are hides to be tanned and deerskins to be dressed and sewn into clothing. A married woman must also pass cold and weary hours in winter watching for seal and walrus, and in summer probe the depths of boredom by fishing with a line for "Tom cod." And from a feminine point of view, there is no reward for her labours, no balls or parties, nor smart hats or gowns to excite the envy of her neighbours; all the Tchuktchi spouse can hope for being a "quid" of tobacco, so rare a luxury that it only reaches her lips when her husband has extracted most of its flavour. While smoking, the Tchuktchis, like the Yakutes, use tiny pipes; the smoke is not ejected or inhaled, but swallowed, and the rankest tobacco is so precious here that it is usually eked out with seal-hairs.

Tchuktchi-land teems with legends and superstitions of which Whalen had its full share. A rock off the coast hard by was said to sing and talk whenever a chief of the village was about to die, and the following curious legend was gravely related to me by Yemanko. Many years ago there lived at Whalen a chief with a wife so pretty that even fish were attracted to the land by her charms. Amongst the dwellers of the sea was a whale, with whom, unknown to her husband, she contracted a union. Eventually a young whale was born to the amazement of the settlement, which, regarding it as a mysterious gift from the spirits, paid the new arrival great homage. A huge tank was dug and contained the monster until it had attained its full growth, when it was marked and turned loose in the sea to decoy other whales. But the natives of Inchaun, an adjoining village, caught and killed the marked whale, which was scaring away all their fish. The Inchaun people were thereupon attacked by the

Whalen men, who slaughtered every soul in their village. There is no doubt that this tribal conflict did take place some time during the eighteenth century, but I cannot say whether the murder of the marked whale was the real cause of the battle.

The Tchuktchis appeared to have no religion, and I never saw any ceremony performed suggestive of a belief in a Supreme Being, although good and evil spirits are believed to exist, and when I was at Oumwaidjik, sacrifices of seal and walrus meat were often thrown into the sea by the medicine men to abate its fury. Three men who died at Whalen during our visit were clad after death in their best deerskins and carried some distance away from the settlement, where I believe they were eventually devoured by the dogs. Several natives told me that a man who dies a violent death ensures eternal happiness, but that an easy dissolution generally means torment in the next world, which shows that the Tchuktchi has some belief in a future state. The theory that a painful death meets with spiritual compensation probably accounts for the fact that loss of life is generally regarded here with utter indifference. A ghastly ceremony I once witnessed at Oumwaidjik is a proof of this. It was called the *Kamitok*, in other words the sacrifice, with the full consent, of the aged and useless members of the community. When a man's powers have decreased to a depreciable extent from age, accident, or disease, a family council is held and a day and hour is fixed for the victim's departure for another world. The most curious feature of the affair is the indifference shown by the doomed one, who takes a lively interest in the preliminaries of his own execution. The latter is generally preceded by a feast where seal and walrus meat are greedily devoured and whisky is consumed until all are intoxicated. After a while the executioner, usually a near relative of the victim, steps forward, and placing his right foot against the back of the condemned, quickly strangles him with a walrus thong. Or perhaps he is shot with a Winchester rifle, this being the usual mode of despatching a friend who has asked another to put him out of the world on account, perhaps, of some trifling but troublesome ailment such as earache or neuralgia, which the sufferer imagines to be incurable.[64] And a request of this kind must be obeyed, or if not lifelong misfortune will attend the man who has refused to fire the fatal shot. Women, however, are never put to death, nor, so far as I could glean, do they ever want to be. The origin of this custom is probably due to the barren nature of this land where every mouthful of food is precious, and where a man must literally work to live.

[64] Mr. Waldemar Bogoras, the Russian naturalist, writes as follows in *Harper's Magazine* of April 1903: "One of the attendants I had with me for two years while in the Kolyma country belonged to a family with a tradition of this kind. He was a man of fifty, and the father and elder brothers had already followed in the way of their ancestors [by the *Kamitok*]. One time, while stricken with a violent fever, instead of taking the medicine that I gave him, he inquired anxiously if I were sure that he would recover at all, otherwise he felt bound to send for his son and ask for the last stroke." —"A Strange People of the North," by Waldemar Bogoras, *Harper's Magazine*, April 1903.

That the *Kamitok* also exists amongst the Eskimo of Alaska is shown by the following anecdote. Captain Healy, of the Revenue cutter *Thetis*, told me that he once inquired of a native near Point Barrow whether one Charlie he had known the previous year was still alive and in good health.

"Oh no," was the reply, "Charlie dead, I shot him."

"Shot him?" said Healy, taken aback. "What did you do that for?"

"Oh, poor Charlie sick, pains all over, he asked me shoot him, so I shot him with his own gun and kept it afterwards!"

The Tchuktchis are by no means an idle race, and whenever I entered a hut I invariably found even the youngest inmates usefully employed; the women busily engaged cooking and sewing, or cleaning and polishing firearms, while the men were away duck-shooting or hunting the seal or walrus. Sometimes we went seal-hunting with our friends, but this is poor sport, especially in damp, chilly weather. The outfit is very simple, consisting of a rifle, snowshoes and spear. A start is made at daylight until a likely-looking hole in the ice is reached, and here you sit down and wait patiently, perhaps for hours, until a seal's head appears above water, which it frequently fails to do. In warm weather this might be an agreeable occupation, but on cold days it seldom induced me to leave even the comfortless shelter of our hut. Most of the seals caught here are hair seals, which must not be confounded with the valuable fur seal, which is used in Europe for wearing apparel, and is seldom found north of the Privilov Islands in Bering Sea. The latter animal is too well known to need description, but the skin of the hair seal is a kind of dirty grey, flecked with dark spots, and is short and bristly. But it is warm and durable and therefore used by the Tchuktchis for breeches and foot wear. Recently, too, it has been introduced into Europe for the use of *chauffeurs* of automobiles, but ten years ago it was practically worthless; although the flesh is preferable as food to that of the more costly species.

A chase after walrus is far more exciting than either a seal or bear hunt, for their capture involves a certain risk and occasionally actual danger. As soon as one of these beasts is sighted four or five *Baidaras* are launched and set out at a terrific pace, for the crew of the first boat up gets the lion's share of the spoil. Winchester rifles are now used instead of the old-fashioned harpoon, so that accidents are rarer than they used to be, although boats are often upset. I have only once seen a walrus: a distorted, shapeless mass of discoloured flesh, sparsely covered with coarse bristles. The one I saw measured about ten feet long, had quite that girth, and must have weighed over a ton. Walrus meat as a diet is less repulsive than seal, for it is not so fishy in flavour and has more the consistency of beef.

We had been here about ten days when a native arrived from East Cape and reported a whaler off that headland. At Whalen the ice still presented a hopelessly unbroken appearance, but low, dark clouds to the eastward looked like open water in the direction of the Straits, and I sent Harding and Stepan, with the East Cape man, to verify his report. He was a silent, sulky brute, and I felt some anxiety until the pair returned the next day after a terrible journey, partly by land but principally over the sea ice across which they had to wade knee deep in water. For about six miles crossing the tundra they floundered in soft snow up to the waist, and finally reached their destination, wet through and exhausted, to find that the ship, probably scared by heavy pack ice, had disappeared to the southward. The natives, however, treated them well, and sent a man to accompany them half way back to Whalen, for the thaw had come so suddenly that he could proceed no further, and our companions only just managed to reach home. This was the last journey made by land between the two settlements, for which I was not sorry, as the undesirable community at East Cape were now as completely cut off from us as the pirates of Oumwaidjik. Harding informed me that at East Cape a totally different dialect was spoken to that at Whalen, but this did not surprise me, as I compiled while at Oumwaidjik a small glossary which completely differed from words in use at Whalen. The natives of the Diomede Island have also a distinctive language, of which, however, I was unable to obtain any words. A reference to the Appendix will show the difference existing between the dialects spoken on the mainland of Siberia. East of Tchaun Bay the same language existed in every village as far as Whalen. The languages spoken by the Reindeer Tchuktchis of the interior and the Eskimo of the Alaskan Coast do not in any way resemble the dialects spoken on the Siberian Coast.

By the end of June the snow on land was fast disappearing, and blue lakes began to appear amongst the white plains and hummocks of the sea. But those were weary days of waiting even when warmer weather enabled us to live altogether in our hut without taking shelter in the chief's malodorous *yarat*. For the former was crowded all day with natives, who used it as a kind of club, and left us souvenirs every night in the shape of a stifling stench and swarms of vermin. As time wore on the heat in our heavy furs became insupportable, but frequent and sudden changes of temperature rendered it impossible to discard them altogether. For often the sun would be blazing at midday with a temperature of 60° in the shade, and a few minutes later we would be cowering over the stove listening to the howling of the wind and the rattle of sleet against the wooden walls. This would last perhaps an hour or two, and then the sky would again become blue and cloudless, the sunshine as powerful as before. One day in early June is thus described in my journal: "Clear, cloudy, warm, cold, windy, calm, sunshine, fog and a little rain!" The wind troubled us most, for here there is no happy medium between a dead calm and a tearing gale, and the latter occurred on an average every second day. Northerly and north-westerly winds prevailed, and we whistled in vain for a southerly buster to clear the coast of ice. And yet notwithstanding our many miseries there were pleasant days, still and sunlit, when I would stroll to the summit of a grassy hill near the settlement, where the sward was carpeted with wild flowers and where the soothing tinkle of many rivulets formed by melting snow were conducive to lazy reverie. From here one could see for a great distance along the coast to the westward, and on bright days the snowy range of cliffs and kaleidoscopic effects of colour cast by cloud and sunshine over the sea ice formed a charming picture. Stepan passed most of his time on these cliffs watching in vain, like a male sister Anne, for ships, for, like most Russians, the Cossack suffered severely from nostalgia.

But the days crawled wearily away, each more dreary than its predecessor, and the eternal vista of ice greeted each morning the anxious gaze of the first man up to survey the ocean. Our Union Jack, now almost torn to shreds by incessant gales, was hoisted on a long stick lent by Teneskin for the purpose, but I began to think that the shred of silk might as well have fluttered at the North Pole for all the attention it was likely to attract from seaward. So passed a month away, and the grey hag Despair was beginning to show her ugly face when one never-to-be-forgotten morning Harding rushed into the hut and awoke me with the joyful news that a thin strip of blue was visible on the horizon. A few hours later waves were seen breaking near the land, for when once ice begins to move it does so quickly. Three days later wavelets were rippling on the beach, and I felt like a man just released from a long term of penal servitude when on the 15th of July the hull of a black and greasy whaler came stealing round the point where Stepan had passed so many anxious hours.

The whaler proved to be the *William Bayliss* of New Bedford. We boarded her with some difficulty on account of the jagged ice floes on the beach to which she was moored. It was an acrobatic feat to jump from the slippery ice, lay hold of a jibboom towering overhead, and scramble over the bows. But once aboard, Captain Cottle loaded us with good things (including a tin of sorely-needed tobacco), and all would now have seemed *couleur-de-rose* had Cottle been able to give us news of the *Thetis*. This, however, he was unable to do, and when that night the whaler had sailed away I almost regretted that I had declined her skipper's offer of a passage across the Straits, which might, however, have been prolonged for an indefinite period as the ship was now bound in an opposite direction. That night was certainly the worst we ever experienced, for even Teneskin was rendered helpless by the pandemonium created by the floods of whisky which had streamed into the settlement from the hold of the *William Bayliss*. Towards evening things looked so ugly that the chief and his sons, armed with Winchester rifles, took up their quarters for the night in our hut, the door of which was barricaded by means of iron bars. Even Yemanko looked pale and anxious, for every man in the village, he said, was mad with drink. The chief's wife and daughters remained in the *yarat*, for a Tchuktchi however drunk has never been known to molest a woman. Singing, shouting and deafening yells were heard during the earlier part of the night, as men reeled about the settlement in bands, and occasionally our door would re-echo with crashing blows and demands for admission. This went on for two or three hours, and when things had quieted down and we were thinking of emerging from the stifling hut for fresh air, a shot rang out on the stillness. We seized our rifles, and not a moment too soon, for simultaneously the door flew open with a crash and half a dozen men reeled into the room. One of them brandished a Winchester, but I noticed with relief that the rest of the intruders were unarmed. The face of another whom I recognised as a medicine man, was streaming with blood from a wound across the forehead. Fortunately all were overcome by the fiery poison they had been greedily imbibing and were therefore as weak as children in the hands of seven sober men. In less time than it takes me to write it the invaders were firmly secured with walrus thongs and thrown out of doors to sleep the drink off. A watch was kept throughout the night in case of an attack by reinforcements, but the deadly "Tangle-foot" had done its work, and the village did not awaken until the following day from its drunken slumbers. Unfortunately a native was killed by the shot we heard.

On the morning of the 18th of July Harding and I, while walking on the beach, remarked a white cloud on the horizon, the only blur on a dazzling blue sky. Presently the vapour seemed to solidify, and assume the appearance of a floating berg, until, a few minutes after, we looked again at the object which had attracted our attention, and lo and behold a thin black thread was now ascending from it into the clear still air. "A steamer!" shouted Harding, rushing back to the hut for a field-glass. But before he could return through the deep heavy shingle doubt had become certainty and I had recognised the Revenue cutter *Thetis*. This is the same vessel, by the way, which rescued Lieutenant Greely and his party on the shores of Smith Sound, but I do not think even they can have been more heartily grateful to see the trim white vessel than we were.

In less than an hour our welcome deliverer had threaded her way through the ice, and we stood on the beach and watched her cast anchor about half a mile off shore. As the chains rattled cheerily through the hawse holes Stepan flew, on the wings of a light heart, to the flagstaff. I am not emotional, but I must confess to feeling a lump in my throat as the Stars and Stripes were slowly dipped in response to a salute from our ragged little Union Jack. For with the meeting of those familiar colours all my troubles seemed to vanish into thin air!

Once aboard the *Thetis* Harding and I, at any rate, were amongst acquaintances who had previously served on the Revenue cutter *Bear*. I also found an old friend, Lieutenant Cochrane, once third officer of the *Bear*, and now second in command of the *Thetis*, which made this sudden change from a life of mental and physical misery to one of security and well-being the more enjoyable. There was nothing to delay the cutter, save farewells to our kind old host and the repayment for the food with which he had provided us, and by midday we were steaming away from the dreary settlement where I had passed so many anxious hours. And then, for the first time in many weary months, we sat down in the ward-room to a decent and well-served meal and enjoyed it beyond description, for are not all pleasures in this world comparative? Success to the Expedition was drunk in bumpers of champagne, and I then adjourned to Cochrane's room for coffee and liqueurs and a talk over old days on the *Bear*. And the afternoon in that cosy, sunlit cabin, the blessed sensation of rest after toil combined with a luxurious lounge and delicious cigar, constituted as near an approach to "Nirvana" as the writer is ever likely to attain on this side of the grave!

PART II
AMERICA

CHAPTER XIV

ACROSS BERING STRAITS—CAPE PRINCE OF WALES

The term "cutter" is somewhat of a misnomer, if literally taken, for the Government vessels which patrol these Northern waters. The *Bear*, for instance, which landed us on the Siberian coast in 1896, was a three-masted screw-steamer of over 600 tons, an old Dundee whaler purchased for the United States for the Greeley Relief Expedition. The *Thetis*, although somewhat smaller, is practically a sister ship of the *Bear*, which latter is regarded as the best and stoutest vessel of the Revenue Cutter Service. And her officers and men are well worthy of her. Three or four years ago no less than eight whalers were hopelessly jammed in the ice off Point Barrow in the Arctic Ocean, and their crews were in imminent danger of starvation. The season was too far advanced for a ship to proceed to their rescue, but a party from the *Bear* managed to carry supplies to the beleaguered ships after a sled journey of almost unparalleled difficulty, and thereby avert a terrible catastrophe. Several of the shipwrecked men had already perished, but the majority were rescued, chiefly through the pluck and perseverance of Lieutenant Jarvis, first lieutenant of the *Bear*, and leader of the expedition.

The *Thetis*, when she called for us at Whalen, was bound on a mission of some peril—the search for two large steamers from San Francisco which, while trying to reach Nome City, had been caught in the pack and swept away by drifting ice into the Polar Sea. Both vessels were crowded with passengers, including many women, and the *Thetis* had already made two unsuccessful attempts to ascertain their whereabouts. Indeed, it was feared that no more would ever be heard of the *Portland* or *Jeannie* which had, as usual, been racing to reach Nome City before any rival liner from the Golden Gate.

When, on that sunlit morning, we left Whalen, a cloudless sky and glassy sea unflecked by the tiniest floe led me to hope that our troubles were at an end. Captain Healey of the *Thetis* had resolved to land us on Cape Prince of Wales, but when, towards evening, that promontory was sighted, my heart sank at the now familiar sight of ice packed heavily around the coast. By nine o'clock we were (to use a whaling term) "up against" the outer edge of the pack, and shortly afterwards the engines of the *Thetis* were slowed down, for the man in the crow's nest reported trouble ahead. And we found it in plenty, for the stout little vessel, after cleaving and crashing her way through the floes for a couple of hours, was finally brought to a standstill by an impassable barrier. We were now about six miles from the land, but an Eskimo village under the Cape was plainly visible across the swirling masses of ice which were drifting to the northward.

"I can't go in any further," cried Healey, and I now had the choice of two evils—to attempt a landing with the aid of the natives, or remain on board the Thetis perhaps for weeks searching for the *Portland* and *Jeannie*.[65] But I quickly decided on the former course, and a signal was run up for assistance from the shore, which was quickly seen by a crowd of natives assembled on the beach. To add to our difficulties a breeze, which had arisen towards evening, was now assuming the proportions of a southerly gale, and Healey impatiently paced the deck, as he watched the Eskimo launch a *baidara*, and cautiously approach us, now threading narrow leads of water, now hauling their skin-boat across the drifting ice.

[65] Both these vessels were eventually rescued without loss of life.

Finally, after a perilous journey, they reached us, and without a moment's delay the expedition was bundled, bag and baggage, into the *baidara*, for the position of the *Thetis* was now not devoid of danger. Amidst hearty cheers from those on board, we pushed off with some misgivings, while the cutter slowly veered away northward on her errand of mercy. I shall never forget that short, but extremely unpleasant journey. At times it seemed as though our frail craft must be overwhelmed and swamped, for it was now blowing a gale. Every moment huge cakes of ice around us were dashed against each other, and splintered into fragments with a report as of a gun. We made way so slowly that the shore seemed to recede instead of to advance, for often boat and baggage had to be hauled across the floes which now travelled so quickly with the wind and tide that it seemed as though we must be carried past our destination and into the Arctic Ocean. Sometimes it looked as though we could never reach the coast, for—

> "The ice was here, the ice was there,
> The ice was all around,
> It cracked and growled, and roared and howled
> Like noises in a swound."

At times the ice-islands we were crossing were tossed to and fro by the waves so violently that it became almost impossible to stand, much less walk, on their slippery surface; at others, while all were paddling for dear life, a towering berg would sail down in perilous proximity, for its touch would have sunk our skin boat like a stone. Once I thought it was all over, when a floe we were on became detached from the main pack, and there was barely time to regain the latter by quickly leaping from one cake of ice to the other as the waves and current tore them apart. It took us four hours to reach land, or rather the foot-ice securely attached to it, and here, worn out after the tough struggle against the forces of nature, every man took a much-needed rest. It was not until 7 A.M. on June 19 that our feet actually touched the soil of America, six months to a day after our departure from the Gare du Nord, Paris.

Cape Prince of Wales is a rocky, precipitous promontory about 2000 ft. high, which stands fully exposed to the furious winds, prevalent at all times on this connecting link between Bering Sea and the Arctic Ocean. Why Bering Straits should be so known remains a mystery, for the explorer of that name only sailed through them in the summer of 1728, while Simeon Deschnev, a Cossack, practically discovered them in the middle of the seventeenth century.[66] Captain Cook, of British fame, who passed through the Straits in 1778, is said to be responsible for the nomenclature, which seems rather an unjust one, but perhaps the intrepid English navigator had never heard of Deschnev.

[66] "On June 20, 1648, Simeon Deschnev, a Cossack trader, sailed from the River Kolyma for the eastward to trade for ivory with the Tchuktchis. His party sailed in three small shallops drawing but little water. After a while the known waters behind them closed up with floes, rendering a return to the Kolyma impossible, but the unknown wastes ahead were open, and invited exploration. Hugging the coast, Deschnev sailed through the Bering Straits, landing there in September. He called the Siberian shore an isthmus, and described the Diomede Islands, which he plainly saw. Although no mention is made by this party of having seen the American continent, it was probably observed by them, for Cape Prince of Wales can easily be seen on a clear day from the Asiatic side. Deschnev's voyage was quite forgotten until discovered by accident amongst some old records in 1774.

"Only in August, 1728, did Bering sail through here, going a short distance into the Arctic Ocean, but returning without giving any sign of the importance of the pass, or its nature, and believing, most likely, that what land he saw on the eastern side was a mere island, and not the great American continent. Captain Cook, who came third, made no mistake, for he fully realised that the division of the two hemispheres was here affected, and gave to these straits the name of Bering, August 1778."—"An Arctic Province," by H. W. Elliott.

The Eskimo settlement which nestles at the foot of Cape Prince of Wales is known as Kingigamoot, and contains about 400 souls. The place looked infinitely drearier and more desolate than the filthy Tchuktchi village which had been our home for so many weary weeks, and it seemed to me at first as though we had stepped, like the immortal Mr. Winkle in "Pickwick," "quietly and comfortably out of the frying-pan into the fire." For our welcome on the shores of America was a terrific gale, and driving sleet against which we could scarcely make headway from the spot where a landing was effected to the village, a distance of perhaps a mile, which took us an hour to accomplish. It was barely eight o'clock, and no one was yet stirring in the settlement, which is only visible a short distance away, for the Eskimo, unlike the Tchuktchis, dwell under the ground.

The sight of a wooden house with glass windows considerably enlivened the dismal and storm-swept landscape, and we made our way to this solitary haven, which proved to be the residence of Mr. Lopp, an American missionary. His home, though snug enough, was too small to contain more inmates, being already occupied by its owner's wife and family, but an empty shed adjoining it was placed at our disposal, and our hospitable friend bustled about to make it as cosy as possible for our reception. The place was cold, pitch dark, and draughty, being only used as a store-house, but by mid-day our tent was pitched inside the building, and a fire was burning merrily in a small stove cleverly fixed up by the missionary, whose kindly assistance was very welcome on this bleak and barren shore. Food is scarce enough here, and had it not been for these good friends in need, we should indeed have fared badly, having landed with but few provisions. But although they could ill afford it, the missionary and school teacher, Mrs. Bernardi, gave freely from their scanty store, thereby rendering us a service which I can never adequately repay.

Nome City was now our objective point, but how to reach it by land was a puzzler, the hundred odd miles of country being flooded by melting snow. Two or three wide rivers must also be crossed, which at this season of the year are often swollen and impassable. It was clearly useless to think of walking, so there was nothing for it but to wait for some passing craft to take us down, a rather gloomy prospect, for whalers were now entering the Arctic, and few other vessels get so far north as this. We were lucky to find a white man at Cape Prince of Wales, for the natives would certainly have afforded us no assistance, and might, indeed, have been actually unfriendly without the firm and restraining hand of Mr. Lopp to keep them in order. A wide and varied experience of savage races has seldom shown me a more arrogant, insolent, and generally offensive race than the Alaskan Eskimo, at any rate of this portion of the country. The Tchuktchis were infinitely superior in every respect but perhaps cleanliness, which, after all, matters little in these wilds. With all their faults our Whalen friends were just and generous in their dealings, though occasionally disquieting during their periods of festivity. The Eskimo we found boorish and surly at all times, and the treachery of these people is shown by the fact that a few years previously they had brutally murdered Mr. Lopp's predecessor by shooting him with a whale-gun. A monument on the cliff facing the Straits bears the following inscription:

> HARRISON R. THORNTON, born January 5, 1858,
> died August 19, 1893.
> A good soldier of Christ Jesus.
> Erected by friends in Southport, Conn.

It is satisfactory to note that the cowardly assassins met with their deserts, for the usual excuse of intoxication could not be pleaded for this foul and deliberate crime.

Although many of the Prince of Wales natives were fairly well educated, thanks to missionary enterprise, the Tchuktchis could certainly have taught them manners, for the latter is a gentleman by nature, while the Eskimo is a vulgar and aggressive cad. Thanks, however, to the untiring zeal and energy of Mr. Lopp, the younger generation here were a distinct improvement upon their elders, and the small school conducted by Mrs. Bernardi had produced several scholars of really remarkable intelligence. Amongst these were the publisher and printer of the most curious little publication I have ever seen, *The Eskimo Bulletin*, a tiny newspaper which is annually published here by the aid of a small printing-press belonging to the missionary. The illustrations were engraved solely by the natives, and were, under the circumstances, very creditable productions. The advertisements in this unique little journal are suggestive of a fair sized town, whereas Kingigamoot resembled a collection of sand-hills, the only visible signs of civilisation being the rather dilapidated huts of the mission.

The ten days we remained here seemed fully as long, if not longer, than the five weeks we had passed at Whalen for the sun only made his appearance twice, for a couple of hours each time, during the whole period of our stay. Most of our time was passed in the cold draughty hut, for it was impossible to face the gales and dense fogs which succeeded each other with startling rapidity, while on gusty days clouds of fine gritty sand would fill the eyes, mouth, and nostrils, causing great discomfort. There is probably no place in the world where the weather is so persistently vile as on this cheerless portion of the earth's surface. In winter furious tempests and snow, in summer similar storms, accompanied by rain, sleet, or mist, are experienced here five days out of the seven. If by accident a still, sunlit day does occur, it is called a "weather-breeder," for dirtier weather than before is sure to be lurking behind it. A howling south-wester on the English coast would be looked upon here as a moderate gale. While walking on the beach one day I was lifted clean off my feet by the wind, although the day was locally called rather a pleasant one.

One would think that this storm-swept, grey-skied region would discourage even the natives after a time and make them pine for a more congenial climate. But to the native of even this bleak and desolate coast there is no place like home. Mr. Elliott, a reliable authority on the subject, writes that cases have come under his notice where whalers have carried Eskimo down to the Sandwich Islands (the winter whaling ground) under an idea that these people would be delighted with the warm climate, fruits and flowers, and be grateful for the trip. But in no instance has an individual of this hyperborean race failed to sigh for his Arctic home after landing at Hawaii. Nor is this nostalgia of the frozen north confined to its aboriginal inhabitants, for most explorers who return from its fastnesses experience sooner or later a keen desire to return. And the majority do so, obedient to an invisible influence as unerring as that of a toy magnet over its fish.

I had little opportunity of studying the manners and customs of the natives while at Kingigamoot. Outwardly the Eskimo differs little from the Tchuktchi, that is, so far as costume is concerned, but the physiognomy and languages essentially differ. That the former is fully as filthy even if more civilised in other ways than the latter I can, from personal experience, testify. Also that the introduction of Christianity has failed to eradicate the love for strong drink, which was quite as prevalent here as at Whalen, although more cunningly concealed. An American explorer, Mr. Eugene McElwaine, who recently travelled extensively throughout these regions, gleaned the following facts, which may interest the reader, but which I am unfortunately unable to furnish from my own personal experience. He writes:

"The average Eskimo is very uncleanly in his personal habits and domestic customs, but is always willing to be taught habits of cleanliness, and is even anxious to change his mode of living when brought to realise its inferiority or repulsiveness. He recognises the white man to be his superior, and his inclination is to better his condition.

"The Eskimo's knowledge of the past is vague and indefinite. Their time is computed by the revolutions of the moon, their distances when travelling by 'sleeps,' and they measure a 'yard' by the length between the two hands with arms stretched horizontally. The Eskimo believe in a power that rewards the good and punishes the bad, indicating by gestures that the former go above and the latter below after death. They bury their dead usually on top of the ground in a box made of small timbers or drift-wood, elevating the box four feet from the surface, and resting it on cross poles. Their meagre belongings are generally buried with them. The small *bidarka* (skin canoe) is not infrequently used for a casket when the head of the household dies.

"Their simple funeral rites are conducted by members of the deceased's own family, no other member of the tribe coming near the house during the time or attending the obsequies at the grave. While the remains are being deposited in the box a member of the family builds a small fire with twigs of willows, and the fire is kept burning until the burial is completed, after which all present march around the fire in single file, chanting a prayer, with bowed heads, and then return to their hut. The household belongings are now removed from the hut and the family move off to build a cabin in another place which the evil spirit will not enter.

"The Eskimo are clever in many ways. Nearly all the men are experts in building canoes, while many are good carvers and draughtsmen. The writer has a map of the Arctic region, drawn by one of the Kowak River natives, which is one of the most complete things of the kind ever made. It shows every river, creek, lake, bay, mountain, village and trail, from the mouth of the Yukon River to Point Hope, and the native drew it in four days.

"A hut here is simply an excavation, about three feet deep, twelve feet long, and sixteen feet wide. Spruce saplings about four feet long and four inches through are set upright side by side around the interior, supported by the beams. Two posts six feet long and one ridge piece support the arched roof, light saplings being used for rafters. An oblique external portal, five feet long, two feet high, and eighteen inches wide is constructed in the same manner as the hut. The opening for the door is about eighteen inches wide by two feet high. This addition has a twofold purpose: it shelters the entrance to the family room of the hut, and the air which passes through the portal into the apartment carries away the smoke and foul air through a hole in the roof. The structure is finally banked and covered with dirt, and more resembles a mound than a human habitation. The interior of these dwellings is not luxurious. The floor is strewn with the pliant branches of the Arctic willow. A few deerskins lie scattered about, and here the men, women, and children of the tribe sit day after day, and month after month, performing their tasks of labour, and it is here when fatigued that they sleep in security and comfort. A miniature camp fire is kept burning day and night during the winter months."

My unfavourable opinion of the specimens of this race whom we met at Cape Prince of Wales is somewhat modified by the following anecdote, also related by Mr. McElwaine:

"An Eskimo lad about sixteen years of age came into my cabin one morning suffering with an acute bowel complaint. I happened to have a preparation for this trouble in my medicine chest, and administered to him a dose according to directions. It relieved him somewhat, and after eating his dinner, he returned home, a distance of some ten miles. In a week or ten days later he came back, bringing with him a number of curios which he had wrapped with care in a piece of deerskin and placed in a small canvas sack. Taking the curios out of the sack one by one, and unwrapping them carefully, he laid them on my table, saying as he did so in his broken English, 'You like 'em?' Receiving an affirmative reply, he said, 'You catch 'em,' at the same time shoving the articles towards me. I thought the young man was bent upon a trade, so, to please him, I laid out upon the table a number of edible articles, together with a red bandana handkerchief (a red handkerchief is prized very highly by all the natives), and awaited his decision. It was soon forthcoming. 'Me no catch 'em,' he said, pointing to the articles which he had placed upon the table; 'me give him you.' He left the trinkets with me, but would not accept a thing in return for them.

"Some four weeks afterwards this Indian boy came to my cabin again. He brought with him on his second visit a pair of small snowshoes and a miniature Eskimo sled. He had been told that I had a little boy at home, and he made me understand that he had made the snowshoes and sled for him, insisting that I should take them, which I did, but he stoutly refused anything in return for them. All this was to show his appreciation of the little act of kindness which I had inadvertently done him."

Mr. McElwaine concludes: "And yet, against the aborigines of Northern Alaska many explorers have charged that they are the most ungrateful wretches in the world."

Personally, I can cordially endorse this statement, but perhaps a very short residence amongst these people has left me ignorant of their real merits, and Mr. McElwaine may be perfectly right when he adds, in connection with the aforesaid explorers: "All such statements are, in my opinion, founded upon a misapprehension of the true character of this peculiar race."

Mr. Henry Elliott thus describes the Eskimo, or Innuit, as he is sometimes called, inhabiting the far northern portions of Alaska: "The average Innuit stands about five feet seven inches in his heelless boots. He is slightly Mongolian in his complexion and facial expression. A broad face, prominent cheek-bones, a large mouth with full lips, small black eyes, prominently set in their sockets, not under a lowering brow, as in the case of true Indian faces. The nose is insignificant, and much depressed, with scarcely any bridge. He has an abundance of coarse black hair, which up to the age of thirty years is cut pretty close; after this period in life it is worn in ragged, unkempt locks. The hands and feet are shapely, the limbs strong and well-formed. An Eskimo woman is proportionately smaller than the man, and when young sometimes good-looking. She has small, tapering hands, and high-instepped feet, and rarely pierces her lips or disfigures her nose. She lavishes upon her child or children a wealth of affection, endowing them with all her ornaments. The hair of the Innuit woman is allowed to grow to its full length and is gathered up behind into thick braids, or else bound up in ropes, lashed by copper wire or sinews. She seldom tattoos herself, but a faint drawing of transverse blue lines upon the chin and cheeks is usually made by her best friend when she is married."

The reader will probably infer, after reading the foregoing notes, that there is really very little difference, broadly speaking, between a Tchuktchi and an Eskimo, and yet the two are as dissimilar in racial characteristics and customs as a Russian and a Turk. Personal experience inclines me to regard the Siberian native as immeasurably superior to his Alaskan neighbours,[67] both from a moral and physical point of view, for the Eskimo is fully as vicious as the Tchuktchi, who frankly boasts of his depravity, while the former cloaks it beneath a mantle of hypocrisy not wholly unconnected with a knowledge of the white man and his methods. But every cloud has its silver lining, and it is comforting to think that even this rapacious and dissipated race can occasionally derive pleasure from the beauties of nature. While strolling round the settlement one day, I gathered a nosegay of wild flowers, including a species of yellow poppy, anent which Kingigamoot cherishes a pretty superstition. This flower blossoms in profusion about mid June around Cape Prince of Wales, and by the end of July has withered away. Simultaneously a tiny golden butterfly makes its appearance for about a fortnight, and also disappears. I was gravely informed by perhaps the greatest inebriate in the village that the poppy and the insect bear a similar name, for when the former has bloomed for a while it develops a pair of wings and flies away to return again the following summer in the guise of a flower.

[67] It is only fair to say that the only Eskimo I met were those at Kingigamoot, and the enmity of these particular natives to most white men is by some ascribed to the following incident. Some thirty years ago a small trading-schooner from San Francisco dropped anchor off the village, and was at once boarded and looted by the natives, who killed two of her crew. The remainder of the white men escaped with their vessel, and returned the following year under

escort of a revenue cutter. Several natives were induced to visit the latter, and when perhaps a score had been lured on board the Government vessel, she steamed away, intending to carry off the Kingigamoot men and punish them for the outrage committed the preceding year. But a fight at once ensued on the deck of the cutter, and every Eskimo was shot down and killed. Relatives of these men are still living at Kingigamoot, and the generally aggressive demeanour of the natives here is often ascribed to this fact, for the vendetta practised amongst both the Tchuktchis and Eskimo is fully as bitter and relentless as that which exists in Corsica.

During my rambles I came across some curious stone erections on the summit of the Cape. They were moss-grown, much dilapidated, and apparently of great age. The tomb-like contrivances are said to have been constructed by the Eskimo as a protection against invaders—the pillars of stone, laid loosely one on the other, about ten feet high, to represent men, and thus deceive the enemy. But for the truth of this I cannot vouch.

The ice remained so thickly piled up around the coast for four or five days after our arrival here that no look-out was kept. No vessel would willingly have approached this part of the coast without a special purpose, and Cape Prince of Wales possesses few attractions, commercial or otherwise. On a clear day the Siberian coast was visible, and the Diomede islands appeared so close with the aid of a field-glass that their tiny drab settlements were distinguishable against the dark masses of rock. The big and little Diomedes are about two miles apart, and the line of demarcation between Russia and America strikes the former off its eastern coast. From the most westerly point of Alaska to the most easterly point of the little Diomede (Ratmanoff) the distance is about fifteen miles, and from the most easterly point of Siberia to the most westerly point of the big Diomede (Krusenstern) the distance is about twenty miles. On the southern extremity of the larger island, a small village is situated, containing about a hundred and fifty natives (Russian subjects), and on the smaller one is another small village, with about the same number of American Eskimo. Fairway rock, a little way east of Ratmanoff island, is not inhabited. The comparatively short distance between the two continents and the intermediate islands has suggested the utilisation of the latter as supports for a leviathan railway bridge, a theory which (as Euclid would remark) is obviously "absurd." For no bridge could withstand the force of the spring ice in Bering Straits for one week. On the other hand, the boring of a tunnel from shore to shore is not entirely without the range of possibility, but of this, and of other matters dealing with the construction of a Franco-American railway, I shall deal fully in the concluding chapter of this work.

CHAPTER XV

AN ARCTIC CITY

"You will find a magic city
  On the shore of Bering Strait,
Which shall be for you a station
  To unload your Arctic freight.
Where the gold of Humboldt's vision
  Has for countless ages lain,
Waiting for the hand of labour
  And the Saxon's tireless brain."
                    S. Dunham.

Billy, the ex-whaleman, accompanied us here on board the *Thetis*, intending to make his way to Nome City. The commander of the cutter had let him go free, thinking, no doubt, that the poor fellow had been sufficiently punished for his misdeeds by a winter passed amongst the savages of Northern Siberia. One day during our stay here a native set out in a skin boat for Nome, and notwithstanding my warnings and a falling barometer Billy resolved to accompany him. But shortly after leaving us the pair encountered a furious gale, which swept them back to the Cape in an exhausted condition, nearly frozen to death after a terrible night in the ice.

By the end of a week the latter had almost disappeared. A vessel could now anchor with ease off the settlement, but it seemed as though we should have to wait until the autumn for that happy consummation. I had therefore decided, after consultation with the missionary, on risking the journey in a *baidara*, when, on the evening of the tenth day, our longing eyes were gladdened by the sight of a small steamer approaching the Cape. She proved to be the *Sadie*, of the "Alaska Commercial Company," returning from her first trip of the year to Candle Creek,[68] a gold-mining settlement on the Arctic Ocean, which had been unapproachable on account of heavy ice. Fortunately for us the Captain had suddenly resolved to call at Kingigamoot in case the missionary needed assistance, and on hearing of our plight at once offered the Expedition a passage to

From Paris to New York by Land

Nome City, whither the *Sadie* was bound. Bidding farewell to our kind friends at the Mission, without whose assistance we should indeed have fared badly, we soon were aboard the clean and comfortable little steamer. A warm welcome awaited us from her skipper, a jovial Heligolander, who at the same time imparted to us the joyful news that the war in South Africa was at an end. Twenty-four hours later we were once more in civilisation, for during the summer there is frequent steam communication between the remote although up-to-date mining city of Nome and our final destination, New York.

[68] In the summer of 1901, $30,000 were taken out of this creek.

Cape Nome derives its name from the Indian word *"No-me,"* which signifies in English, "I don't know." In former days, when whalers anchored here to trade, the invariable answer given by the natives to all questions put by the white men was *"No-me,"* meaning that they did not understand, and the name of the place was thus derived. On Cape Nome, four years ago an Arctic desert, there now stands a fine and well-built city. In winter the place can only be reached by dog-sled, after a fatiguing, if not perilous, journey across Alaska, but in the open season you may now travel there almost any week in large liners from San Francisco. It seemed like a dream to land suddenly in this modern town, within a day's journey of Whalen with all its savagery and squalor, and it was somewhat trying to have to walk up the crowded main street in our filthy, ragged state. Eventually, however, we were rigged up at a well-stocked clothing establishment in suits of dittos which would hardly have passed muster in Bond Street, but which did very well for our purpose. And that evening, dining at a luxurious hotel, with people in evening dress, palms, and a string band around us, I could scarcely realise that only a few days ago we were practically starving in a filthy Siberian village. Handsome buildings, churches, theatres, electric light and telephones are not usually associated with the ice-bound Arctic, but they are all to be found in Nome City, which is now connected by telegraph with the outside world.

And yet the first log-cabin here was only built in the winter of 1898. This formed the nucleus of a town of about three thousand inhabitants by August of the following year, which by the middle of July 1900 had grown into a colony of more than twenty thousand people. As sometimes happens, the first discoverers of gold were not the ones to profit by their lucky find, for this is what happened. Early in July 1898 three prospectors, one Blake, an American, and his two companions, were sailing up the coast in a small schooner, when, abreast of Cape Nome, a storm struck their tiny craft and cast her up on the beach. The gale lasted for several days, and the men made use of the time prospecting in the vicinity of the Snake River, which now runs through the city. At the mouth of Anvil Creek, good colours were found at a depth of one foot, the dirt averaging from fifty cents to one dollar the pan. Satisfied that they had made an important discovery, the men returned as soon as the weather would permit to their permanent camp in Golovin Bay, down coast, for provisions and mining tools, and thus lost, perhaps, the richest gold-producing property yet discovered in Alaska. How the secret got about was never known (perhaps "tanglefoot" was not unconnected with its disclosure), but three Swedes (one of whom was then a reindeer-herder and is now a millionaire), got wind of the news, and quickly and quietly set out for Cape Nome, which they reached late in September of the same year. Ascending Snake River, they prospected Anvil and other Creeks, and in three days took out $1800 (nearly £400). After staking all the claims of apparent value, the Swedes returned to Golovin Bay, and having staked their ground, were not afraid to communicate the news of their discovery. It was, therefore, only after all the good claims had been appropriated that poor Blake and his associates discovered that their anticipated golden harvest had been reaped by the energetic Scandinavians.

Fresh finds speedily followed, notably of one rich spot about five miles west of Nome, where $9000 was rocked out of a hole twelve foot square and four feet deep in three days. Then gold began to appear on the beach. Small particles of it were found in the very streets, so that this Arctic township may almost be said to have been at one time literally paved with gold. In 1899 the seashore alone produced between $1,750,000 and $2,000,000.

The presence here of a numerous and influential Press astonished me more than anything else. Nome City can boast of no less than three newspapers, and no sooner was the Expedition comfortably installed in the "Golden Gate Hotel" than it was besieged by the usual reporters. The rapidity with which the interviews were published would have done credit to a London evening paper, and I could only admire the versatility of the gentleman who, only four hours after our arrival, brought out a special edition of the *Nome Nugget*, containing a portrait of His Royal Highness the Duke of the Abruzzi in full naval uniform, which was described as his humble servant: the writer! The jealousy amongst these Arctic editors is as keen and bitter as it ever was in Eatanswill, and the next day the following paragraph appeared in the *News*, a rival publication:

"One of our contemporaries has celebrated the rescue of some explorers from starvation by publishing the picture of Prince Louis of Savoy under the caption 'Harry de Windt.' But the Italian prince is also an explorer, and probably all explorers look alike to the *Nugget*!"

Nome City impressed me at first as being a kind of squalid Monte Carlo. There is the same unrest, the same feverish quest for gold, and the same extravagance of life as in the devil's garden on the blue Mediterranean. On landing, I was struck with the number of well-dressed men and women who rub shoulders in the street with the dilapidated-looking mining element. In the same way palatial banks and prim business houses are incongruously scattered amongst saloons and drinking bars. Front Street, facing the sea, is the principal thoroughfare, so crowded at midday that you can scarcely get along. It is paved with wood, imported here at enormous expense, and a pavement of the same material is raised about two feet above the roadway. Here are good shops where everything is cheap, for during the great gold-rush Nome was over-stocked. Wearing apparel may be purchased here even cheaper than in San Francisco, and everything is on the same scale; oranges, for instance, which two years ago cost one dollar apiece and which are now sold in the streets for five cents. Luxurious shaving saloons abound, also restaurants—one kept by a Frenchman who is deservedly reaping a golden harvest.

In summer there is no rest here throughout the twenty-four hours. People wander aimlessly about the streets, eternally discussing quartz and placer-claims, and recent strikes, which here form the sole topic of conversation, like a run on zero or the cards at Monaco. Port Said is suggested by the dusty, flashy streets and cosmopolitan crowd, also by the fact that gambling saloons and even shops remain open all night, or so long as customers are stirring, which is generally from supper until breakfast-time, for at this season of perpetual daylight no one ever seemed to go to bed. The sight of the principal street at four in the morning, with music halls, restaurants, drinking and dancing saloons blazing with electricity in the cold, grey light of a midnight sun was both novel and unique. At this hour the night-houses were always crowded, and you might re-visit them at midday and find the same occupants still out of bed, drinking, smoking, and gambling, yet as quiet and orderly in their demeanour as a company of Quakers. For, notwithstanding its large percentage of the riff-raff element, crime is very rare in Nome. I frequently visited the gambling saloons, where gum-booted, mud-stained prospectors elbowed women in dainty Parisian gowns and men in the conventional swallowtail, but I never once saw a shot fired, nor even a dispute, although champagne flowed like water. These places generally consisted of a spacious and gaudily decorated hall with a drinking bar surrounded by various *roulette, crap*, and *faro* tables. The price of a drink admitted you to an adjoining music hall, where I witnessed a variety entertainment that would scarcely have passed the London County Council. But gambling was the chief attraction, and it seemed to be fair, for cheating is clearly superfluous with three zeros! Many of the frequenters of these night-houses appeared to be foreigners, chiefly Swedes and Germans, and a few Frenchmen, and the company was very mixed, Jews, Greeks, and Levantines being numerous amongst the men, whilst the ladies were mostly flashily dressed birds of passage from San Francisco, only here for a brief space before flitting South, like the swallows, at the first fall of snow.

There was a delightfully free-and-easy, *laisser-aller* air about everybody and everything at Nome City, which would, perhaps, have jarred upon an ultra-respectable mind. Most of the ladies at the Golden Gate Hotel were located there in couples, unattended, permanently at any rate, by male protectors. The bedroom adjoining mine was occupied by two of these Californian *houris*, whose habits were apparently not framed on Lucretian lines. For the manager appeared at my bedside early one morning with a polite request that I would rise and dress as quietly as possible, as the "ladies" next door had just gone to bed for the first time in three days, and rather needed a rest!

A stroll through the streets of Nome at midday was also amusing, although the sun blazed down with a force which recalled summer-days in Hong-kong or Calcutta. It was then hard to picture these warm and sunlit streets swept by howling blizzards and buried in drifts which frequently rise to the roofs of the houses, until their inmates have to be literally dug out after a night of wind and snow. But when we were at Nome, Cairo in August would have seemed cool by comparison, and I began to doubt whether ice here could ever exist, for nothing around was suggestive of a Northern clime. The open-air life, muslin-clad women, gaily striped awnings, and Neapolitan fruit-sellers seemed to bear one imperceptibly to some sunlit town of Italy or Spain, thousands of miles away from this gloomy world (in winter) of cold and darkness. Only occasionally a skin-clad Eskimo from up coast would slouch shyly through the busy throng, rudely recalling the fact that we were still within the region of raw seal-meat and walrus-hide huts.

Most of the prospectors I met here had no use for the place as a gold-mining centre, but I should add that these grumblers were usually inexperienced men, who had come in with no knowledge whatever of quartz or placer-mining. On the other hand, fortunes have been made with remarkable ease and rapidity, as in the case of one of the first pioneers, Mr. Lindeberg, a young Swede (already mentioned), who arrived here as a reindeer-herder and now owns the largest share of Anvil Creek. From this about $3,000,000 have been taken in two years, and the lucky proprietor has recently laid a line of railway to his claims, about seven miles out of Nome. Anvil Creek has turned out the largest nugget ever found in Alaska.

Generally speaking, however, Nome is no place for a poor man, although when we were there five dollars a day (and all found) could be easily earned on the Creeks. I invariably found men connected with large companies enthusiastic, and grub-stakers down on their luck. Lack of water in this district has proved a stumbling block which will shortly be dispelled by machinery. Anvil Creek will probably yield double the output hitherto extracted when this commodity has been turned on, and this is now being done at an enormous cost by its enterprising proprietors. But the days are past when nuggets were picked up here on the beach, for it now needs costly machinery to find them in the interior. Even during the first mad rush, when Nome was but a town of tents, many who expected to find the country teeming with gold were disappointed. In those days men would often rush ashore, after restless nights passed on board ship in wakeful anticipation, catch up half a dozen handfuls of earth, and finding nothing, cry, "I told you it was all a fake," and re-embark on the first steamer for San Francisco. It therefore came to pass that patient, hard-working men like Lindeberg, inured to hardship and privation, whose primary object in the country was totally unconnected with mining, have made colossal fortunes solely by dogged perseverance and the sweat of their brow. The general opinion here seemed to be that at the present time a man with a capital of, say, £10,000 could succeed here, but even then it was doubtful whether the money could not be more profitably invested in a more temperate clime, and one involving less risk to life and limb.

Although epidemics occasionally occur, Nome cannot be called unhealthy. The greatest variation of temperature is probably from 40° below zero in winter to 90° above in summer, and the dry, intense cold we experienced in Northern Siberia is here unknown. Only a short time ago the sea journey to Nome was no less hazardous than the land trip formerly was over the dreaded Chilkoot Pass and across the treacherous lakes to Dawson City. In those days catastrophes were only too frequent in that graveyard of the Pacific, Bering Sea, and this was chiefly on account of unseaworthy ships patched up for passenger-traffic by unscrupulous owners in San Francisco. Nome City can now be reached by the fine steamships of the "Alaska Commercial Company" as safely and comfortably as New York in an Atlantic liner, but these boats are unfortunately in the minority, and even while we were at Nome, passengers were arriving there almost daily on board veritable coffin-ships, in which I would not willingly navigate the Serpentine.

Shipping disasters have been frequent not only at sea, but also while landing here, for Nome has no harbour, but merely an open, shallow roadstead, fully exposed to the billows of the ocean. There is therefore frequently a heavy surf along the beach, and here many a poor miner has been drowned within a few yards of the Eldorado he has risked his all to reach.

Intending prospectors should know that nearly every available mile of country from Norton Sound to the Arctic Ocean has now been staked out, and before claims are now obtained they must be paid for. American missionaries have not been behind-hand in the race for wealth, and in connection with this subject, the following lines by a disappointed Klondiker are not without humour:

> "Then we climbed the cold creeks near a mission
>   That is run by the agents of God,
> Who trade Bibles and Prayer-books to heathen
>   For ivory, sealskins and cod.
> At last we were sure we had struck it,
>   But alas! for our hope of reward,
> The landscape from sea-beach to sky-line
>   Was staked in the name of the Lord!"[69]

[69] "The Goldsmith of Nome," by Sam Dunham. (Neale Publishing Company, Washington, D.C.)

That these lines, however, do not apply to *all* Alaskan missionaries I can testify from a personal knowledge of our good friend Mr. Lopp's comfortless, primitive life, and unselfish devotion to the cause of Christianity.

CHAPTER XVI

A RIVER OF GOLD

The heading of this chapter is not suggested by a flight of fancy, but by solid fact, for there is not a mile along either bank of the Yukon River, over 2000 miles long from the great lakes to Bering Sea, where you cannot dip in a pan and get a colour. Gold may not be found in paying quantities so near the main stream, but it is there.

From Nome to Dawson City is about 1600 miles, the terminus of the Yukon River steamers being St. Michael, on Bering Sea. When I was at this place in 1896, it consisted of two or three small buildings of the "Alaska Commercial Company," a Russian church and ruined stockade, and about a dozen Eskimo wigwams. During my stay there, on that occasion, one small cargo-boat arrived from the South, and a solitary whaler put in for water, their appearance causing wild excitement amongst the few white settlers.

Although the civilisation of Nome City had somewhat prepared me for surprises, I scarcely expected to find St. Michael converted from a squalid settlement into a modern city almost as fine as Nome itself. For here also were a large hotel, good shops, electric light, and a roadstead alive with shipping of every description from the Eskimo *kayak* to the towering liner from 'Frisco. We arrived at 6 A.M. after a twelve hours' journey from Nome, but even at that early hour the clang of a ship-yard and shriek of steam syrens were awakening the once silent and desolate waters of Norton Sound. St. Michael feeds and clothes the Alaskan miner, despatches goods and stores into the remotest corner of this barren land, and has thus rapidly grown from a dreary little settlement into a centre of mercantile activity. Seven years ago I journeyed down the Yukon towards Siberia and a problematical Paris in a small crowded steamer, built of roughly hewn logs, and propelled by a fussy little engine of mediæval construction. We then slept on planks, dined in our shirt-sleeves, and scrambled for meals which a respectable dog would have turned from in disgust. On the present occasion we embarked on board a floating palace, a huge stern-wheeler, as large and luxuriously appointed as the most modern Mississippi flyer. The *Hannah's* airy deck-halls were of dainty white, picked out with gold, some of the well-furnished state-rooms had baths attached, and a perfect *cuisine* partly atoned for the wearisome monotony of a long river voyage.

A delay here of twenty-four hours enabled me to re-visit the places I had known only too well while wearily awaiting the *Bear* here for five weeks in 1896. But everything was changed beyond recognition. Only two landmarks remained of the old St. Michael: the agency of the "Alaska Commercial Company," and the wooden church built by the Russians during their occupation of the country.[70] A native hut near the beach, where I was wont to smoke my evening pipe with an old Eskimo fisherman, was now a circulating library; the ramshackle rest-house, once crowded with "Toughs," a fashionable hotel with a verandah and five o'clock tea-tables for the use of the select. And here I may note that tea is, or was, all that the traveller can get here, for St. Michael is now a military reservation, where even the sale of beer or claret is strictly prohibited. My old friend Mikouline would have fared badly throughout this part of the journey, for from here on to Dawson City alcoholic refreshment of any kind was absolutely unprocurable, and although the heat was tropical, iced water, not always of the purest description, was the only cold beverage obtainable at St. Michael or on the river. I was afterwards informed that the initiated always carry their own cellar, and having a rooted antipathy to tea at dinner (especially when served in conjunction with tinned soup), regretted that I had not ascertained this fact before we left Nome.

[70] The Russo-Greek religion is still maintained throughout Alaska, and nearly a hundred of its churches and chapels still exist throughout the country and in the Aleutian Islands.

ESKIMO GIRLS.

From Paris to New York by Land

But although this liquor law was enforced with severity ashore its infringement afloat was openly winked at by the authorities. Soldiers were stationed night and day with loaded rifles on the beach to prevent the importation of spirits, and yet within half a mile of them, anchored in the roadstead, were four or five hulks, floating public-houses, where a man might get as drunk as he pleased with impunity, and often for the last time, especially when a return to the shore had to be made through a nasty sea in a skin *kayak*. It was even whispered that "Hootch" (a fiery poison akin to "Tanglefoot") was manufactured at the barracks, and retailed by the soldiers to the natives, the very class for whose protection against temptation the prohibitive law was framed.

"All my men are intoxicated," the Commandant at St. Michael was said to have exclaimed. "So I suppose I had better get drunk myself."

But there was little love lost here between the civil and military element, and these were probably libels, for I have seldom seen a better drilled or disciplined set of men, although the hideous uniform of the American linesman is less suggestive of a soldier than of a railway guard.[71]

[71] Permanent military posts of the United States have been established as follows, throughout Alaska: Fort Egbert at Circle City, Fort Gibbon on the Tanana River, Fort Valdez on Prince William Sound, Fort Davis at Nome, and Fort St. Michael on the island of that name.

The heat at St. Michael was even more oppressive than at Nome, and it was impossible to stir out of doors at midday with any comfort. We were therefore not sorry to embark on board the *Hannah*, of the "Alaska Commercial Company," which contained one hundred state-rooms, of which barely a dozen were occupied, for at this season of the year travellers are mostly outward bound. The White Pass railway has practically killed the Yukon passenger trade, for people now travel to Dawson by rail, and to Nome by sea direct. They used to go by ocean steamer to St. Michael, and thence ascend the river to Dawson, for in those days the perilous Chilkoot Pass was the only direct way from the South into the Klondike region. Our fellow travellers, therefore, lacked in numbers but not in originality, for they included a millionaire in fustian, who preferred to eat with the crew; a young and well-dressed widow from San Francisco, who owned claims on the Tanana and worked them herself; a confidence-man with a gambling outfit, who had struck the wrong crowd; and last, but not least, Mrs. Z., recently a well-known *prima donna* in the United States, who, although in the zenith of her youthful fame and popularity, had abandoned a brilliant career to share the fortunes of her husband, an official of the "Alaska Commercial Company," in this inartistic land. I found the conditions of travel on the Yukon as completely changed as everything else. Even the technical expressions once used by the gold-mining fraternity were now replaced by others. Thus the "Oldtimer" had become "a Sourdough," and his antithesis, the "Tenderfoot," was now called a "Chechako." A word now frequently heard (and unknown in 1896) was "Musher," signifying a prospector who is not afraid to explore the unknown. This word is of Canadian origin, and probably a corruption of the French *"Marcheur."* Various passengers on board the *Hannah* were said to be returning to their homes with "Cold feet," also a new term, defining the disappointed gold-seeker who is leaving the country in disgust.

But a change which excited both my admiration and approval was that in the accommodation provided on board the *Hannah* and the really excellent dinner to which we sat down every day, although enforced teetotalism was somewhat irritating to those accustomed to wine with their meals. It is no exaggeration to say that an overland journey may now be made from Skagway to Nome City with as little discomfort as a trip across Switzerland, if the tourist keeps to the beaten track by rail and steamer. But the slightest deviation on either side will show him what Alaskan travel really was, and he will then probably curse the country and all that therein lies. The tourist may even experience some trying hours on the river-boat, for although the latter is fitted with cunning contrivances for their exclusion, mosquitoes invariably swarm, and the Yukon specimen is so unequalled for size and ferocity that I once heard an old miner declare that this virulent insect was "as big as a rabbit and bit at both ends." But this is about the only discomfort that travellers by the main route through Alaska need now endure. Otherwise the path of travel has been made almost as smooth as Cook's easiest tours.

As the reader may one day summon the courage to visit this great Northern land, it may not be out of place to give a brief history of Alaska, which, only thirty years ago, was peopled solely by Indians and a few Russian settlers, and was practically unknown to the civilised world.

It has always seemed strange to me that Russia, a country with a world-wide reputation for diplomatic shrewdness, should have made such an egregious error as to part with Alaska at a merely nominal price,[72] the more so that when the transfer took place gold had long been known to exist in this Arctic province. Vitus Bering discovered traces of it as far back as the eighteenth century. William H. Seward, Secretary of State under President Johnson, was mainly responsible for the purchase of this huge territory, which covers an area of about 600,000 square miles, measuring 1000 miles from north to south and 3500 miles from east to west. It is said that the coast line alone, if straightened out, would girdle the globe.

[72] The word "Alaska" is derived from the Indian "Al-ay-eksa," which signifies a great country.

The formal transfer of Alaska to the United States was made on October 18, 1867, and its acquisition was first regarded with great disfavour by the majority of the American public. Although only $7,200,000 was paid for the whole of Russian America,[73] the general opinion in New York and other large cities of the Union was that "Seward's ice-box," as it was then derisively termed, would prove a white elephant, and that the statesman responsible for its purchase had been, plainly speaking, sold. It was only when the marvellous riches of Nome were disclosed that people began to realise what the annexation of the country really meant, although even at this period Alaska had already repaid itself many times over. Klondike had already startled the civilised world, but this is, of course, in British territory. Nevertheless, between the years 1870 and 1900 Secretary Seward's investment had returned nearly $8,000,000, and within the same period fisheries and furs had yielded no less than $100,000,000. Gold and timber had produced $40,000,000 more, making a clear profit of nearly $200,000,000 in thirty years.

[73] It is said that most of this was used in Petersburg to satisfy old debts and obligations incurred by Alaskan enterprises, attorneys' fees, &c., so in short Russia really gave her American possessions to the American people, reaping no direct emolument whatsoever from the transfer. ("Our Arctic Province," by Henry W. Elliott.)

It is sad to think that the once maligned politician who acquired this priceless treasure did not live to see his golden dream realised. A few days before his death the Secretary was asked what he considered the most important measure of his official career.

"The purchase of Alaska," was the reply, "but it will take the people a generation to find it out."

Alaska may be divided into two great south-east and western districts. Mount St. Elias, nearly 20,000 ft. high, marks the dividing line at 141° west long., running north from this point to the Arctic Ocean. The diversity of climate existing throughout this huge province from its southern coast to the shores of the Polar Sea is naturally very great, and the marvellous contrast between an Alaskan June and December has nowhere been more picturesquely and graphically described than by General Sir William Butler in his "Great Lone Land": "In summer a land of sound—a land echoed with the voices of birds, the ripple of running water, the mournful music of the waving pine branch; in winter a land of silence, its great rivers glimmering in the moonlight, wrapped in their shrouds of ice, its still forests rising weird and spectral against the auroral-lighted horizon, its nights so still that the moving streamers across the Northern skies seem to carry to the ear a sense of sound!"

On the North Pacific coast densely wooded islands are so numerous that from Victoria in British Columbia to the town of Skagway at the head of the Lynn Canal there are but a few miles of open sea. Inland, almost as far as the Arctic Circle, mountain ranges, some of great altitude, are everywhere visible. There are also many large lakes, surrounded by the swamps, and impenetrable forests, that formerly rendered Alaska so hard a nut for the explorer to crack. Only a few miles north of the coast range fertile soil and luxuriant vegetation are replaced by Arctic deserts. Here, for eight months of the year, plains and rivers are merged into one vast wilderness of ice, save during the short summer when dog-roses bloom and the coarse luxurious grass is plentifully sprinkled with daisies and other wild flowers. In Central Alaska the ground is perpetually frozen to a depth of several inches, and in the North wells have been sunk through forty feet of solid ice.

Alaska is fairly healthy, although the temperature in the interior ranges from 90° in the shade to over 60° below zero Fahr. May, June, and July are the best months for travelling, for the days are then generally bright and pleasant and the heat tempered by a cool breeze. On the coast during the summer rain and fogs prevail, and the sun is only occasionally visible, for there are on an average only sixty-six fine days throughout the year. In 1884, a rainfall of sixty-four inches was registered at Unalaska. The rain seldom pours down here, but falls in a steady drizzle from a hopelessly leaden sky, under which a grey and sodden landscape presents a picture of dreary desolation. But this damp cheerlessness has its advantages, for incessant humidity sheds perpetual verdure over the coast-districts, where the thermometer rarely falls as low as zero Fahr. Winter only sets in here about the 1st of December, and snow has vanished by the end of May, while in the interior lakes and rivers are still in the grip of the ice. Near the sea the soil is rich and root-crops are prolific, while horses and cattle thrive well, also the ports as far north as Cook's Inlet are open to navigation all the year round, so that, taking all these facts into consideration, coast settlements are preferable as a permanent residence to those of the interior, with the exception, perhaps, of Dawson City.

It is said that the mild climate of Southern Alaska is due to the Japan Gulf Stream, which first strikes the North American continent at the Queen Charlotte Island in latitude 50° north. At this point the stream divides, one part going northward and westward along the coast of Alaska, and the other southward along the coast of British Columbia, Washington territory, Oregon, and California. Thus the climate of these states is made mild and pleasant in precisely the same way as the shores of Spain, Portugal and France by the ocean currents of the Atlantic.

Notwithstanding the society of pleasant fellow travellers, life on board the *Hannah* became intolerably tedious after the first few days. The Lower Yukon is not an attractive river from a picturesque point of view, and only the upper portion of its two thousand odd miles possesses any scenic interest. Grey and monotonous tundra rolling away to the horizon, and melancholy, grey-green shrubs lining the stream formed the daily and dismal landscape during the first week. There is literally nothing of interest to be seen along the banks of the Yukon from its mouth to Dawson City, save perhaps the Catholic mission of the Holy Cross at Koserefski; which is prettily situated within a stone's throw of the river, and consists of several neat wooden buildings comprising a beautiful little chapel and school for native children. The *Hannah* remained here for some hours, which enabled me to renew my acquaintance with the good nuns, and to visit the schoolhouse, where some Indian children of both sexes were at work. French was the language spoken, and it seemed strange to hear the crisp, clear accent in this deserted corner of civilisation. An old acquaintance of my former voyage, pretty Sister Winifred, showed us around the garden, with its smooth green lawns, bright flower-beds, and white statue of Our Lady in a shrine of pine boughs. All the surroundings wore an air of peace and homeliness suggestive of some quiet country village in far-away France, and I could have lingered here for hours had not large and bloodthirsty mosquitoes swarmed from the woods around and driven me reluctantly back to the steamer.

At Koserefski we bade a final farewell to the "Tundra" and its Eskimo, and from here onwards encountered only dense forests and the unsavoury and generally sulky Alaskan Indian. They are not a pleasing race, for laziness and impudence seemed to be the chief characteristics of those with whom we had to deal throughout the former journey. On this occasion we met with very few natives, who have apparently been driven out of the principal towns by the white man. The Alaskan Indian's once picturesque costume is now discarded for clothes of European cut, which render him even more unattractive than ever. Moccasins and his pretty bark-canoe are now the only distinctive mark of the *Siwash*, who is as fond of strong drink as the Eskimo, and also resembles the latter in his boundless capacities for lying and theft. But there are probably not more than

From Paris to New York by Land

1500 natives in all inhabiting the Yukon region, and these are rapidly decreasing. I do not think I saw more than fifty Indians throughout the journey from Cape Nome to Skagway, the terminus of the "White Pass" railway. South of this, along the coast to Vancouver, they were more numerous, and apparently less lazy and degraded than the Indians of the interior.

On board the *Hannah* the talk was all of gold, and every one, from captain to cook, seemed indirectly interested in the capture of the precious metal. The purser had claims to dispose of, and even your bedroom steward knew of a likely ledge of which he would divulge the position—for a consideration. The Koyukuk and Tanana rivers on this part of the Yukon are new ground, and are said to be promising, but I could hear of no reliable discoveries of any extent on either of these streams.

"Cities" on the American Yukon consist of perhaps a score or more of log huts, which Yankee push and enterprise have invested with the dignity of towns. "Rampart City," for instance, which the *Hannah* reached on the sixth day in from the coast, consisted of only about thirty one-storied wooden dwellings, the erection of which had been due to the discovery of gold in the vicinity, although during the previous year (1901) the claims around had only produced £40,000. And yet even this tiny township could boast of two hotels, five or six saloons, electric light and two newspapers: the *Alaska Forum* and *Rampart Sun*. The circulation of these journals was not disclosed to the writer, who was, however, gravely interviewed by the editors of both publications. Just before leaving Rampart City news of the postponement of the coronation of his Majesty King Edward VII. on account of serious illness, reached us, and it was gratifying to note the respectful sympathy for the Queen of England displayed by the American inhabitants of this remote Alaskan settlement.

Four days after this the hideous Yukon flats were reached, a vast desert of swamp and sand dunes, through which the great river diffuses itself, like a sky-rocket, into hundreds of lesser streams, lakes, and aqueous blind alleys, which severely taxed the skill and patience of our skipper. Here the outlook was even more depressing than on the dreary Lena. Before reaching Circle City the Yukon attains its most northerly point and then descends in a south-easterly direction for the remainder of its course. At the bend it is joined by the Porcupine River; and here is Fort Yukon, once an important trading coast of the Hudson Bay Company, but now an overgrown clearing in the forest, of which a few miserable Indians in grimy tents disputed the possession with dense clouds of mosquitoes. But even the appearance of Circle City,[74] once a prosperous mining town and now a collection of ruined log-huts, was hailed with delight by the hopelessly bored passengers in the *Hannah*, for it meant the end of another stage in this wearisome journey.

[74] In 1901 the diggings around Circle City produced about £30,000.

There is nothing exciting or even picturesque about a modern Alaskan mining camp. Bowlers and loud checks have superseded the red flannel shirt and sombrero, and while missions and libraries abound, Judge Lynch and the crack of a six-shooter are almost unknown in these townships, the conventional security of which would certainly have amazed and disgusted the late Bret Harte. When last I travelled down the Yukon, Circle City (now called Silent City) was known as the "Paris of Alaska," and there was certainly more gaiety, or rather life, of a tawdry, disreputable kind here than at Forty Mile, the only other settlement of any size on the river, for Klondike was not then in existence. Circle City could then boast of two theatres, a so-called music hall, and several gambling and dancing saloons, which, together with other dens of a worse description, were now silent heaps of grass-grown timber. In those days the dancing rooms were crowded nightly, and I once attended a ball here in a low, stuffy apartment, festooned with flags, with a drinking bar at one end. The orchestra consisted of a violin and guitar, the music being almost drowned by a noisy crowd at the bar, where a wrangle took place on an average every five minutes. One dollar was charged by the saloon-keeper for the privilege of a dance with a gaily painted lady (of a class with which most mining camps are only too familiar), who received twenty-five cents as her share of the transaction. The guests numbered about sixty, and about a third that number of dogs which had strayed in through the open doorway. When an attendant (in shirt-sleeves) proceeded to walk round and sprinkle the rough boards with resin, the dancers fairly yelled with delight, for a hungry cur closely followed him, greedily devouring the stuff as it fell! But although in those days the Yukon gold-digger was as tough a customer as ever rocked a cradle in the wildest days of Colorado, there was a rough and friendly *bonhomie* amongst the inhabitants of Circle City which is now lacking in the Klondike metropolis.

Between Rampart and Circle Cities we experienced an annoyance almost as great as that caused by the mosquitoes, in the shape of clouds of pungent smoke caused by forest fires. In these densely wooded regions a smouldering match dropped by a careless miner often sets hundreds of square miles of timber ablaze. As the natives are also constantly clearing and burning the woods for cultivation, the air was seldom entirely clear, and often so thick as to cause irritation in the eyes, especially after suffering, as most of us had, from snow blindness and incipient ophthalmia. On still, sultry days the pain resulting from smoke and the glare off the river was almost as severe as that which I had experienced in the Arctic. Mosquitoes now attacked us in myriads, and the heat was insupportable, but the cooler air of the upper deck was rendered unattainable by showers of sparks which constantly issued from the funnels of the hard-driven *Hannah*.

At Eagle City, consisting of about thirty log-huts, we reached for the first time the end of a telegraph wire,[75] and I was able to cable home the safe arrival in Alaska of the Expedition; and none too soon, for the total loss of the latter had already been reported in London. How this baseless rumour was spread remains a mystery, but fortunately the wire announcing our safety was published in the London newspapers only three days after the public had read of a probable disaster. Eagle City, although even smaller than Rampart, also boasted of a newspaper, the enterprising owner of which made me a tempting offer for the tiny silk banner which had shared our fortunes all the way from France. But "the flag which braved a thousand years" was not for sale, and it now adorns the walls of the author's smoking-room, the only Union Jack which, so far as I know, has safety accomplished the journey from Paris to New York by land.

[75] This has since been extended and telegraphic messages may now be sent through from Europe to Nome City.

Above Eagle City the journey was rendered even more weary by frequent stoppages. Once we tugged for twenty-four hours at a stranded steamer, and finally got her off a sand-bank at considerable risk to ourselves. Every hundred miles or so the *Hannah* would tie up to take in fuel at some wood-cutter's shanty, where the cool, green forest, with its flowers and ferns, looked inviting from the deck, but to land amongst them was to be devoured by clouds of ferocious mosquitoes. De Clinchamp was the happiest being on board, for his days were passed in developing the hundreds of photographs taken since our departure from Yakutsk; and Stepan was perhaps the most forlorn, amongst strangers unacquainted with his language. The poor fellow had been as gay as a cricket amidst the dangers of the Arctic, but here he was as timid as a lost child, gazing hour by hour into the water, smoking endless cigarettes, and thinking, perhaps, of his wife and little "Isba" in now distant Siberia.

On July 15 we passed the boundary into British North-west territory, and shortly afterwards hailed the British flag fluttering from the barracks at Forty Mile City as an old and long-lost friend. This was the chief town of the Upper Yukon in the palmy days of the Hudson Bay Company when furs rather than gold were the attraction to these gloomy regions. In 1896 this was the highest point reached by the larger river-boats, and here, on that occasion, we left the tiny skiff in which we had travelled for over a month on the great lakes, and boarded the steamer for St. Michael. Forty Mile then consisted of eighty or ninety log-huts on a mud bank, where numerous tree-stumps, wood-shavings, empty tins, and other rubbish littered the ground amongst the houses, adding to the general appearance of dirt and neglect. But now several neat, new buildings have arisen from the ashes of the old; streets have been laid out with regularity; and a trim fort is occupied by a khaki-clad detachment of the North-west Mounted Police. Forty Mile is more of a military post than anything else, most of its prospectors having left the place for the Klondike, although a few years back this was the chief rendezvous of Yukon pioneers. These, however, were mostly "grub-stakers," quite content if enough gold-dust was forthcoming to keep the wolf from the door.

From Paris to New York by Land

In those days a nugget of any size was a rarity, and fortunes were made here, not by the miner, but by those who fed and clothed him. For instance, in 1886 Forty Mile Creek yielded less than £30,000, but at this time the total number of prospectors in the entire territory of the Upper Yukon was under 250, and very few of these who could avoid it wintered in the country.

At last, on the thirteenth day, we neared our destination. "It seems a month since we left St. Michael," says the confidence-man as for the last time we watch the pine forest darken and the great river fade into a silvery grey in the twilight. From the brightly lit saloon come the tinkle of a piano and the clear notes of Mrs. Z.'s voice. Her pathetic little melody is familiar to the wanderer in every lonely land:

> "All the world am sad and dreary
> Everywhere I roam!"

But, fortunately for us, the Yukon, like the Suwanee River, must have an ending, and I am awakened early next morning to find the *Hannah* moored alongside a busy wharf at Dawson City.

CHAPTER XVII

DAWSON

"The Yukon district is a vast tract of country which forms the extreme north-westerly portion of the north-west territories of Canada. It is bounded to the south by the northern line of British Columbia, to the west by the eastern line of the United States territory of Alaska, to the east by the Rocky Mountains, and to the north by the Arctic Ocean. The district has an area of 192,000 square miles, or about the size of France. The region, as a whole, is mountainous in character, but it comprises as well an area of merely hilly or gently undulating country, besides many wide and flat bottomed valleys. It is more mountainous in the south-east and subsides generally and uniformly to the north-westward, the mountains becoming more isolated and separated by broader tracts of low land. The Yukon or Pelly River provides the main drainage of this region, passing from Canadian into American territory at a point in its course 1600 miles from the sea. The two hundred miles of its course in Canada receives the waters of all the most important of its tributaries—the Stewart, Macmillan, Upper Pelly, Lewes, White River, &c., each with an extensive subsidiary river system, which spreading out like a fan towards the north-east, east, and south-east facilitate access into the interior." So writes my friend Mr. Ogilvie, the Dominion Surveyor, who has an experience of over twenty years of this country and who is probably better acquainted with its natural characteristics and resources than any other living white man.

On the occasion of my last attempt to travel overland from New York to Paris the spot upon which Dawson City now stands was occupied by perhaps a dozen Indian wigwams.[76] The current was so strong that we only landed from our skiff with difficulty and the timely assistance of some natives in birch bark canoes, the first of these graceful but rickety craft we had yet encountered. Just below the village a small river flows into the Yukon from the east, and the water looked so clear and pure that we filled our barrels, little dreaming that in a few months this apparently insignificant stream would be the talk of the civilised world. For this was the Throndiuck,[77] a word eventually corrupted into "Klondike" by the jargon of many nationalities. Then we visited the village, in search of food; finding in one hut some salmon, in another a piece of moose meat, both of venerable exterior. Most of the braves of the tribe were away hunting or fishing, but the old men and maidens were eager for news from up river, the sole topic of interest being, not the finding of nuggets, but the catching of fish. Strange as it may seem the name of Klondike is to this day associated in my mind with comparatively clean Indians and a good square meal. But hardly a year had elapsed before I discovered that on that quiet, sunlit evening, I was carelessly strolling about over millions of money without being aware of the fact.

[76] Dawson City is named after Dr. Dawson who first established the boundary between Alaska and British north-west territory.

[77] An Indian word signifying "Plenty of fish." On old maps the place is marked "Tondack."

Dawson City stands on the right bank of the Yukon on a plain almost surrounded by picturesque and partly wooded hills. There are towns existing much further north than this notwithstanding all that has been written to the contrary. Many a cheap tripper from Aberdeen or Newcastle has been a good deal nearer the Pole, so far as actual latitude is concerned, for Dawson is south of the Norwegian towns of Hammerfest and Tromsö; Archangel—on the White Sea—being situated on about the same latitude as the Klondike metropolis. The latter was founded shortly after the first discovery of gold in 1896, and a few months afterwards seven or eight thousand people were living there in tents and log huts. In 1898 a fire occurred and the whole town was rebuilt on more business-like lines, buildings, streets, and squares being laid out with regularity. The fire had not been wholly disastrous, for before its occurrence typhoid fever was raging amongst the miners, chiefly on account of improper food, impure water, and the miasma arising from the marshy, undrained soil. But when the town was restored, these evils were remedied, and, at the present day, Dawson contains about 30,000 inhabitants (probably more in summer), who, save for a rigorous winter, live under much the same conditions as the dweller in any civilised city of England or America. Out on the creeks, the life is still rough and primitive, but all the luxuries of life are obtainable in town, that is if you can afford to pay for them, for prices here are, at present, ruinous. This is chiefly due to the almost prohibitive tariff imposed upon everything, from machinery to cigars, by the Canadian Government. During our stay much discontent also prevailed in consequence of the vexatious gold-mining regulations which had lately come into operation and which had already compelled many owners of valuable claims to sell them at a loss and quit the country. An Englishman residing here told me that so long as the present mining laws exist prospectors will do well to avoid Canadian territory, and this I could well believe, for while we were there, Dawson was, on this account, in a ferment of excitement which threatened shortly to blaze into open rebellion unless the tension was removed.

The natural charms of Dawson have hitherto been sadly neglected by writers on Klondike, and yet it is in summer one of the prettiest places imaginable. Viewed from a distance on a still July day, the clean bright looking town and garden-girt villas dotting the green hills around are more suggestive of a tropical country than of a bleak Arctic land. An interesting landmark is the mighty landslip of rock and rubble which defaces the side of a steep cliff overlooking the city, for this avalanche of earth is said to have entombed some fifty or sixty Indians many years ago, and is of course therefore, according to local tradition, haunted. Notwithstanding its remoteness Dawson may almost be called a gay place. Stroll down the principal street at mid-day and you will find a well-dressed crowd of both sexes, some driving and cycling, others inspecting the shops or seated at flower-bedecked tables in the fashionable French "Restaurant du Louvre" with its white aproned *garçons* and central snowy altar of silver, fruit, and *hors-d'œuvres* all complete. Everything has a continental look, from the glittering jewellers' shops to the flower and fruit stalls, where you may buy roses or strawberries for a dollar apiece. I recollect discussing a meal of somewhat rusty bacon and beans (or Alaska strawberries as they were then called) when we landed for the first time amongst the Indians of Thron-diuck, and it seemed like some weird dream when

From Paris to New York by Land

one sultry afternoon during my recent stay I was invited by a party of smartly dressed ladies to partake of ices in a gilded *café* with red-striped sun-blinds on the very same spot. But you can now get almost anything here by paying for it, on a scale regulated by the local daily newspapers, which are sold for a shilling and sometimes more. Even in the cheaper eating-houses, where sausages steam in the window, the most frugal meal runs away with a five dollar note, while at the Regina Hotel (by no means a first-class establishment) the price charged for the most modest bedroom would have secured a sumptuous apartment at the Ritz palaces in Pall Mall or the Place Vendôme! On the day of our arrival I thought a bar-tender was joking when he charged me three dollars for a pint of very ordinary "Medoc," but quickly discovered that the man was in sober earnest. Nevertheless, only big prices are to be expected in a region almost inaccessible ten years ago. And what a change there is since those days. In 1896 it took us two months to reach Thron-diuck from the coast, and on the last occasion I received a reply from London to a cable within seven hours! This new era of progress and enlightenment seemed to have scared the insect creation, for, in 1896, "smudges" were lit here to drive away the clouds of mosquitoes which mingled with our very food; and now not a gnat was to be seen in Dawson, although the creeks around were said to be alive with them.

This is essentially a cosmopolitan city, and you may hear almost every known language, from Patagonian to Chinese, talked in its streets. "First Avenue," about a mile long and fronting the river, is the finest thoroughfare, and the high-sounding title is not incongruous, for several handsome stone buildings now grace this street which in a few years will doubtless be worthy of Seattle or San Francisco. One side of the road is lined by busy wharves, with numberless steamers ever on the move, the other by shops of every description, restaurants, and gorgeous drinking-saloons. A stranger here cannot fail to be struck with the incongruity with which wealth and squalor are blended. Here a dainty restaurant is elbowed by a cheap American *gargote*, there a plate-glass window blazing with diamonds seems to shrink from a neighbouring emporium stocked with second-hand wearing apparel. Even the exclusive Zero Club with its bow window generally crowded with fashionable loungers, is contaminated by the proximity of a shabby drinking-bar, which, however, does not impair the excellence of its internal arrangements, as the writer can testify. For a Lucullian repast, of which I was invited to partake at this hospitable resort of good fellows of all nationalities, yet lingers in my memory!

But hospitality seems ingrained in the nature of the Klondiker high or low, and during its short stay here the Expedition was regally received and entertained. A wood-cut, which appeared in the principal newspaper representing "Dawson City extending the glad hand of welcome to Explorer De Windt" was no mere figure of speech, for we were seldom allowed to pay for a meal, while the refreshments and cigars lavished upon me by total strangers at every moment of the day would have set up a regimental mess. My host here was the manager of the "Alaska Commercial Company," which has practically ruled the country from the year of its annexation, and without whose assistance I should often have fared badly during my travels in the interior. Mr. Mizner, the agent, occupied one of the newest and finest houses in Dawson, but I was awakened the first night by a sound suggestive of a spirited wrestling bout in an adjoining apartment. The noise continued almost without cessation, and only ceased when the business of the day recommenced in the streets. Then the mystery was explained; my imaginary wrestlers were rats, which are not, I believe, indigenous to Alaska. Originally brought to St. Michael during the gold rush by an old and patched-up barque from San Francisco, the enterprising rodents boarded a river steamer and landed here, where conditions appear especially favourable to their reproduction. Scarcely a house in the place was free from them, and at night, or rather through its twilight hours, the streets swarmed with the disgusting brutes who seemed to regard human beings with supreme indifference. From latest advices this annoyance still exists and a fortune therefore awaits a good London rat-catcher in Dawson.

Dissipation used to reign here supreme as it does to-day at Nome, but the Canadian authorities have now placed a heavy heel upon gambling-saloons, dancing-halls, and similar establishments. And although the closing of these places has caused much dissatisfaction amongst those who profited by them, the measure has undoubtedly been for the general good of the community. Many a poor miner has come in from the creeks with gold-dust galore, the result of many months of hard work and privation, and found himself penniless after a single night passed amongst the saloons, dives, and dens of an even worse description which formerly flourished here. In those days the place swarmed with women of the lowest class, the very sweepings of San Francisco, and with them came such a train of thieves and bullies that finally the law was compelled to step in and prevent a further influx of this undesirable element. Dawson is now as quiet and orderly as it was once the opposite, for ladies unable to prove their respectability are compelled to reside in a distant suburb bearing the euphonious name of Louse-Town. This place is probably unique, at any rate amongst civilised nations, although the Japanese Yoshiwara, outside Tokio, where every dwelling is one of ill-fame, is, although, much larger, almost its exact prototype.

Crime in and about Dawson is now rare thanks to that fine body of men, the North-west Mounted Police. Piccadilly is no safer than the streets here, which, during the dark winter months, blaze with electricity. The Irish ruffian, George O'Brien, who, a couple of years ago, built a shanty in a lonely spot and robbed and murdered many prospectors, was arrested and hanged with a celerity which has since deterred other evil doers. For the system of police surveillance here is almost as strict as in Russia, and although passports are not required the compulsory registration of every traveller at the hotels and road houses answers much the same purpose.

Although rowdy revelry is discountenanced by the authorities Dawson City can be gay enough both in summer and winter. In the open season there is horse-racing along First Avenue, where notwithstanding the rough and stony course and deplorable "crocks" engaged, large sums of money change hands. There are also picnics and A. B. floaters, or water parties organised by a Society known as the "Arctic Brotherhood," who charter a steamer once a week for a trip up or down river, which is made the occasion for dancing and other festivities entailing the consumption of much champagne. At this season there is also excellent fishing in the Yukon and its tributaries, where salmon, grayling, and trout are plentiful. The first named run to an enormous weight, but are much coarser and less delicate in flavour than the European fish. The Fourth of July is a day of general rejoicing, for there are probably as many, if not more, Americans than Canadians here. There is good rough shooting within easy distance of Dawson, and the sporting fraternity occasionally witnesses a prize fight, when Frank Slavin (who owns an hotel here) occasionally displays his skill.

The history of the Klondike gold-fields has so often been told that I shall not weary the reader by going over old ground: how George Cormack made his lucky strike on Bonanza Creek, taking out £240 of gold in a couple of days from a spot which, with proper appliances, would have yielded £1000, or how the steamship *Excelsior* arrived in San Francisco one July day in 1897 with half a million dollars and thirty old timers whose tales of a land gorged with gold were almost universally discredited. But these were confirmed by the arrival of the *Portland* a few days later with over a million dollars' worth of dust stowed away in oil cans, jam-tins, and even wrapped in old newspapers, so desolate and primitive was the region from whence it came.[78] Then, as every one knows, the news was flashed over the world and was followed by a stampede the like of which had not been witnessed since the days of '49. Unfortunately, the simple and primitive way in which the gold was gained seemed suggestive of a poor man's "El Dorado," and consequently many of those who went into the Klondike with the first batch of gold seekers were small tradesmen, railway officials, clerks, and others, whose sedentary occupation had rendered them quite unfit for a life of peril and privation in the frozen north. The tragic experiences of these first pilgrims to the land of gold are probably still fresh in the mind of the reader—the deaths by cold and hunger on the dreaded Chilkoot Pass, or by drowning in the stormy lakes and treacherous rapids of the Yukon. The death list during the rush of 1897 will long be remembered in Dawson City, for many of those who survived the dangers of the road were stricken down on arrival by typhoid fever, which allied to famine, claimed, in those days, a terrible percentage of victims. And yet if the risks were great, the rewards were greater for those blessed with youth, perseverance and, above all, a hardy constitution. Perhaps the most notable case of success in the early days was that of Clarence Berry (then known as the "Barnato of the Klondike"). When Berry left California his capital consisted of £20 which enabled him to reach the scene of operations and to take £26,000 out of the ground within six months of his departure from home. Mrs. Berry, who pluckily joined her husband at Dawson, is said to have lifted no less than £10,000 from her husband's claims in her spare moments. About this period many other valuable discoveries took place and amongst them may be mentioned MacDonald's claim on "El Dorado" which yielded £19,000 in twenty-eight days, Leggatt's claims on the same creek which in eight months produced £8400 from a space only twenty-four square feet, and Ladue, a Klondike pioneer, who for seven consecutive days took £360 from one claim and followed his good fortune with such pluck and persistency that he is now a millionaire. Of other authentic cases I may mention that of a San Francisco man and his wife who were able to secure only one claim which to their joy and surprise yielded £27,000, and that of a stoker on board a Yukon river boat who in 1896 was earning £10 a month and who, the following summer, was worth his £30,000!

[78] In view of the eventual development of this region it is interesting to note Mr. Ogilvie's report of his explorations in 1887 which runs thus:

"The Thron-diuck river enters the Yukon from the east, it is a small stream about forty yards wide at the mouth and shallow; the water is clear and transparent and of a beautiful blue colour, the Indians catch great numbers of salmon here. A miner had prospected up this river for an estimated distance of forty miles in the season of 1887. I did not see him."

But the foregoing are only individual cases which have come under my personal notice. There were, of course, innumerable others, for it was a common thing in those days for a man to return to California after a year's absence with from £5000 to £10,000 in his pocket. Take, for instance, the case of the lucky bar-tender of Forty Mile City who joined the general exodus from that place which followed Cormack's first discovery. This man came out of the country with $132,000 in gold dust which he had taken out of his stake, and after purchasing an adjoining claim for another $100,000 (all taken from his original claim), it is said (though I cannot vouch for this statement) that the fortunate cock-tail mixer eventually sold his property to a New York Syndicate for £400,000. Of course at this time fairy tales were pretty freely circulated; how, for instance, one man with very long whiskers had been working hard in his drift all through the winter and, as was the custom, neither washed nor shaved. In the spring when the whiskers were shaved off his partner is said to have secured them, washed them out in a pan, and collected $27 as the result! This is of course absurd, but facts in those days concerning discoveries were so marvellous that they were easily confused with fiction. Thus Mr. Ogilvie, the Dominion Surveyor and a personal friend of mine, told me that he went into one of the richest claims one day and asked to be allowed to wash out a panful of gold. The pay streak was very rich but standing at the bottom of the shaft, and looking at it by the light of a candle, all that could be seen was a yellowish looking dirt with here and there the sparkle of a little gold. Ogilvie took out a big panful and started to wash it out, while several miners stood around betting as to the result. Five hundred dollars was the highest estimate, but when the gold was weighed it came to a little over $590, or nearly £120. This I can vouch for as a fact.

A coach runs daily out from Dawson to the diggings about fifteen miles away, but although the famous Bonanza and El Dorado Creeks are still worth a visit,[79] I fancy the good old days are over here when fortunes were made in a week and saloon keepers reaped a comfortable income by sweeping up spilt gold dust every morning. Klondike is no longer a region of giant nuggets and fabulous finds, for every inch of likely ground has been prospected over and over again. Nevertheless many of the creeks are doing well, notably that of "Last Chance," which may even eclipse El Dorado when machinery has been brought to bear. Almost any claim on "Last Chance" is now a sound investment, but this was about the only creek which, during our stay, was attracting any serious attention from outside.

[79] Professor Angelo Heilprin has reported that El Dorado and Bonanza gold generally assays but about $15.50 or $15.80 to the ounce. Dominion gold shows as high as $17.80, while the gold of Bear Creek, a minor tributary of the Klondike, is reported to give $19.20 to the ounce.

It is probably unnecessary to explain that, with one or two exceptions, the gold in Alaska is obtained by placer-mining. This consists simply in making a shaft to bedrock[80] and then tunnelling in various directions. The pay dirt is hauled out by a small hand-windlass and piled up until it is washed out. I am indebted to my friend Mr. Joseph Ladue, for the following description of the various processes which follow excavation.

[80] The depth to bedrock varies from fourteen to twenty feet.

"The miner lifts a little of the finer gravel or sand in his pan. He then fills the latter with water and gives it a few rapid whirls and shakes. This tends to bring the gold to the bottom on account of its greater specific gravity. The pan is then held and shaken in such a way that the sand and gravel are gradually washed out, care being taken as the process nears completion, to avoid letting out the finer and heavier parts that have settled to the bottom. Finally all that is left in the pan is gold and some black sand, which is generally pulverised magnetic iron-ore. Should the gold thus found be fine, the contents of the pan are thrown into a barrel containing water and a pound or two of mercury. As soon as the gold comes in contact with the mercury it combines with it and forms an amalgam. The process is continued until enough amalgam has been formed to pay for roasting or firing.

"It is then squeezed through a buckskin bag, all the mercury that comes through the bag being put into the barrel to serve again, and what remains in the bag is placed in a retort, if the miner has one, or if not, on a shovel, and heated until nearly all the mercury is vaporised. The gold then remains in a lump with some mercury still held in combination with it.

"This is called the 'pan,' or 'hand-method,' which is only employed when it is impossible to procure a rocker or to make and work sluices.

"The latter is the best method of placer-mining, but it requires a good supply of water with sufficient head or falls. The process is as follows: Planks are secured and made into a box of suitable depth and width. Slats are fixed across the bottom of the box at intervals, or holes bored in the bottom in such a way as to preclude the escape of any particle of gold. Several of these boxes are then set up with a considerable slope, and are fitted into one another at the ends like a stove pipe. A stream of water is then thrown into the upper end of the highest box, the dirt being shovelled in and washed downwards, at the same time. The gold is detained by its weight, and is held by the slats or in the holes aforementioned. If it be fine, mercury is placed behind the slats or in these holes to catch it. After the boxes are done with they are burnt and the ashes washed for the gold held in the wood."

These methods seem simple enough and, no doubt, would be in more temperate regions, but the mines of the Yukon are of a class by themselves, and the rigorous climate here necessitates entirely new methods for getting the gold. It was formerly considered impossible to work after the month of September, but experience has now conclusively proved that much may be accomplished during the winter months. The working year is therefore three times as long as it used to be, and the time formerly wasted in idleness is now profitably employed. The difficulty of winter mining is, of course, enormously increased by the fact that the ground is frozen. Every foot of it must be thawed, either in sinking or drifting, by small fires. The shallower mines are worked during the summer in the open air, but when the gravel is more than six feet deep a shaft is sunk, and dirt enough removed to allow space to work in. Thus the gold seeker with a log hut close to the mouth of his shaft and provided with plenty of food and fuel may pass a whole winter in comparative comfort. About a ton of dead ground can be dumped daily, and a few hundred pounds of pay gravel. The latter is piled up until the spring when the thaw comes. It is then "panned" or "rocked" without difficulty, for here, unlike Western Australia, there is no lack of water.[81]

[81] For further particulars anent gold-mining in the Klondike, see "Through the Gold Fields of Alaska," by Harry de Windt.

Steam power has now supplanted these more or less primitive methods on the most important claims, but here again the enormous duty levied by the Canadian Government on machinery of all kinds, was, while we were at Dawson, causing universal indignation. A single visit to the creeks sufficed for me, for although Dawson was free from mosquitoes, the diggings swarmed with them. And, talking of mosquitoes, no one unacquainted with Alaska can be aware of the almost unbearable suffering which they are capable of inflicting upon mankind. Brehm, the famous naturalist, has furnished about the best description of a luckless prospector caught in the toils. "Before a man knows," says the professor, "he is covered from head to foot with a dense swarm, blackening grey cloths and giving dark ones a strange spotted appearance. They creep to the unprotected face and neck, the bare hands, and stockinged feet, slowly sink their sting into the skin, and pour the irritant poison into the wound. Furiously the victim beats the blood-sucker to a pulp, but while he does so, five, ten, twenty other gnats fasten on his face and hands. The favourite points of attack are the temples, the neck, and the wrist, also the back of the head, for the thickest hair is of no protection. Although the naturalist knows that it is only the female mosquitoes which suck blood, and that their activity in this respect is connected with reproduction and is probably necessary to the ripening of the fertilised eggs, yet even he is finally overcome by the torture caused by these demons, though he be the most equable philosopher under the sun. It is not the pain caused by the sting, or still more by the resulting swelling; it is the continual annoyance, the everlastingly recurring discomfort under which one suffers. One can endure the pain of the sting without complaint at first, but sooner or later every man is bound to confess himself conquered, and all resistance is gradually paralysed by the innumerable omnipresent armies always ready for combat."

Although the climate of Dawson is naturally severe a man may live with proper precautions through a dozen winters comfortably enough in Alaska. Many people are under the impression that the winters here are of Cimmerian darkness, with no daylight for weeks at a time, whereas, even on the shortest day of December, there are still two hours of sunlight. 75° F. below zero is about the coldest yet experienced, but this is very rare, and here, unlike Canada, there is seldom the wind which makes even 20° below almost unbearable. Winter generally commences in October, but often much earlier, and the Yukon is generally clear of ice by the beginning of June. The snowfall is not excessive, three feet being considered deep. In summer the temperature often exceeds 90° F. but the nights are always cool and pleasant.

The Klondike district had, up to the time of the great gold strike, borne the reputation of being an arid ice-bound waste, incapable of producing anything more nutritious than trees, coarse grass, and the berries peculiar to sub-Arctic regions. On the occasion of my first stroll down First Avenue I was scarcely surprised to find all kinds of fruit and vegetables exposed for sale, the transit now being so rapidly accomplished (in summer) from California. But ocular proof was needed to convince me that potatoes, radishes, lettuce, cucumbers, indeed almost every known vegetable, is now grown around Dawson and on the opposite side of the river. Strawberries and nectarines (Klondike-grown) were served at the restaurants, of course at stupendous prices, as hundreds of acres of glass and costly artificial heat had been needed for their production. Hot-house flowers are now grown here and also sold at a ruinous cost, but the lucky prospector will cheerfully part with $5 for a rose, or five times the amount for a puny gardenia, and some of the market gardens around Dawson are almost as profitable as a fairly rich claim. High prices here even extended to the commonest furs judging from the price I obtained for a tattered deerskin coat which had cost me only eighty roubles at Moscow. But although the garment was now almost unpresentable I sold it to a bar-tender for its original price, and heard, on the same evening, that it had again been disposed of to a "Chechako" from up country for over $200!

Klondike is generally associated in the public mind with intense cold. We suffered from a perpetual and stifling heat which necessitated the wearing of tropical tweeds, a sartorial luxury here where a summer suiting costs about six times as much as in Savile Row. Once there was a sharp thunderstorm and the rain came down in sheets, somewhat cooling the atmosphere, but only for a short time, for when the sky cleared a dense mist arose from the swampy ground, and the air became as heavy and oppressive as I have known it during the hottest season of the year in Central Borneo. But the nights were always cool and delicious, and these moreover were now gradually darkening, an ineffable blessing which can only be duly appreciated by those who have experienced the miseries of eternal day. The English tourist who in July races northwards in the "Argonaut" to behold the midnight sun should pass a summer or two in Northern Alaska. He would never wish to see it again!

CHAPTER XVIII

THE UPPER YUKON AND LEWES RIVERS.
THE WHITE PASS RAILWAY.

The steamer *White Horse*, in which we travelled from Dawson City up the Yukon to the terminus of the White Pass Railway was, although much smaller than the *Hannah*, quite as luxuriously fitted as that palatial river boat. There is now, in the open season, daily communication between Dawson and the coast, and the journey to Vancouver may now be accomplished under six days. In winter-time closed and comfortable sleighs, drawn by horses, convey the traveller to rail-head. There are post-houses with good accommodation every twenty miles or so, and this trip, once so replete with hardships, may now be undertaken at any time of the year by the most inexperienced traveller. In a couple of years the Alaskan line from Skagway will probably have been extended as far as Dawson City, which will then be within easy reach of all civilised centres.

The three days' journey on the Upper Yukon (or rather Yukon and Lewes, for above its junction with the Pelly River the Yukon is known by the latter name), was not devoid of enjoyment, for the scenery here is as mountainous and picturesque as that of the lower river is flat and dreary. Settlements are more numerous, and the trip is not without interest, and even a spice of danger when the rapids are reached. The last of these down stream, although insignificant when compared with the perilous falls up river, are sufficiently swift and voluminous to cause considerable anxiety to a nervous mind. The five granite pillars which here span the Yukon, at intervals of a few feet, from shore to shore, are known as the "Five Fingers," and here the steamer must be hauled up the falls through a narrow passage blasted out of a submerged rock. A steel hawser attached to a windlass above the falls is used to tow the vessel up the watery incline, and were the cable to snap, a frightful disaster would certainly ensue. At this spot, the billows and surf raging madly round our tiny craft, the dark, jagged rocks threatening her on every side, and the deafening roar of foam and breakers were a novel experience which some of our passengers would apparently have cheerfully dispensed with. There was an awkward moment when the cable got foul of a snag, and the *White Horse* swerved round and lay broadside to the torrent, which for several minutes heeled her over at a very uncomfortable angle. "Something will happen here some day," coolly remarked the pilot, a long, lanky New Englander, lighting a fresh cigarette, and viewing the wild excitement of men afloat and ashore with lazy interest, and although, on this occasion, we escaped a catastrophe, and got off easily with shattered bulwarks, I have no doubt he was right. Going down stream steamers shoot these rapids, which entails a considerable amount of coolness and courage on the part of the steersman, for the slightest mistake would send the vessel crashing into the rocks on either side of the narrow passage.

Six years ago the rapids of the Yukon formed one of the most serious obstacles to Alaskan travel, and I retain a vivid recollection of the "Grand Cañon" and "White Horse" rapids during our journey through the country in 1896. These falls are beyond Lake Le Barge, and about two hundred miles above Five Fingers. At first sight of the Grand Cañon I wondered, not that accidents often took place there, but that any one ever ran it in safety, for the force of the current through the dark, narrow gorge is so tremendous that the stream is forced to a crest about four feet high, like a sloping roof, in the centre of the river. It is essential to keep on the summit of this crest, or be instantly dashed to pieces on the rocks. The strongest swimmer would stand no chance here, and no man who has ever got in has lived to relate his experiences. The Grand Cañon is nearly a mile in length, but our boat ran through it in less than two minutes.

The first plunge into the White Horse Rapid, only a few miles below the Grand Cañon, is even more abrupt and dangerous than that into the latter, and here the water dashes down with an appalling roar. The foaming crest of the wave, following the first downward sweep, is supposed to resemble a white horse's mane, which circumstance christened the fall. The latter was also formerly known as the "Miner's Grave," which, seeing that at one time a yearly average of twenty men were drowned here, seems a more suitable title. But these death-traps are now happily perils of the past, both being now avoided by the new rail and steamboat route into the Klondike.

Shortly after negotiating Five Fingers, we passed the mouth of the Nordenskiold River, which enters the Yukon from the west. This is an insignificant stream, although coal has lately been discovered in its vicinity, a fact which may shortly lower the now outrageous price of that commodity in Dawson. Above this the river widens, and occasionally expands into a series of lakes, studded with prettily wooded islands, perfect gardens of wild flowers, but fruitful breeding-places of our implacable foes, the mosquitoes. A few hours of this, and the river narrows again, and is fringed by low banks of sand and limestone, riddled by millions of martin's nests, while inshore a vista of dark pine forests and grassy, undulating hills stretches away to a chain of granite peaks, still streaked in places with the winter snow. Towards evening we tie up for fuel at the mouth of the Hootalinqua River, which drains Lake Teslin, the largest in the Yukon basin. The mountains at the head of Teslin form part of the now well-known Cassiar range, where the rich mines of that name are worked. On board were two prospectors who had passed several months in the Hootalinqua district, and who predicted that its mineral wealth would one day surpass that of Bonanza and El Dorado. But this I am inclined to doubt, as the river was apparently little frequented, and my friends, although so sanguine of its bright future, were leaving the country for British Columbia. So far as I could ascertain, throughout the journey up the Yukon, the immediate neighbourhood of Dawson City is about the only district in the North-west Province where a prospector may hope to meet with anything like success. When this country is opened up, things will, no doubt, be very different, and new fields of wealth will await the gold-seeker, but the cold fact remains that at present there is no indication whatever that such fields exist, outside of Nome and the Klondike, with one exception. I know Alaska far too well to advise any one to go there who can possibly find any other outlet for his energy and capital, but if any man is bent on staking his all, or part of it, in this country, then let him try the Copper River district, which up till now is practically unknown to the outside world. Mr. J. E. Bennett, of Newcastle, Colo., a passenger on the *White Horse*, showed me a nugget worth fifty pounds which he had picked out of a stream there the previous year. He is now in the district in question prospecting, and from his last advices had struck indications of very rich ground. Many have been scared away from this part of Alaska by reports of dangerous natives, but although the Indians here were formerly ugly customers, there is now little to fear on that score. There are very few people there as yet, and it is a poor man's country with boundless possibilities, one great advantage being that its chief sea-port is open to navigation all the year round. At the newly built town of Valdes on the coast, stores of all kinds can be purchased at reasonable prices, the place being easy of access. I should add that the Copper River and its affluents are in American territory, and that it is therefore exempt from the now vexatious mining laws of Canada.[82]

[82] Ocean steamers landing at Orca station, in Prince William Sound, give miners the chance of reaching Copper River, by a 30-mile trail over Valdes Pass, at a point above the Miles Glacier and the other dangerous stretches near the mouth of that stream. Rich placer-regions have been found along the Tonsino Creek, which empties into Copper River about 100 miles from the sea. The route up the Copper River across a low divide to the Tanana and down that stream was explored and first followed by Lieutenant Allen, U.S.A., in 1885.

Should any of my readers decide to take a prospecting trip to this newly discovered northern El Dorado, it may not be out of place to furnish a description of the kind of outfit required for a year's residence there. Mr. Bennett was good enough to give me a list of requisites which an experience of two years in the Copper River district had shown him were essential to the comfort and health of the prospector. They are as follows:

CLOTHING.

Three thick tweed suits.
Three suits heavy woollen underwear.
Six pairs wool stockings.
Two pairs fur mits.
Two heavy Mackinaw suits.[83]
Four woollen shirts.

From Paris to New York by Land

Two heavy sweaters.
One rubber lined top-coat.
One fur Parka and hood.[83]
Two pairs high rubber boots.
Two pairs shoes.
Two pairs heavy blankets.
One fur-lined sleeping-bag.
One suit oilskins.
One suit buckskin underwear.
Towels, needles, thread, wax, buttons.

[83] Procurable at Valdes.

MINING TOOLS.

One long-handled shovel.
One pick.
One axe (duplicate handles).
Five lbs. wire nails.
Three lbs. oakum.
Two large files.
Two hammers.
One jack blade.
One large whip saw.
One hand saw.
One hundred and fifty feet ⅝" rope.
A draw knife.
Two chisels.
One jack knife.
One whetstone.
Two buckets.
Two miner's gold-pans.
One frying-pan.
One kettle.
One Yukon stove.
One enamelled iron pot.
Two plates.
One cup.
One teapot.

Three knives.
Three forks.
Three spoons.

Food.

Three hundred and fifty lbs. flour.
Two hundred lbs. bacon.
One hundred and fifty lbs. beans.
Ten lbs. tea.
Seventy-five lbs. coffee.
Five lbs. baking powder.
Twenty-five lbs. salt.
Five lbs. sugar.
One hundred and fifty lbs. dried vegetables and meats.
One hundred lbs. assorted dried fruits.
Ten lbs. soap.
Three tins matches.

Armament.

One gun (to fire shot or bullets).
One hundred rounds shot and bullet cartridges.
Re-loading tools.
One large hunting knife.
Fishing tackle.
Snow goggles.

Camping Outfit.

One canvas tent, 8 ft. by 10 ft., in one piece, with floor-cloth.
Spare pegs and guy ropes.
Mosquito netting.

Medicine Chest.[84]

Quinine pills.
Calomel.
Compound catharic pills.
Chlorate of potash.
Mustard plasters.

Belladonna plasters.
Carbolic ointment.
Witch hazel.
Essence of ginger.
Laudanum.
Tincture of iodine.
Spirits of nitre.
Tincture of iron.
Cough mixture.
Elliman's embrocation.
Toothache drops.
Vaseline.
Iodoform.
Goulard water.
Lint.
Bandages.
Adhesive rubber plasters.
Cotton wool.

[84] Best procurable at Burroughs & Welcome, Snow Hill, London.

A few cheap knives, compasses, &c., may be taken as presents for the natives. All these supplies will weigh, roughly speaking, 1400 lbs., and the whole outfit may be purchased at San Francisco, or any other city on the Pacific slope, for about £60.

Above the Hootalinqua the Lewes is known as the thirty-mile river, that being about the distance from the mouth of the first-named stream to the foot of the lake. This is a dangerous bit of navigation, for the Thirty Mile rushes out of Le Barge like a mill sluice and the little *White Horse* panted and puffed and rained showers of sparks in her frantic efforts to make headway. Several steamers which have been lost here perpetually menace the safety of others. It is impossible to raise the sunken vessels, the force of the current here being so great that it seemed when standing on the deck of the steamer as though one were looking down an inclined plane of water. The stream here runs through pine forests, ending at the river's edge in low, sandy cliffs, portions of which have been torn bodily away by the force of the ice in springtime to form miniature islands some yards from the shore.[85] A characteristic of this stream is its marvellous transparency. On a clear day rocks and boulders are visible at a depth of twenty to thirty feet. I have observed a similar effect on the River Rhone and other streams fed to a large extent by glaciers and melting snow.

[85] The fall from Lake Lindemann at the head of the lake and river system is about 800 ft. in a distance of about 540 miles.

The afternoon of the third day found us entering Lake Le Barge,[86] a sheet of water thirty-one miles in length, which stands over two thousand feet above the sea-level, and is surrounded by precipitous mountains, densely wooded as far as the timber line, with curiously crenelated limestone summits. The southern shores of the lake are composed of vast plains of fertile meadow land, interspersed with picturesque and densely wooded valleys, a landscape which, combined with the blue waters of Le Barge and snowy summits glittering on the horizon, reminds one of Switzerland. Le Barge has an evil reputation for storms, and only recently a river steamer had gone down with all hands in one of the sudden and violent squalls peculiar to this region. To-day, however, a brazen sun blazed down upon a liquid mirror, and I sat on the bridge under an awning with a cool drink and a cigar, and complacently watched the glassy surface where five years before we had to battle in an open skiff against a stiff gale, drenched by the waves and worn out by hard work at the oars. To-day the *White Horse* accomplished the passage from river to river in about three hours, while on the former occasion it took us as many days!

[86] Lake Le Barge was named after Mike Le Barge, of the "Western Union Telegraph Company," who was employed in constructing the overland telegraph line from America to Europe (*viâ* Bering Straits) in 1867. The completion of the Atlantic cable about this period put an end to the project.

There is, on portions of Lake Le Barge, a curiously loud and resonant echo. A cry is repeated quite a dozen times, and a rifle shot awakens quite a salvo of artillery. This is especially noticeable near an island about four miles long near the centre of the lake, which for some obscure reason is shown on Schwatka's charts as a peninsula. The

American explorer named it the "Richtofen Rocks," but as the nearest point of this unmistakable island to the western shore is but half a mile distant, and as the extreme width of the lake is only five miles, I cannot conceive how the error arose.

Towards evening we reached the Fifty Mile River, noted for the abundance and excellence of its fish. A few miles above the lake the Takheena flows in from the west. This river, which rises in Lake Askell, derives its name from the Indian words, "Taka," a mosquito, and "Heena," a stream, and it is aptly named, for from here on to White Horse City we were assailed by myriads of these pests. Indeed the spot where the town now stands was once a mosquito swamp in which I can recall passing a night of abject misery. It was past midnight before the *White Horse* was safely moored alongside her wharf, but electric light blazed everywhere, and here, for the first time since leaving Irkutsk, more than seven months before, clanking buffers and the shriek of a locomotive struck pleasantly upon the ear.

White Horse City is a cheerful little town rendered doubly attractive by light-coloured soil and gaily painted buildings. There is a first-rate hotel adjoining the railway station, which contained a gorgeous bar with several billiard and "ping-pong" tables, the latter game being then the rage in every settlement from Dawson to the coast. I mention the bar, as it was the scene of a somewhat amusing incident, which, however, is, as a Klondiker would say, "up against me." About this period a "desperado" of world-wide fame named Harry Tracy was raising a siege of terror in the State of Oregon, having committed over a dozen murders, and successfully baffled the police. We had found Dawson wild with excitement over the affair, and here again Tracy was the topic of the hour. Entering the hotel with some fellow passengers, I took up a Seattle newspaper and carelessly glancing at the portrait of a seedy-looking individual of ferocious exterior, passed it on to a neighbour, remarking (with reference to Tracy), "What a blood-thirsty looking ruffian!" "Why, it's yourself!" exclaimed my friend, pointing to the heading, "A Phenomenal Globe-trotter," which, appearing above the wood-cut, had escaped my notice. I am glad to be able to add that the portrait was not from a photograph!

As an instance of engineering skill, the "White Pass" is probably the most remarkable railway in existence, and the beauty and grandeur of the country through which it passes fully entitles it to rank as the "Scenic railway of the world." In 1896, I was compelled to cross the Chilkoot Pass to enter Alaska (suffering severely from cold and hunger during the process), and to scramble painfully over a peak that would have tried the nerves and patience of an experienced Alpine climber. Regarding this same Chilkoot a Yankee prospector once said to his mate: "Wal, pard, I was prepared for it to be perpendicular, but, by G—d, I never thought it would lean forward!" And indeed my recollections of the old "Gateway of the Klondike" does not fall far short of this description. And in those days the passage of the White Pass, across which the line now runs, was almost as unpleasant a journey as that over the Chilkoot judging from the following account given by Professor Heilprin, who was one of the first to enter the country by this route. The professor writes:

"It is not often that the selection of a route of travel is determined by the odorous, or mal-odorous qualities pertaining thereto. Such a case, however, was presented here. It was not the depth of mud alone which was to deter one from essaying the White Pass route. Sturdy pioneers who had toiled long and hard in opening up one or more new regions had laid emphasis on the stench of decaying horseflesh as a first consideration in the choice of route. And so far as stench and decaying horseflesh were concerned they were in strong evidence. The desert of Sahara with its lines of skeletons, can boast of no such exhibition of carcasses. Long before Bennett was reached I had taken count of more than a thousand unfortunates whose bodies now made part of the trail. Frequently we were obliged to pass directly over these ghastly figures of hide, and sometimes, indeed, broke into them. Men whose veracity need not be questioned assured me that what I saw was in no way the full picture of the 'life' of the trail; the carcasses of that time were less than one-third the full number which in April and May gave grim character to the route to the new 'El Dorado.' Equally spread out this number would mean one dead animal for every sixty feet of distance! The poor beasts succumbed not so much to the hardships of the trail as to lack of care and the inhuman treatment which they received at the hands of their owners. Once out of the line of the mad rush, perhaps unable to extricate themselves from the holding meshes of soft snow and of quagmires, they were allowed to remain where they were, a food-offering to the army of carrion eaters which were hovering about, only too certain of the meal which was being prepared for them."

It will be seen by the foregoing accounts that only a short time ago the journey across this coast range was anything but one of unalloyed enjoyment, and even now, although the White Pass Railway is undoubtedly a twentieth-century marvel, and every luxury is found on board the train, from a morning paper to "candies" and cigars, the trip across the summit is scarcely one which I should recommend to persons afflicted with nerves. The line is a narrow gauge one about 110 miles in length, which was completed in 1899 at a cost of about $3,000,000, and trains leave the termini at Skagway and White Horse simultaneously every day in the year at 9 A.M., reaching their respective destinations at 4 P.M. For a couple of hours after leaving White Horse the track skirts the eastern shores of Lakes Bennett and Lindemann, through wild but picturesque moorland, carpeted with wild flowers,[87] and strewn with grey rocks and boulders. A species of pink heather grows freely here, the scent of which and the presence of bubbling fern-fringed brooks, and crisp bracing air, recalled many a pleasant morning after grouse in Bonnie Scotland. A raw-boned Aberdonian on the train remarks on the resemblance of the landscape to that of his own country and is flatly contradicted by an American sitting beside him, who, however, owns that he has never been there! The usual argument follows as to the respective merits, climatic and otherwise, of England and the United States, which entails (also as usual) a good deal of forcible language. Shortly after this, however, the train begins to ascend, and its erratic movements are less conducive to discussion than reverie. For although the rails are smooth and level enough, the engine proceeds in a manner suggestive of a toy train being dragged across a nursery floor by a fractious child. At midday Bennett station is reached, and half an hour is allowed here for lunch in a cheerful little restaurant, where all fall to with appetites sharpened by the keen mountain air, and where the Scot and his late antagonist bury the hatchet in "Two of whisky-straight."

[87] Lake Lindemann is about five miles, and Bennett twenty-five miles in length.

Bennett is buried in pine forests, but here the real ascent commences, and we crawl slowly up an incline which grows steeper and steeper in proportion as trees and vegetation slowly disappear, to give place to barren rocks, moss, and lichens. Towards the summit (over two thousand feet high) the scene is one of wild and lonely grandeur, recalling the weirdest efforts of Gustave Doré. Nothing is now visible but a wilderness of dark volcanic crags with here and there a pinnacle of limestone, towering perilously near the line, and looking as though a puff of wind would dislodge it with disastrous results. The only gleam of colour in the sombre landscape are numerous lakes, or rather pools, of emerald green, perhaps extinct craters, which, shining dimly out of the dark shadows cast by the surrounding cliffs, enhance the gloom and mystery of the scene. Nearing the summit, the road has been blasted out of many yards of solid rock, a work entailing fabulous cost and many months of perilous and patient labour. The Chamounix railway in Switzerland was, at the time of its construction, considered the king of mountain railways, but it becomes a very humble subject indeed when compared with the White Pass line.

At Summit we cross the frontier into American territory, and here my thermometer marks a drop of 25° F. since our departure this morning. Although this rapidly constructed line is admirably laid, portions of the ascent from White Horse are anything but reassuring to those averse to high altitudes, but they are not a circumstance to those on the downward side. On leaving Summit station the train enters a short tunnel, from which it emerges with startling suddenness upon a light, iron bridge which spans, at a giddy height, a desolate gorge. This spidery viaduct slowly and safely crossed, we skirt, for a while, the mountain side, still overhanging a perilous abyss. Every car has a platform, and at this point many passengers instinctively seek the side away from the precipice, which would in case of accident benefit them little, for there is no standing room between the train and a sheer wall of overhanging rock, the crest of which is invisible. Here the outlook is one which can only really be enjoyed by one of steady nerves, for the southward slope of the mountain is seen in its entirety, giving the impression that a hardy mountaineer would find it a hard job to scale its precipitous sides, and that this railway journey in the clouds cannot be reality but is probably the result of a heavy supper. Perhaps the worst portion of the downward journey is at a spot where solid foothold has been found impracticable, and the train passes over an artificial roadway of sleepers, supported by wooden trestles and clamped to the rock by means of iron girders. Here you may stand up in the car and look almost between your toes a sheer thousand feet into space. While we were crossing it, this apparently insecure structure shook so violently under the heavy weight of metal that I must own to a feeling of relief when our wheels were once more gliding over *terra firma*. The men employed in constructing this and other parts of the track were lowered to the spot by ropes, which were then lashed to a place of safety while they were at work. But although the construction of this line entailed probably as much risk to life and limb as that of the Eiffel Tower, only one death by accident is recorded during the whole period of operations here, while it cost over a hundred lives to erect the famous iron edifice in Paris.

The gradient of this railway is naturally an unusually steep one, and should, one would think, necessitate the utmost caution during the descent, but we rattled down the mountain at a pace which in any country but happy-go-lucky Alaska would certainly have seemed like tempting Providence, especially as only brakes are used to check the speed of the train. However, the fact that two passenger trains are run daily (also a goods train), and that not a single accident has occurred during the four years the line has been in operation, are sufficient proof that the officials of the White Pass Railway know what they are about, and are not lacking in care and competence. I can speak from personal experience as to their civility and also punctuality, for, towards three o'clock, the silvery waters of the Lynn Canal were disclosed through a rift in the mountains, and an hour later we were steaming into the town of Skagway, within half a minute of the scheduled time.

CONSTRUCTING THE WHITE PASS RAILWAY.

CHAPTER XIX

THE FRANCO-AMERICAN RAILWAY—SKAGWAY—NEW YORK

While on the subject of railways a few remarks anent the projected line from France (*viâ* Siberia and Bering Straits) to America may not be amiss. As the reader is already aware, the main object of our expedition was to determine whether the construction of such a line is within the range of human possibility. The only means of practically solving this question was (firstly) to cover the entire distance by land between the two cities, by such primitive means of travel as are now available, and (secondly) to minutely observe the natural characteristics of the countries passed through, in order to ascertain whether these offer any insuperable obstacle to the construction of a railway.

I would again remind the reader that the overland journey from Paris to New York had never been made, or even attempted, until it was accomplished by ourselves. This is the more necessary in so far as, before our departure from Paris, the project of an All-World railway was freely discussed in the English and French Press by persons with no practical experience whatsoever of either Siberia or Alaska. Their opinions would, therefore, have been equally valuable with reference to a railway across the moon or planet Mars. From a humorous point of view, some of the letters published were well worth perusal, notably those of a French gentleman, who, in the Paris *New York Herald,* repeatedly drew my attention to the fact that he "claimed the paternity of the scheme to unite France and America by rail," and this being so, apparently strongly resented my making a preliminary trip over the ground with dogs and reindeer. Having ascertained, however, that M. de Lobel had never visited Arctic Siberia, and had not the remotest intention of doing so, I scarcely felt justified in abandoning the overland journey on his account. This ridiculous but somewhat amusing incident was therefore brought to an end by the following letter:

From Paris to New York by Land

"To the Editor of the *New York Herald*, Paris.

"Sir,—May I briefly reply to M. Loicq de Lobel's letter which appeared in your issue of November 23rd. Your correspondent has already violently attacked me in the Paris *Journal*, his grievance being that he 'claims the paternity' of the projected Trans-Siberian and Alaskan Railway. This fact is probably as uninteresting to your readers and to the world in general as it is to myself, and so far as I am concerned M. de Lobel is also welcome to annex (in his own imagination) the countries through which the proposed line may eventually pass.

"But this is not the point. According to his own showing, M. de Lobel only 'conceived the project' of uniting Paris and New York by rail in the year 1898. As I left New York in 1896 for Paris by land, with the object of ascertaining the practicability of this gigantic enterprise, I think that I may, with due modesty, dispute the shadowy 'paternity' of the scheme, which, after all, is worth nothing from a theoretical point of view.

"The American and British Press of March, April, and May 1897 will fully enlighten your correspondent as to the details of my last attempt, which unhappily met with disaster and defeat on the Siberian shores of Bering Straits. But I trust and believe that a brighter future is in store for the 'Daily Express' Expedition of 1901, which I have the honour to command, and which leaves Paris for New York by land on the 15th of next month.

"If, as M. de Lobel writes, 'the Englishman thought best not to answer' it was simply because the former's childish tirades seemed to me unworthy of a reply. If, however, you will kindly insert this brief explanation, you may rest assured that, so far as I am concerned, this correspondence is closed.

"I am, yours faithfully,
"Harry de Windt.

"Royal Geographical Society,
London,
November 26, 1901."

With regard to the projected railway, let me now state as briefly and as clearly as I can the conclusion to which I was led by plain facts and personal experience. To begin with, there are two more or less available routes across Siberia to Bering Straits, which the reader may easily trace on a map of Asia. The city of Irkutsk is in both cases the starting-point, and the tracks thence are as follows:

No. 1 Route. To Yakutsk, following the course of the Lena River, and thence in an easterly direction to the town of Okhotsk on the sea of that name. From Okhotsk, northward along the coast to Ola and Gijiga, and from the latter place still northward to the Cossack outpost of Marcova on the Anadyr River. From Marcova the line would proceed northward chiefly over tundra and across or through one precipitous range of mountains, to the Siberian terminus, East Cape, Bering Straits.

The second route is practically the one we travelled, viz., from Irkutsk to the Straits *viâ* Yukutsk, Verkhoyansk, and Sredni-Kolymsk.

From a commercial point of view, route No. 1 would undoubtedly be the best, for of late years a considerable trade has been carried on between Vladivostok and the Sea of Okhotsk. The latter only twenty years ago was visited solely by a few whalers and sealing schooners, but a line of cargo steamers now leaves Vladivostok once a month throughout the open season (from June to September) and make a round trip, calling at Petropaulovsk (Kamchatka), Okhotsk, Yamsk, and Ayan.[88] There is now a brisk and increasing export trade in furs, fish, lumber, and whalebone from these ports, the imports chiefly consisting of American and Japanese goods.

[88] These vessels also carry passengers.

It has already been shown in a previous chapter that the natural resources of the Yakutsk district would probably repay an extension of the Trans-Siberian line to this now inaccessible portion of the Tsar's dominions. Indeed it is more than probable that in a few years the mineral wealth of this province, to say nothing of its agricultural possibilities, will render the construction of a line imperative, at any rate as far as the city of Yakutsk. The prolongation of this as far north as Gijiga is no idle dream, for I have frequently heard it seriously discussed, and even advocated, by the merchant princes of Irkutsk. A railway to Gijiga would open up Kamtchatka, with its valuable minerals, furs, and lumber, and also Nelkan, near Ayan, where gold has lately been discovered in such quantities that a well-known Siberian millionaire has actually commenced a narrow-gauge railway about two hundred miles in length, to connect the new gold-fields with the sea. Even this miniature line is to cost an enormous sum, for it must pass through a region as mountainous and densely wooded as the eight hundred odd miles which separate Yakutsk from the coast. But although this latter section of the Franco-American line, short as it is, would entail a fabulous outlay, there is here, at any rate, some *raison-d'être* for a railway, viz., the vast and varied resources of the region through which it would pass, whereas to the north of Gijiga on the one hand, and Verkhoyansk on the other, we enter a land of desolation, thousands of miles in extent, chiefly composed of tundra, as yet unprospected, it is true; but probably as unproductive, minerally and agriculturally, as an Irish bog. The reader is already aware that tundra is impassable in summer, for its consistency is then that of a wet bath sponge. The foot sinks in over the knee at every step, and a good walker can scarcely cover a mile within the hour. In winter the hard and frozen surface affords good going for a dog-sled and could, no doubt, be made to support a rolling mass of metal; but even then I doubt whether the thaws and floods of springtime would not find the rails and sleepers at sixes and sevens. This opinion is, of course, purely theoretical, for the experiment of laying a line of such magnitude under such hopeless conditions has yet to be tried.

Chat Moss in England is the nearest approach I can think of to these Siberian swamps, but the railway across the former is only four miles long, and cost, I am told, something like thirty thousand pounds. At this rate the tundra section of the Bering Straits Railway would alone involve an outlay of twenty million sterling; probably far more, for every foot of timber for the roadway would have to be imported into this treeless waste. And how is this expenditure going to be repaid by these barren deserts, in winter of ice, and in summer of mud and mosquitoes. Let another Klondike be discovered near, say, Sredni-Kolymsk, and I have no doubt that surveys for a line to this place would be commenced to-morrow by the Russian Government, but neither gold, not any other mineral has yet been found so far north in anything like paying quantities. Draw a straight line on the map from Verkhoyansk to Gijiga and it will divide the southern (or productive) portion of Siberia from the northern (and useless) wastes about three thousand miles in length, which a Paris-New York railroad would have to cross.[89]

[89] "Around the North Pole lies a broad belt of inhospitable land, a desert which owes its special character rather to water than to the sun. Towards the Pole this desert gradually loses itself in fields of ice; towards the south in dwarfed woods, becoming itself a field of snow and ice when the long winter sets in, while stunted trees struggle for existence only in the deepest valleys or on the sunniest slopes. This region is the tundra. Our language possesses no synonym for the word tundra. Our fatherland possesses no such track of country, for the tundra is neither heath nor moor, neither marsh nor fen, neither highlands nor sand-dunes, neither moss nor morass, though in many places it may resemble one or other of these. 'Moss Steppes' some one has attempted to name it, but the expression is only satisfactory to those who have grasped the idea of steppe in its widest sense." —*Brehm*.

A so-called prospectus issued by a syndicate, inviting the public to subscribe for a "preliminary survey" for a Franco-American line, came under my notice the other day. Here is an extract:

"Ten years ago the name Siberia called up a picture of wastes of snow and ice. To-day the same Siberia is a land filled with thriving villages, producing grain and various vegetables; that great compeller of civilisation, the railway, has broken down the bars between the world and Siberia. Besides its countless resources of the soil, besides its rivers filled with valuable fish, and its forests inhabited by fur-bearing animals, Siberia is now beginning to show to the world its resources of gold, iron, copper, manganese, quicksilver, platinum, and coal, the yearly output of which is but a feeble index of what it will be when the deposits are developed."

All this is very true regarding certain portions of Siberia. The Amur, Altai, Yenesei, and even Yakutsk provinces. But although the writer

From Paris to New York by Land

goes on to enlarge upon the boundless possibilities which would be opened up by the construction of a railway from Europe to America, he fails to mention that it would have to traverse an Arctic and unproductive Sahara thousands of miles in extent.

Some enthusiastic visionaries mentioned in an earlier portion of this chapter have laid stress on the fact that the passenger traffic over this portion of the line would be enormous, that surging crowds of sea-sick victims would gladly endure even three weeks in a train in preference to a stormy passage across the Atlantic, and so forth. But I fancy a moment's serious thought will show the absurdity of this theory. In the first place a journey by rail from Paris to New York would certainly occupy over a month under the most favourable conditions, for while in summer time all might be comparatively plain sailing, gales, snow-drifts, and blizzards would surely, judging from our own experiences, seriously hamper the winter traffic, especially along the coast. If this leviathan railway is ever constructed it must, in the opinion of the ablest Russian engineers, depend solely upon (1) the transport of merchandise, and (2) the development of the now ice-locked regions it will traverse. The scheme has never been, as many people seem to imagine, simply to convey passengers and their belongings from one terminus to the other, for even Jules Verne would probably hesitate to predict the existence of this line as one of restaurants and sleeping-cars.

But let us assume that the railway has actually reached East Cape at a cost of, say, fifty millions sterling from Irkutsk, which is probably a low estimate. Here we are confronted by another colossal difficulty, the passage of Bering Straits, which (at the narrowest part) are forty miles across. Here my friends the theorists have again been very busy, and all kinds of schemes have been suggested for the negotiation of this stumbling-block, from a bridge to balloons. Both are equally wild and impracticable, although the former has been warmly advocated by a Parisian gentleman, who never having been nearer even Berlin than the Gare du Nord, can scarcely be expected to know much about the climatic conditions of North-Eastern Siberia. As a matter of fact, the mightiest stone and iron structure ever built would not stand the break-up of the ice here in the spring time for one week. A tunnel could no doubt be made, for the depth of the Straits nowhere exceeds twenty-seven fathoms, and the Diomede Islands could be conveniently utilised for purposes of ventilation. But what would such a subway cost? And above all, where is the money coming from to repay its construction?

In Northern Alaska almost the same difficulties would be met with as in Arctic Siberia, for here also spongy tundra covers enormous tracts of country. A company has, however, been formed for the purpose of laying a line between Iliamna on Cook's Inlet and Nome City which will, when completed, be really useful and profitable. Cook's Inlet is navigable throughout the year, and it is proposed to run a line of steamers from Seattle on Puget Sound to this port, where passengers will be able to embark on a comfortable train for Nome instead of facing a long and painful journey by dog-sled. I understand that this work has actually been commenced by the "Trans-Alaskan Railway Company," but not with any idea of connection with a possible Siberian system. This will be merely a local railway, which, judging from the increasing prosperity of Nome, and the fact that the line will pass through the rich Copper River country, should certainly repay its shareholders with interest. The extension of the White Pass Railway as far as Dawson City is only a question of time, but the idea of prolonging it to Bering Straits was not even hinted at when I was in Alaska.

All things considered I cannot see what object would be gained by the construction (at present) of a Franco-American railway. That the latter will one day connect Paris and New York I have little doubt, for where gold exists the rail must surely follow, and there can be no reasonable doubt regarding the boundless wealth and ultimate prosperity of those great countries of the future; Siberia and Alaska. But it is probably safe to predict that the work will not be accomplished in the lifetime of the present generation, or even commenced during the existence of the next. When, at the conclusion of the journey, I arrived at New York, I was asked by reporters whether I considered it possible to connect the latter city by rail with Paris. Most certainly it would be possible with unlimited capital, for this stupendous engineering feat would assuredly entail an expenditure (on the Siberian side alone and not including a Bering Straits tunnel), of fifty to sixty millions sterling. It seems to me that the question is not so much, "Can the line be laid?" as "Would it pay?" In the distant future this question may perhaps be answered in the affirmative, but at present nothing whatever is known of the mineral resources of Arctic Siberia, a practical survey of which must take at least fifteen to twenty years. If reports are then favourable, Russia may begin to consider the advisability of a line to America, but, notwithstanding the fact that an attempt has been made in certain quarters to obtain money from the public for this now extremely shadowy scheme, I can only say that all the prominent Russian officials whom I have met simply ridicule the project.

Skagway is pleasantly situated on the shores of the Lynn Canal, in an amphitheatre formed by precipitous cliffs, the granite peaks of which almost overhang the little town. A curious effect is produced here by rudely coloured advertisements of some one's chewing gum, or somebody's else cigars with which the rocky sides of the nearest hills are defaced. But there is nothing new in this, for, as far back as 1887, the name of a well-known American pill and ointment vendor met my astonished gaze on the Great Wall of China. The North Pole will soon be the only virgin field left open to the up-to-date advertiser. Skagway is now a quiet, orderly township, and a favourite resort of tourists, but shortly after it was founded, in 1898, a band of swindlers and cut-throats arrived on the scene, and practically held the place at their mercy for several weeks. The leader of this gang was one "Soapy Smith," a noted "confidence man," whose deeds of violence are still spoken of here with bated breath. This impudent scoundrel (said to have been a gentleman by birth) was clever enough to become mayor of the town, and was thus enabled to commit robberies with impunity. Many a poor miner leaving the country with a hardly earned pile has been completely fleeced, and sometimes murdered, by the iniquitous and ubiquitous "Soapy," who is said to have slain, directly or indirectly, over twenty men. Finally, however, a mass meeting was held, where Smith was shot dead, not before he had also taken the life of his slayer.

Southern Alaska is the Switzerland of America, and every summer its shores are invaded by hordes of tourists. There was, therefore, little room to spare in the steamer in which we travelled down the Lynn Canal, one of the grandest fjords on the coast, which meanders through an archipelago of beautiful islands, and past a coast-line of snowy peaks and glaciers of clear, blue crystal washed by the waves of the sea. Its glaciers are one of the wonders of Alaska, for nowhere in the world can they be witnessed in such perfection. According to a talented American authoress, "In Switzerland a glacier is a vast bed of dirty, air-holed ice, that has fastened itself like a cold, porous plaster to the side of an alp. Distance alone lends enchantment to the view. In Alaska a glacier is a wonderful torrent that seems to have been suddenly frozen when about to plunge into the sea," and the comparison, although far-fetched, is not wholly devoid of truth.

Nearing Juneau we passed the Davidson glacier sufficiently near to distinguish the strange and beautiful effects produced upon its white and glittering surface by cloud and sunshine. This is the second largest ice-field in Alaska, the finest being its immediate neighbour, the Muir glacier, which drains an area of 800 square miles.[90] The actual ice surface covers about 350 square miles, the mass of it, thirty-five miles long and ten to fifteen miles wide, while surrounding it on three sides are mountains averaging 4000 to 6000 ft. in height. Vessels dare not approach the ice wall, about 250 ft. high, nearer than a quarter of a mile, as masses of ice continually fall from its surface, and submarine bergs, becoming detached from its sunken fore-foot rise to the surface with tremendous force. The colour of the ice on the Muir glacier is as curious as it is beautiful, varying from the lightest blue to dark sapphire, and from a dark olive to the tenderest shades of green. Although the feat has been often attempted no one has yet succeeded in crossing the Muir from shore to shore.[91]

[90] The Jostedalbrae in Norway, the largest glacier in Europe, only covers 470 square miles.

[91] See "Studies of Muir Glacier, in Alaska," by Harry Fielding Reid, *National Geographic Magazine*, March 1892.

The captain of the *Topeka* informed me that glaciers and canneries are the chief attractions of this coast. I assumed that it could not be the climate, for rain drizzled persistently from a grey and woolly sky nearly all the way from Skagway to Port Townsend, and this was regarded as "seasonable summer weather." With bright sunshine this journey through a calm inland sea, gliding smoothly through fjords of incomparable beauty, surrounded by every luxury, would be idyllic. As it is, cold, rain and mist generally render this so-called pleasure trip one of monotony and discomfort, where passengers are often compelled to seek shelter throughout the day in smoke-room or saloon. Swathed in oil-skins, however, I braved the downpour, and visited one of the numerous canneries to which the *Topeka* tied up for a few minutes, and here I was surprised to find that Chinese labour is almost exclusively employed. And the ease and celerity with which a fish was received, so to speak, fresh from the sea, cleaned, steamed, and securely soldered in a smartly labelled tin, all by machinery, within the space of a few minutes, was marvellous to behold. Before the days of Klondike, the fisheries of this coast were the chief source of wealth in Alaska, where sea-board, lakes, and rivers teem with fish, the wholesale netting of which seem in no way to diminish the number. The yearly output of these coast canneries is something stupendous, and they are, undoubtedly, a far better investment than many a claim of fabulous (prospective) wealth in the gold-fields of the interior. For the establishment of a cannery is not costly, labour and taxes are low, and fish of every description, from salmon and trout to cod and halibut, can be caught without difficulty in their millions. Codfish which abound in Chatham Creek are the most profitable, also herrings, of which six hundred barrels were once caught in a single haul, off Killisnoo. But the number of canneries on this coast is increasing at a rapid rate, and five or six years hence large fortunes will be a thing of the past. The now priceless sea-otter was once abundant along the south-eastern coast of Alaska, the value of skins taken up to 1890 being thirty-six million dollars, but the wholesale slaughter of this valuable animal by the Russians, and later on by the Americans, has driven it away, and almost the only grounds where it is now found are among the Aleutian Islands and near the mouth of the Copper River. A good sea-otter skin now costs something like £200 in the European market.

Juneau and Port Wrangell were the only towns of any size touched at during the two days' trip from Skagway to Port Townsend. The former was once the fitting-out place for miners bound for the Yukon, but Skagway has now ruined its commercial prosperity, and it is now a sleepy, miserable settlement which appeared doubly unattractive viewed through a curtain of mist. The rain poured down here in such sheets that Douglas Island, only a couple of miles away, was invisible. Here is the famous Treadwell mine, where the largest quartz mill in the world crushes six hundred tons in the twenty-four hours. This mine has already yielded more gold than was paid for the whole of Alaska.

Fort Wrangell is more picturesque than Juneau, although perhaps this was partly due to the cessation (for exactly half an hour) of the rain, which enabled our hitherto cooped-up tourists to enjoy a stroll, and a breath of fresh air ashore. Wrangell was once, like Juneau, a thriving town, when the Cassiar mines in British Columbia were a centre of attraction. Between four and five thousand miners passed through every spring and autumn, travelling to and from the diggings, and the usual hotels, saloons, and stores sprang up on all sides. Then came a period of stagnation, till the last gold rush to Klondike, when it seemed as though Wrangell would rise from its ashes. But the proposed route into the country by way of the Stikine River was finally abandoned for the White Pass, and dealt the final *coup de grâce* to the little town, which is now merely a decaying collection of wooden shanties and ruined log huts, tenanted chiefly by Indians, of whom we met more here than at any other point throughout the Alaskan journey. The natives of this part of the coast are called Thlinkits, a race numbering about 7000, and once numerous and powerful. But the Siwashes of Wrangell were a miserable-looking lot, the men apparently physically inferior to the women, some of whom would not have been ill-favoured, had it not been for the disgusting habit of daubing their faces with a mixture of soot and grease, which is supposed to keep off mosquitoes, and which gives them the grotesque appearance of Christy Minstrels. Tattooing no longer prevails amongst the Thlinkits, but the men still paint their faces and discard ragged tweeds and bowlers for the picturesque native dress on the occasion of a dance, or the feast known as a "Potlatch." The Thlinkits are not hardy, nor, as a rule, long-lived, and diseases due to drink and dissipation are rapidly thinning them out. Shamanism exists here, but not to such an extent as amongst the Siberian races, and the totem poles, which are met with at every turn in Wrangell, are not objects of worship, but are used apparently for a heraldic purpose. Some of the ancient war canoes of this tribe are still in existence, but they are only brought out on the occasion of a feast, when a chief and his crew appear in the gaudy panoply of war-paint and feathers.

On July 28, Seattle was reached, and here we met with a reception worthy of far doughtier deeds than we had accomplished. In 1896, Seattle was a country town of some 30,000 inhabitants, and I could scarcely recognise this fine modern city of over 100,000 souls which may shortly rival San Francisco as a commercial and social centre. This wonderful change is partly due to discoveries in the Klondike, but chiefly perhaps to the increasing trade of Puget Sound with the East. Fine Japanese liners now run direct every fortnight from Seattle to Japan, and on one of these a passage was obtained for my faithful friend and comrade, Stepan Rastorguyeff, whose invaluable services I can never repay, and to whom I bade farewell with sincere regret. I am glad to add that the plucky Cossack eventually reached his home in safety (*viâ* Yokohama and Vladivostok) arriving in Yakutsk by way of Irkutsk and the Lena River early in the new year of 1902. Vicomte de Clinchamp also left me here, to return direct to France *viâ* New York and Le Havre.

There is little more to tell. Travelling leisurely in glorious weather through the garden-girt towns and smiling villages of the "Rouge-River" Valley, perhaps the most picturesque and fertile in the world, a day was passed at Shasta Springs, the summer resort of fashionable Californians, where the sun-baked traveller may rest awhile in a little oasis of coolness and gaiety, cascades and flowers, set in a desert of dark pines. A week with old friends in cosmopolitan, ever delightful San Francisco, a rapid and luxurious journey across the American continent, land on August 25, 1902, New York was reached, and the long land journey of 18,494 miles from Paris, which had taken us two-thirds of a year to accomplish, was at an end.

From Paris to New York by Land

PART III

APPENDIX I

EUROPE AND ASIA

	E. M.
Paris to Moscow (rail)	1,800
Moscow to Irkutsk (rail)	4,000
Irkutsk to Yakutsk (employed 720 horses)	2,000
Yakutsk to Verkhoyansk (employed 80 horses and 240 reindeer)	623
Verkhoyansk to Sredni-Kolymsk (employed 620 deer)	1,006
Sredni-Kolymsk to Nijni-Kolymsk (employed 8 horses, 27 reindeer, 50 dogs).	334
Nijni-Kolymsk to Bering Straits (started with 64 dogs, arrived at Bering Straits with 9)	1,500
English miles: Europe and Asia	11,263

(Employing 808 horses, 887 reindeer, and 114 dogs.)

AMERICA

East Cape, Bering Straits to Cape Prince of Wales, Alaska	60
Cape Prince of Wales to Nome City	140
Nome City to St. Michael's	120
St. Michael's to Dawson City	1,200
Dawson City to White Horse Rapids	450
White Horse Rapids to Skagway	110
Skagway to Seattle	1,041
Seattle to San Francisco	1,000
San Francisco to New York	3,110
Total mileage: Paris to New York	18,494

APPENDIX II

LIST OF POST-STATIONS BETWEEN IRKUTSK AND YAKUTSK

	Versts.
Irkutsk to Koulinskaya	23
Koulinskaya to Jerdovskaya	21
Jerdovskaya to Ust-Ardinsk	21½
Ust-Ardinsk to Alzonovskaya	31
Alzonovskaya to Bandevskaya	25
Bandevskaya to Hagatovskaya	29
Hagatovskaya to Manzourskaya	30
Manzourskaya to Malo-Manzoursk	31½
Malo-Manzoursk to Katchugaskaya	24½
Katchugaskaya to Verkolensk	28¾
	265¼

To Verkolensk, 3 kopeks a verst per horse.
From Verkolensk to Yakutsk, 4½ kopeks a verst per horse.

Verkolensk to Tumentsofskaya	25
Tumentsofskaya to Korkinskaya	16
Korkinskaya to Petrofskaya	19½
Petrofskaya to Panamarefskaya	22
Panamarefskaya to Jigalovskaya	21
Jigalovskaya to Ust-Ilginsk	30½
Ust-Ilginsk to Grousnovskaya	26
Grousnovskaya to Zakamenska	19
Zakamenska to Shamanovskaya	16¾
Shamanovskaya to Golovskaya	18
Golovskaya to Sourovskaya	16
Sourovskaya to Diadinskaya	15½
Diadinskaya to Basovskaya	22
Basovskaya to Orlinsk	21
Orlinsk to Tarasovskaya	17¼
Tarasovskaya to Skokinskaya	22
Skokinskaya to Boyarsky	20

From Paris to New York by Land

Boyarsky to Omolevskaya	23
Omolevskaya to Riskaya	18
Riskaya to Bania	17¾
Bania to Touroutskaya	16¾
Touroutskaya to Ust-Kutsk	16
Ust-Kutsk to Yakurimsk	18½
Yakurimsk to Kazarkinskaya	28
Kazarkinskaya to Kokiskaya	20¼
Kokiskaya to Sukhovskaya	25¾
Sukhovskaya to Nazarovskaya	25½
Nazarovskaya to Markovskaya	23
Markovskaya to Oulkanskaya	21
Oulkanskaya to Krasnoyarskaya	17½
Krasnoyarskaya to Potapovskaya	14
Potapovskaya to Makarovskaya	22¾
Makarovskaya to Zaborskaya	15
Zaborskaya to Bezroukov	31
Bezroukov to Kirensk	31
	————
	997½ — 732¼
Kirensk to Alexeieff	21
Alexeieff to Garbovsk	21
Garbovsk to Vishniakovskaya	28
Vishniakovskaya to Spalashinsk	25
Spalashinsk to Ilinsk	24¼
Ilinsk to Darinskaya	22
Darinskaya to Itcherskaya	28½
Itcherskaya to Montinskaya	22½
Montinskaya to Ivanoushkofskaya	28
Ivanoushkofskaya to Tchastinsk	29
Tchastinsk to Pianovkovskaya	18½
Pianovkovskaya to Dulrovskaya	18½
Dulrovskaya to Kireisk	30
Kireisk to Solianskaya	26
Solianskaya to Parshinsk	18¼
Parshinsk to Risinsk	26½
Risinsk to Tchuskaya	26

From Paris to New York by Land

Tchuskaya to Vitimsk	22½

1433—435½

Vitimsk to Polovinaya	13
Polovinaya to Peledonskaya	15¼
Peledonskaya to Krestovskaya	28½
Krestovskaya to Peskovskaya	28
Peskovskaya to Graditsa	25
Graditsa to Khamrinsk	31¼
Khamrinsk to Kukinskaya	26
Kukinskaya to Terechinskaya	20½
Terechinskaya to Mukhtomskaya	29½
Mukhtomskaya to Murinsk	22½
Murinsk to Batamaiskaya	20
Batamaiskaya to Sadkolskaya	21½
Sadkolskaya to Niouskaya	25½
Niouskaya to Turuklinsk	17½
Turuklinsk to Jerbinsk	17½
Jerbinsk to Tinnaiya	17¾
Tinnaiya to Kamenskaya	21
Kamenskaya to Jeloiskaya	23
Jeloiskaya to Noktinskaya	30

1866¼—433¼

Noktinskaya to Gotchilnaya	30
Gotchilnaya to Beresovzskaya	22
Beresovzskaya to Inniakskaya	17½
Inniakskaya to Delgeskaya	22
Delgeskaya to Katchegarskaya	20
Katchegarskaya to Naleskaya	21
Naleskaya to Tcherendeskaya	32½
Tcherendeskaya to Birioutskaya	22½
Birioutskaya to Berdianskaya	20
Berdianskaya to Dourdousovskaya	20
Dourdousovskaya to Olekminsk	18

From Paris to New York by Land

2111¾—245½

Olekminsk to Solyanskaya	26
Solyanskaya to Harialakskaya	22¼
Harialakskaya to Namaminskaya	24
Namaminskaya to Russkaya	18
Russkaya to Tchekurskaya	32½
Tchekurskaya to Billaya	17
Billaya to Hat-Tumulskaya	71
Hat-Tumulskaya to Marhinskaya	22¼
Marhinskaya to Marchihanskaya	22½
Marchihanskaya to Samatatskaya	25½
Samatatskaya to Elovskaya	25
Elovskaya to Malikanskaya	25½
Malikanskaya to Tchuriskaya	22
Tchuriskaya to Isitzkaya	17½
Isitzkaya to Krestinskaya	17¾
Krestinskaya to Jurninsk	18¾
Jurninsk to Oïmurdusk	26½
Oïmurdusk to Ad-Dabausk	16
Ad-Dabausk to Sinskaya	19
Sinskaya to Batamaïskaya	27¾
Batamaïskaya to Tit-Arinsk	24½
Tit-Arinsk to Elanskaya	22
Elanskaya to Tun-Arinsk	22
Tun-Arinsk to Bulguniatatskaya	15
Bulguniatatskaya to Bestiatskaya	15½
Bestiatskaya to Pokrovskaya	23¾
Pokrovskaya to Ulak-Ansk	18½
Ulak-Ansk to Tektiurskaya	21¾
Tektiurskaya to Tabaginskaya	17
Tabaginskaya to Yakutsk	25

701¾

Total versts, 2813½
(A verst is two-thirds of an English mile.)

APPENDIX III

	Versts.
Yakutsk to Turutskaya	20
Turutskaya to Makarinsk	30
Makarinsk to Hatustatskaya	22
Hatustatskaya to Eleginiakskaya	25
Eleginiakskaya to Hagaraderdinsk	20
Hagaraderdinsk to Taraïskaya	45
Taraïskaya to Khatignak	37
Khatignak to Tandinskaya	30
Tandinskaya to Sanga-Ali (*Pov.*)	30
Sanga-Ali to Sordonakia (*Pov.*)	50
Sordonakia to Beté-Kül	50
Beté-Kül to Anna-Sük (*Pov.*)	50

VERKHOYANSK PASS.

Anna-Sük to Kangerak	40
Kangerak to Mollahoï (*Pov.*)	65
Mollahoï to Suruktutskaya	65
Suruktutskaya to Suruktak (*Pov.*)	50
Suruktak to Siremskaya	35
Siremskaya to Golova-Medvied (*Pov.*)	60
Golova-Medvied to Tsissibas	60
Tsissibas to Yuk-Tak (*Pov.*)	50
Yuk-Tak to Kurinskaya	70
Kurinskaya to Verkhoyansk	30
Total versts	934

Pov. — *Povarnia.*

APPENDIX IV

YAKUTE SETTLEMENTS BETWEEN VERKHOYANSK AND SREDNI-KOLYMSK

	Versts.
Verkhoyansk to Lang-Lor (Y.)	60
Lang-Lor to Batagaï (Pov.)	45
Batagaï to Aditschá (S.)	150 v. —45
Aditschá to Bür-Alü (Pov.)	45
Bür-Alü to Tostach (S. *)	115 v. —70
Tostach to Kürtas (Pov.)	85
Kürtas to Siss (Pov.)	45
Siss to Tiriak-Hureya (Pov.)	45
Tiriak-Hureya to Sordak (Pov.)	45
Sordak to Kurelach (S. *)	270 v. —50
Kurelach to Sarok-Kalak (Pov.)	45
Sarok-Kalak to Ustin (Pov.)	50
Ustin to Bachaol-Buta (Y.)	30
Bachaol-Buta to Ebelach (S. *)	175 v. —50
Ebelach to Khatignak-Kül (Y.)	60
Khatignak-Kül to Haras-Kül (Y.)	50
Haras-Kül to Keni-Kül (S. *)	150 v. —40
Keni-Kül to Ari-Tumul (Y.)	25
Ari-Tumul to Khatignak (S. *)	100 v. —75
Khatignak to Shestakova (Pov.)	80
Shestakova to Siss-Ana (Pov.)	50
Siss-Ana to Tsiganak (Y.)	50
Tsiganak to Sokurdakh (Pov.)	20
Sokurdakh to Andylakh (S. *)	250 v. —50
Andylakh to Ultum (S. *)	60
Ultum to Utchugoi-Kel (Y.)	40
Utchugoi-Kel to Malofskaya (S. *)	50
Malofskaya to Ehelakh (Pov.)	60
Ehelakh to Yatetsia (Y.)	30
Yatetsia to Sredni-Kolymsk	300 v. —60
Total versts	1510

From Paris to New York by Land

(*)—Change reindeer.
(Y.)—*Yurta*.
(S.)—Station.
(*Pov.*)—*Povarnia*.

APPENDIX V

SETTLEMENTS ON KOLYMA RIVER BETWEEN SREDNI-KOLYMSK AND NIJNI-KOLYMSK

	Versts.
Sredni-Kolymsk to Botolakh	50
Botolakh to Silgisit	40
Silgisit to Olbut	60
Olbut to Pamaskina	60
Pamaskina to Yuguz-Tamak	40
(*Horses*)	
Yuguz-Tamak to Krest	30
Krest to Gornitza	60
(*Reindeer*)	
Gornitza to Omolonskaya	60
Omolonskaya to Lakeyevskaya	40
Lakeyevskaya to Kimkina	40
Kimkina to Nijni-Kolymsk	40
(*Dogs*)	
Total versts	520

APPENDIX VI

A SHORT GLOSSARY OF YAKUTE WORDS

	Yakute.	Turkish
1	Bir	*Bir*
2	*Iki*	*Iki*
3	Us	*Utch*
4	Tar	*Dort*
5	Bar	*Besh*
6	Ali	*Alti*
7	Sekki	*Yedi*
8	Ahuse	*Sekis*
9	*Too-oose*	*Dokus*
10	Ohn	*Ohn*
20	Shirbeh	
30	Olût	
100	Sūs	

A man — *Kehé*
A woman — *Diak-Tar*
Yes — *Da*
No — *Sok*
Good — *Yutchingan*
Bad — *Koosahan*
Big — *Lohan*
Little — *Atchu-bui*
A horse — *Atté*
A dog — *Ut*
A house — *Djiéh*
A fire — *Wat*
A gun — *Sar*
Meat — *Ette*
A mouse — *Kugak*
A rat — *Kutchas*

Quick — *Turganik*
A door — *Ana*
Water — *Ou*
The sea — *Bayahel*
A river — *Uriakh*
The face — *Surei*
The hands — *Ili*
The arms — *Khari*
The feet — *Atakh*
Rain — *Sammor*
Wind — *Tül*
Snow — *Har*
The sun — *Kün*
The moon — *Oui*
To go — *Sullar*
To give — *Bier*

From Paris to New York by Land

A wolf—*Bireh*
A bear—*Ehä*
A cow—*Anakh*
Beautiful—*Utchingoi*
Ugly—*Kouhahan*
Dry—*Kuranak*
Wet—*Nitchagaï*
Dear—*Garāhan*
Cheap—*Tcheptchiki*
Far—*Gurach*
Near—*Tchugoss*

To speak—*Etter*
To ask—*Orjitar*
To ride—*Miner*
To buy—*Atlahar*
To eat—*Ahukka*
To drink—*Ihiéka*
To smoke—*Tardar*
A month—*Ui*
A week—*Nediélia*
A day—*Boikun*
An hour—*Birtchas*

APPENDIX VII

GLOSSARY OF VARIOUS DIALECTS IN USE AMONGST THE TCHUKTCHIS INHABITING THE COASTS OF N.E. SIBERIA

Cape Shelagskoi to Whalen.	East Cape.	Oumwaidjik.
There is: *Warkin*	*Warkin*	
There is not: *Winga*	*Winga*	
No: *Winga*	*Winga*	*Naka*
Yes: *Ee-ee*	*Ee-ee*	*Ah-ah*
All right: *Metchinki*		
Here: *Utku*		
I—my: *Mori*	*Wee*	*Kwanga*
You—your: *Turginian*		
A deer: *Korang*	*Kashinat*	*Guwiniak*
A house: *Yarat*	*Muntarak*	*Muntarak*
Far: *Yar*		
By-and-bye: *Yo-yo*		
A walrus: *Durka*	*Ibok*	*Ayivak*
Wood: *Ut-Tut*	*Naksiet*	
To sleep: *Zipiska*		
Keep still: *Deakarikti*	*Sien*	*Napéré*
I don't know: *Ko*		
A dog: *At-Tau*	*Kokmarok*	*Klikmak*
A man: *Katowvak*		*Yuk*
A woman: *Nawonskat*		*Aranak*
To drink: *Megwesiak*		*Mugwe*
A bear: *Umhang*	*Nanok*	*Nanok*
A seal: *Memet*	*Nahksak*	*Maklak*
A sled: *Urgur*	*Kaimukshik*	*Kamiyak*
A steamer: *It-Kowat*	*Toroma*	*Amakpawit*
A knife: *Vallia*	*Sinkat*	
A duck: *Gallia*	*Tigumak*	*Kawak*
Ice: *Ilgil*	*Sikok*	*Siku*
Snow: *Alash*	*Ani*	*Anio*
Wind: *Yu-yo*	*Anok*	*Anokiva*
Good-day: *Ta-oom*	*Taham*	*Tanakhoom*
You lie:	*Eklang*	*Eklima-Kotung*

From Paris to New York by Land

The hand:	*Askak*	*Eehit*
To smoke: *Takwaigen*	*Aptiok*	*Meluktok*
1: *Nerisha*	*Atajak*	*Atajak*
2: *Irak*	*Mailop*	*Mailop*
3: *Nerok*	*Piniayut*	*Piniayut*
4: *Nirak*	*Shtemet*	*Shtemet*
5: *Metch-Tinga*	*Taklimat*	*Taklimat*
6: *No-Metch-Tinga*	*Awindlit*	*Awindlit*
7: *Nera-Ah*	*Mara-Awindlit*	*Mara-Awindlit*
8: *Angero-Utkui*	*Pinia-Unlulut*	*Pinia-Unlulut*
9: *Onasinki*	*Shtema-Unlulut*	*Shtema-Unlulut*
10: *Menitku*	*Kullia*	*Kullia*

From Paris to New York by Land

APPENDIX VIII

METEOROLOGICAL RECORD OF THE DE WINDT EXPEDITION
PARIS TO NEW YORK, 1901-1902

Date.	Place.		Remarks.	8 A.M.	6 P.M.
Dec.					
19	Paris		Dull—some snow		40°
20	Berlin	Nord Express	Clear—sunshine	42°	50°
21	Warsaw		Clear	41°	33°
22	Viazma		Dull—snow	20°	22°
23	Moscow		""	22°	19°
24	"		Dull	17°	12°
25	"		"snow	-2°	5°
26	"		""	-8°	-5°
27	"		Fog and snow	-10°	5°
28	"		Dull	14°	21°
29	"		Dull—snow	6°	15°
30	"		Dull	11°	12°
31	"		Dull—fog	20°	22°
Jan.					
1	"		Dull	20°	22°
2	"		"	30°	33°
3	"		"	32°	33°
4	"		"	37°	18°
5	"		"	30°	28°
6	"		"	32°	29°
7			"LIST OF POST-STATIONS BETWEEN IRKUTSK AND	19°	29°
8	Trans-Siberian Railway		Bright—some clouds	21°	25°
9			Bright sunshine	12°	0°
10			Fine	-15°	-9°
11			"	-14°	2°
12			Dull—snow	7°	5°
13	Irkutsk		Fine	8°	15°
14	"		Dull	-2°	10°
15	"		"	0°	15°
16	"		Bright sunshine	10°	22°
17	"		Fog and snow	15°	11°
18	"		Bright sunshine	-8°	6°

263

From Paris to New York by Land

Date	Location	Weather		
19	"	Dull	-2°	-10°
20	Alzonovskaya	Bright sunshine	-31°	-35°
21		Fog	-65°	-30°
22		"	-50°	-32°
23		"	-50°	11°
24		"	-12°	1°
25		Dull—snow and gale N.E.	0°	8°
26		Clear	-8°	5°
27		Snow	12°	5°
28		Clear	-5°	-14°
29		"	-35°	-30°
30		Fog	-51°	-35°
31		Snow	-10°	-5°
Feb.				
1	Lena Post-Road	"	-2°	-2°
2		"	-2°	-5°
3		Bright sunshine	2°	5°
4		Dull	10°	12°
5		"	15°	15°
6		Fog	2°	-5°
7		"	-5°	-4°
8		Fine	-12°	-28°
9		Bright sunshine	-40°	-32°
10		""	-30°	-10°
11		""	-25°	-16°
12		""	-28°	-35°
13		""	-34°	-25°
14	Yakutsk	Snow	-15°	-24°
15	"	Bright sunshine	-24°	-24°
16	"	""	-32°	-34°
17	"	""	-34°	-24°
18	"	""	-32°	-26°
19	"	""	-20°	-14°
20	"	""	-24°	-30°
21	"	""	-41°	-2°
22		Dull	-12°	-10°
23		Bright sunshine	-45°	-20°
24		""	-41°	-23°
25	Yakutsk to	""	-45°	-30°
26	Verkhoyansk	""	-42°	-40°
27		""	-75°	-75°
28		Dull—snow	-35°	-37°
Mar.				

From Paris to New York by Land

1		Bright sunshine	-45°	-63°
2	Verkhoyansk	""	-65°	-50°
3	"	""	-40°	-62°
4	"	""	-66°	-65°
5		""	-73°	-10°
6		""	-30°	-35°
7		""	-30°	-25°
8		Fog	-10°	-78°
9		"	-30°	-30°
10		"	-30°	-0°
11	Verkhoyansk to Sredni-Kolymsk	Bright sunshine	-55°	-60°
12		""	-35°	-40°
13		""	-34°	-25°
14		""	-40°	-30°
15		""	-25°	-25°
16		""	-10°	-20°
17		""	-15°	0°
18	Sredni-Kolymsk	""	-15°	-10°
19	""	""	-20°	-10°
20	""	Fog	-10°	-18°
21	""	"	-38°	-25°
22	""	Bright sunshine	-35°	-30°
23		""	-40°	-25°
24	Sredni-Kolymsk— Nijni-Kolymsk	Dull	0°	-10°
25		Dull—gale S.W.	-5°	-15°
26		Fine	-20°	-5°
27		Dull—gale S.E.	5°	-15°
28	Nijni-Kolymsk	Dull	-20°	-15°
29	""	Fine	-30°	-8°
30	""	Bright sunshine	-35°	-10°
31	""	""	-30°	-25°
Apr.				
1	""	""	-26°	-30°
2	""	Fine—some snow	-18°	-20°
3	""	Fine	-20°	-14°
4	Sukharno	Strong gale N.W.	-16°	-20°
5	"	""""	-15°	-22°
6	"	""""	-20°	-20°
7	Camp 1	Bright sunshine	-16°	-20°
8		Dull	0°	0°
9[92]		Strong gale N.	0°	-2°
10	Arctic Coast	Snow	20°	-10°
11		Strong gale N.W.	-10°	-10°

265

From Paris to New York by Land

12		""E.	5°	15°
13		Poorga N.W.	12°	25°
14		""	12°	9°
15		""	4°	-7°
16		"S.E.	-2°	5°
17		""	10°	5°
18		"E.	0°	4°
19		Strong gale N.E.	0°	0°
20		""W.	-5°	2°
21		Fine—N.E. light	6°	10°
22		Gale S.W.	0°	0°
23		Snowstorms	30°	5°
24		"	25°	5°
25		Dull—snow	12°	19°
26		Strong gale N.W.	22°	15°
27		Gale N.W.	20°	15°
28		Light breeze N.	14°	10°
29		Dull	25°	-2°
30		Bright sunshine	-8°	10°
May				
1		Dull—gale N.	18°	16°
2		Snowstorms	22°	0°
3		Gale N. and snow	25°	15°
4		Strong gale N.W.	20°	20°
5[93]		""N.E.	22°	20°
6		Dull	55°	24°
7		Gale N.E.	32°	28°
8		"S.W.	38°	26°
9		Fog	26°	20°
10		Bright and clear	15°	28°
11		""	18°	25°
12		""	23°	17°
13		Dull—strong breeze S.W.	22°	25°
14		""	22°	15°
15		Poorga N.E.	15°	15°
16		Dull—strong gale N.E.	20°	18°
17		Strong gale N.W.—snow	20°	18°
18		Snow	25°	20°
19	Whalen—Bering Straits	Dull—still	32°	25°
20	""	""	45°	25°
21	""	""	50°	34°
22	""	""	32°	31°

From Paris to New York by Land

23	″″″″	Snow	44°	45°
24	″″″″	Fog	44°	39°
25	″″″″	Strong breeze S.—dull	36°	40°
26	″″″″	Gale S.E. and sleet	35°	36°
27	″″″″	Fine	36°	39°
28	″″″″	Dull—fog	42°	40°
29	″″″″	Dull	43°	40°
30		″	49°	34°
31		″	38°	46°
June				
1		Bright and clear	34°	28°
2		Gale S.	32°	32°
3		Dull—rain	42°	34°
4		Bright and clear	56°	51°
5		Clear	38°	52°
6		Fine—hazy	56°	68°
7		Clear	47°	65°
8	Bering Straits	″	46°	55°
9		″	48°	88°
10		″	48°	60°
11		″	45°	38°
12[94]		Rain	46°	36°
13		″	46°	40°
14[94]		″	43°	40°
15		Fog	40°	42°
16		Clear	40°	55°
17		Still	53°	55°
18		″	51°	50°
19		Gale S.—dull—rain	42°	41°
20		Strong gale S.W.	34°	40°
21	Cape Prince of	″″″″	33°	36°
22	Wales—Alaska	Gale N.W.—dull	45°	42°
23		"S.W.—dull	36°	38°
24		"S.W.—dull	38°	38°
25	Nome City	Clear and bright	45°	65°
26	″″″	″″″″	45°	62°
27	″″″	″″″″	55°	70°
28	″″″	″″″″	62°	64°
29	″″″	″″″″	60°	64°
30	Saint Michael's	″″″″	62°	73°

[92] 40° below zero inside tent for three hours at night.

[93] Dates from this must be set back one day on account of crossing 180° long.

[94] Sea ice opened.

THE END.